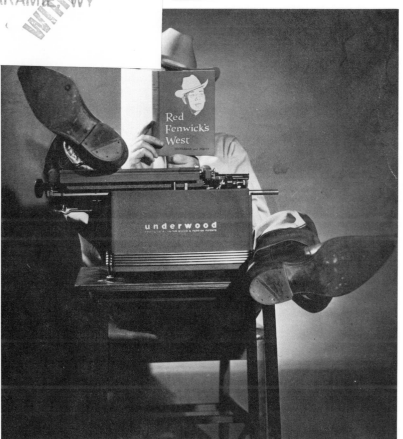

Tilted hat with worn cowboy boots, for once resting on his trusted typewriter, Red as he reviews his 1956 edition of *Red Fenwick's West, Yesterday and Today*.

WEST
Red Fenwick's
YESTERDAY AND TODAY

Robert W. (Red) Fenwick
❧ *Memorial Edition* ❧

Foreword by Pete Smythe • Preface by Willard Simms
Introduction by Mrs. Red (Donelle) Fenwick

PRUETT **P** *PUBLISHING COMPANY*
Boulder, Colorado

Memorial Edition
ISBN: 0-87108-658-1
1 2 3 4 5 6 7 8 9

Printed in the United States of America

Foreword

By
Pete Smythe

Some wise man once said, "I am persuaded that every time a man smiles, but much more when he laughs, it adds something to his fragment of life." Red and I must have shared a million laughs together. Whenever we came in sight of one another the electricity would begin generating humor of some kind. And so it was a coincidence that electricity once shocked us out of business.

It all began with a brilliant idea, the Jackalope races. Each summer for several years, we promoted them in *The Denver Post* and over the Barbwire Network, the East Tincup Broadscattering Situation and 50 thousand watts of KOA, Denver.

A Jackalope is a cross between a Jackrabbit and an Antelope, and mighty swift they are. We usually started the event at Chugwater and headed west toward Rock Springs, reporting the results each day. The race never ended. Jackalopes are strange creatures. They breed only during a lightning flash. And every season our racers were enveloped in a torrential Wyoming gullywasher and an eye-blinking electric display.

Nature giveth and she taketh away. The leaping Jackalopes lost all interest in the race and began leaping at each other. The end.

But the hilarity continued. I smile and chuckle when I recall our wild arena show at the Wyoming State Fair in Douglas; the bronc team that ran away with our rig in the parade at Cheyenne; riding with the Roundup Riders of the Rockies; judging the horses in the St. Patrick's Day Parade in Denver; the meetings of the Evil Companions at the Auditorium Hotel Saloon.

Even Red's funeral was laced with humor. I'll bet there'll be some grins in heaven.

Pete Smythe

Preface

By

Willard E. Simms

There's been no writer more qualified, as factually entertaining, nor as widely known from the grassland plains to the snowy mountain tops or from the skyscraper canyons to suburban town houses as the late "Red" Fenwick in chronicling the true West. It is most fitting that select columns and newspaper reports from his first seventeen years on *The Denver Post* are revived in book form.

What Charley Russell did to keep the West alive with paint brush, Red Fenwick did with his typewriter.

This offers an unusual opportunity for those who knew Red in person and in *The Denver Post* to relive and re-read his colorful stories and observations from years gone by. And it provides those who did not know Red or his writing in the past the unusual current opportunity to capture real tales and accounts of the West in the moving prose and vernacular of the region in the style that was only Fenwick's.

Red knew how to write to be read because he had lived the hard life on the range, in sheep camps, at cow towns, during drouth and blizzard, in good times and bad.

He traveled thousands of miles covering the West, picked up hundreds of real life stories, covered dozens of events and knew how to tell them so every reader could understand.

His name was synonomous with every western "going on." Walk into any cowboy bar, hotel, rodeo, county or state fair, stock show, Indian reservation, parade, cattle association or water meeting — and everybody there knew the name Red Fenwick. He had either been there, was there, or would be coming there later.

If there ever was a full-blooded, practicing, preaching, writing, living and breathing, loyally sincere, fiercely ardent exponent of the true West in word, life, manner and dress, it was Red Fenwick.

The proof is on the pages of this most worthwhile book.

Willard E. Simms

Red Fenwick

By

Mrs. Red (Donelle) Fenwick

It has been said the only friends Red Fenwick never had were those he never met.

Yet the country gentleman who rode the West with his typewriter felt every one of his readers — whom he lived to share this great West with — was his friend.

Red didn't write to them, he wrote for them. He talked with them, as he did each individual he personally met.

This is what made Red Fenwick the West's best loved representative — because he never forgot he was one of the "folks."

There probably isn't a rock in this part of the country Red didn't either walk on, ride over or pick up and look at.

Red's devotion and zest for life spanned from the golden burst of the sun glittering across the Rockies; to the candid curiosity of a child; to heralding our western heritage, crusty cowpunchers and cowboys; to the love of his ancestry — the mighty Irish.

As his country-raised child bride, I witnessed the gentle, caring attributes of a man who in the eyes of others, achieved greatness.

But in the eyes of my husband, he was merely the local yokel.

"Just an ole country gaffer," he'd say, "gettin' long in the tooth."

Red left each of us many trails to ride in our minds. The legend we call Fenner and friend tipped his hat to every story afforded him.

I see Red in the winter wheat leaning gently on the Wyoming hillside; in knarled posts lining mountain ranges now reminiscent of bygone wars fought over cattle and sheep; in the birth of a bull calf in early spring whose eyes yearn to experience a life of peace and rambling.

And I see Red in the sunset along a cool stream, where the rays dance reflectively upon the water recalling the shimmering life Red so generously shared with each of us.

As Red left this north forty, in my arms, to ride other ranges, I promised him I would finish his work.

Republishing *Red Fenwick's West, Yesterday and Today* was a project foremost on Red's mind because of the numerous requests from his readers.

A portion of the proceeds from this book will be designated to the Red Fenwick Memorial Journalism Scholorship Fund at the University of Wyoming where Red received his Honorary Doctorate of Laws Degree in 1976. Red's scholorship fund will aid in the education of our western students who desire to pursue a journalism career here in the West. Even in his final hours, Red was thinking of others.

As you relive the West Red gathered his zeal for life and appreciation from, do not let history close with the passing of the page.

When you wish to recall your childhood or seek the life you've never known — travel to the places Red wrote about: the small towns, ranches and farms, the mountain ranges non pareil.

It was the experience of such magnificent moments which manifested the salt of the earth in the man called "Red."

Remembering Red's words as you drive our western by-ways, look over yonder to the serenity of the country side.

There you just may see a shadow high on the hillside astride a paint horse, loping down across the prairie — bidding you to come join him.

The shadow you most likely see is Red Fenwick on his beloved G-Boy, at home, out Ridin' the Range . . . forever . . .

Right cordially yours,
Mrs. Red (Donelle) Fenwick

Table of Contents

INTRODUCTION, *by Palmer Hoyt*   9

ABOUT PLACES

My Heart's in Wyoming   13
Hurrah for Santa Fe!   20
The Death of the CY   21
Truth or Subsequences   23
Ah, Yellowstone   24
Alpha and Omega   25
I Like a Uke, Myself   27
Name of a Name!   28
The Saga of Newcastle   30
A Tale of Two Cities   32
Don't Feed the Animals   33
T-Days A-comin!   35
The Ghost's Gold   37
Over the Pass   38
'Vegas Was Wide Open   40
When Yellowstone Is White   42
Rough-ridin' Rawlins   43
Up in Dubois, Wyo., Everybody's a Friend   45
"Daddy of 'em All"   46
"High on the Hawg"   48
I'll Take Chugwater   50
The Big Horn Country   52

ABOUT PEOPLE

A Wild Goose Guy   57
T-Joe's Busy Season   58
Big, Tough and 76   60
Just Act Normal   61
The Speedy Salesman   63
Sold Again   64
It's Called Crow Soup   66
Just Call Me Irish   67
Why Ed Missed Supper   69
Jennie Was a Lady   71

Schoolmarm and a King   73
Dorothea at the Amador   74
Cow Country Doc   76
Wyoming Safari   77
Sam Sees Trouble Ahead for Humanity   78
Crisis on the Range   80
When Tony Got Mad   81
On Taking Up a Collection   83
Desert Business Woman   84
Canterbury Tale   85
"A Man Who. . ."   88
Maybe Next Year   90
Honest Ed Shows Up   91
Leave 'Em Smiling   93
Fast on the Drawers   95
Doc Said a Mouthful   96
The Undefeated Champ   98
Otto's Steamboat Ride   100
McFaddlefoot the Diviner   102
These Rugged Pioneers   103
Preacher on Horseback   105
Dick Jewell's Downfall   107
Sober Smith's Roan   109
The Lemon Peel Kid   110
The Amiable Amicks   112

SOME PERSONAL SLANTS

The Sun Worshiper   117
A Hick at Heart   118
Lost: A Place to Sit   120
She's a Jagalope   121
Dennis the Menace   123
Patrick Dennis Rebutts   125
Windy McCabe, Drummer   126
Saved by the Lens   128
He Didn't Stay Long   130
Pass the Biscuits   131
Our Daily Bread?   132
Encounter with the East   134
Blessed Are the Meek   135
Make Mine Winter   136

The Lucky Stiff 141
Firemen's Trumpet 143
AWOL for 80 years? 144
Funereal Fun 146
Mabel's Had Enough 147
How Sheep Tick Tom Got the Bird. . . 148
Too Proud to Walk 150
Sagebrush Robin Hood 151
Intelligence from Tolliver 153
Never Say Buy 154
Whose Rats? 155
Man of Courage 157
No Place Like Home 158
G.T.C.A.T.H.W.T. 159
Soft-Boiled Cop 161
The Heart Lake Monster 162
One Word of Caution 163
"Sure-Thing" Gamble 165
Blackie's Last Stand 166
The $3 Epitaph 168
Old Tip on Traffic 169
Such Interesting People 170
Pioneers from the Orient 172
The Last Stronghold 173
Seth Gets an Earful 175
Winner by a Natural 177
Old Fashioned Xmas 178
Grampf Loft Hif Teece 180
New Year at Poison Spider 182
Christmas on the Range 183
Zeb Rankin's Thanksgiving 185
Sheepherder's Eulogy 187
Where'd the Color Go? 189
These Changing Times 190

The West—As She Is

Schoolboy Spellbinder 195
Eau de Schoolroom 196

In Love with a School Marm 197
Lingo Learnin' 199
Who's Underprivileged? 201
Asafetida Time 203
Mother's Little Helper 204
Ladies' Home Companion 205
Oh, My Aching Epitaph! 207
Introduction to G-Boy 208
Love Comes to G-Boy 210
Consternation in Kansas 212
How Much Car-Power in a Horse? 213
No Limit on Jackalopes! 215
More about Jackalope 216
Proof, at Last! 218
Derby Day 220
"Here Comes Trusty" 222
Bush Time Coming Up 224
They're Off and Running! 225
Derby's Dastardly Disaster 227
Bores-a-Hole with Bullet 229
The Indian Wheel Mystery 231
Dance of the Man God 233
Ancient Wisdom 235
White Crow's Downfall 236
Miss White Eyes Would Baffle Brooklyn 237
Why I Don't Fish 239
The TRUTH about Fishing 240
For Good Old Dad 242
For A.A.-uld Lang Syne 243
Street Scene, Dec. 24 245
Words without Music 246
Comes the Resolution! 248
Cook's Christmas Comments 249
All Hail the Horse 250
Godiva of the Corrals 252
How to Get Along with Horses 253
Good for a Man 255
Saddle Savvy 257
Science Goes Too Far in Aiding Fair Sex 259
Pal Had Faith in Ab, and Bet $4 on It 261

Introduction

Shortly after I became editor and publisher of *The Denver Post* a decade ago, I had occasion to address the national convention of the National Editorial Association at Estes Park. Robert Wesley Fenwick, better known as Red for the hair which at that time still grew abundantly on his scalp, covered the meeting at which I spoke.

My talk was good if I do say it and made a good impression on the audience. It also made a considerable impression on Fenwick. After the meeting he came up to me, shook my hand and said with genuine admiration showing in his face: That was a great speech, Boss, who wrote it?

It happens that I write my own speeches, and I was obliged to inform Fenwick of this fact.

A lesser personality than Fenwick might have considered his utterance a major faux paus. But not Red. He was simply being his normal, candid, enthusiastic, completely honest self.

Fenwick has demonstrated these characteristics on many an occasion during his 15 years as a *Denver Post* reporter, columnist and emissary at large. He has distinguished himself in each of these capacities. I am sure that it is these very traits that have endeared him—with a few notable exceptions—to the people of the Rocky Mountain Empire. The exceptions are inevitable and to be expected in the case of any reporter worth his salt.

For some five years the 13 states of the Rocky Mountain Empire were Fenwick's beat. This is one-third the area of the United States. He traveled it incessantly. He talked to hundreds of persons each week, and each of them was a potential news source. In the far reaches of his beat he ferreted out stories of scope and significance that were unknown even to local reporters.

Today, years after we brought him into the home office, Fenwick is still as well known in Great Falls, Mont., or Las Cruces, N. M., as he is in Denver. This wide acquaintanceship with people and the land they live in is the secret of the popularity of Fenwick's weekly *Empire* magazine column, "Ridin' the Range."

We know that the column is read as faithfully in Denver as in Pinedale, Wyo., and Moab, Utah. When he wrote about picking up a stray pup and asked his readers to suggest a name, hundreds of children wrote in. His columns have been pinned up on the bulletin boards of such varied places as the old folks home in Thermopolis, Wyo., and W.C.T.U. headquarters at Scottsbluff, Neb., in miners' cabins, in livery stables and grade school classrooms.

Red was born in Indiana, spent his early childhood in Kentucky, but moved to Wyoming as a youngster. When he writes about "Douglas (my old home town), Wyo.," everybody in that section of the state talks about it. When he recalls working as a telephone lineman or riding in the horse cavalry, he gets immediate response from oldtime pole-jumpers and soldiers.

In his time Fenwick has covered some major stories for the *Post*. During the war he flew to Alaska, discovered waste on the Alcan highway and wrote a series which launched a congressional investigation. His probing uncovered facts which proved a convict's innocence and won him a pardon from a life term. His reports on the plight of the Navajos led to a nation-wide drive to help this unfortunate minority. He speaks the cattleman's language and he shares the dryland farmer's despair in drouth and joy in rainfall, for he has lived with them, reported intimately of them.

Of all Fenwick's writing assignments, he's proudest, I suspect, of the columns he turns out each week. That's why I am especially happy to see the best of "Ridin' the Range" assembled in this book. It makes a warm and fascinating record of one intensely vital mans' travels, thoughts, experiences and friends in what, to me, is the most wonderful region in the world.

PALMER HOYT
Editor and Publisher
The Denver Post

ABOUT PLACES

HRB

My Heart's in Wyoming

Ask most any oldtimer up in Wyoming what he thinks about the state and chances are he'll haul off and cuss up a purple storm. But suggest that he move elsewhere and you've a fight on your hands. To the ground-tied, raised-in-the-rough Wyomingite, there simply isn't any other place fit for human habitation unless, maybe, it's Colorado or Montana and there's some doubt about these two.

It's perfectly all right for the native Wyomingite to run down his state, but don't you try it. Not up in Wyoming, unless you're hankering to get your nose bloodied.

Two easterners (the dern furriners) learned this the hard way in a Thermopolis bar not long ago. They were abusing the Equality state with superlative invective: The wind blew too much; it was too hot; too cold; the people were clannish and unfriendly.

The last complaint did it. A tall cowpuncher standing nearby unlimbered two arms knotty as fenceposts. He rolled up his sleeves and threw both men out on the sidewalk. Then, as he planted a boot toe into their hinds, he sobbed, "Iffn you don't like Wyoming, go on back to New York. We don't stand for any remarks about our hospitality."

Wyoming is fiercely proud of its history, traditions, customs, people, resources, scenery and its own distinctive way of life. You have to ram around Wyoming a while and know it intimately to understand it. Some of the little amenities of life are revealing.

When you buy a round of drinks, you leave the change on the bar to demonstrate that your hospitality hasn't ended and that you respect the integrity of your friends, old or new-found. And you can expect any blue-jeaned cowpuncher to "spring back" with a round of his own, too, whether in the company of millionaires or oil field roustabouts. He's as good as anybody and so is his money.

The out-of-stater unfamiliar with Wyoming may gather the erroneous impression at this point that this is a somewhat sudsy report on the state. But it must be understood that in hale and hearty Wyoming the bar occupies a high place in the social life of most communities. Not a few businessmen refer to it only half jokingly as "the office." It is common practice for livestockmen to meet there and agree on stock and wool transactions approximating a million dollars while enjoying the favorite drink—a shot and ditch (bourbon with water chaser).

It must be remembered, too, that the bar may be the only public place open after the sun goes down on a little prairie or mountain town. Not many years ago refusal to drink with a man was an insult that called for gun pulling.

Wind-burned, sun-tanned Wyoming lives outdoors more than most states. The elements are strangers to no one. Everyone has battled a blizzard at one time or another and some, if pressed, can relate hair-raising accounts of their experiences. The pleasant soda jerker may have grown up on a ranch. The banker may have been a cowpuncher. A doctor may yet spend much of his time riding on inspections of his cattle or sheep.

Many men frequently are alone for months in the wide open spaces. They learn to cook their own bacon and beans and to make delicious biscuits merely by dumping the ingredients into the flour sack and working the dough with their hands. They wash their own dishes and hang their laundry on sagebrush. Needless to say, such living is conducive to the most fervent idolatry of all womanhood. It is accountable for the traditional gentle respect which range folk hold for their women and, paradoxically, it is directly responsible for the tolerant attitude toward prostitution.

Although the disparity between men and women has been reduced considerably since the 1880's when men outnumbered women better than two-to-one, there still are 114 men to every 100 women in Wyoming. (Go west, young woman. Go west!)

Self reliance runs strong in the state. A boy at 12 used to take a .30-.30 rifle, four horses and a wagon and freight the winter's supplies 60 or 70 miles from town. Today he handles a tractor at that

14

age if he's a ranch boy, and by the time he's 14 he can take down the motor and make repairs. He thinks nothing of handling the family jeep at 10, and I've seen 5-year-olds on horseback jingling the milk cows. Youths mature to firm flesh and much muscle at an early age in Wyoming.

They're not crowded for space, either. The 1950 census rated Wyoming next to Nevada as lowest of all the states in population (290,529), which averages out to three persons to every square mile.

There's an emptiness and timelessness to Wyoming that's difficult to describe. The vast distances create an illusion of complete removal from the rest of the world. The past still crowds in on the present so closely that "progress" vital to the city dweller is shrugged off in the cactus country. The rest of the world can go hang.

Because of these many influences, Wyoming has developed a rugged individualism all its own—not like the stanch conservatism of Kansas or like the righteous Republicanism of North Dakota. A Wyoming rancher may be broke, but he's never beaten. His range may be shriveling in the sun, but he'll swear that all he needs is rain. He usually gets it in time, too. Financially he might be pretty badly busted up, but there's something in the rough humor of Wyoming that causes him to see something funny in the fractures.

It is this spirit which accounts for the Wyomingite's freehandedness with money. (What the hell, the gov'ment's got lots of it.) This country has been the scene of some of the most fantastic booms and busts in the nation's history. Broke today? Tomorrow is a new day. Maybe it will bring something better—possibly even sudden riches. It has happened before and certainly no native lacks confidence that Wyoming can produce magically.

Paradoxically, Wyomingites like to carry silver dollars around in their pockets. The firmness and weight of cartwheels give them a feeling of substance that paper bills never can supply.

Currently, Wyoming is enjoying a boom that reminds folks vividly of the days immediately after World War I when Casper reached metropolis proportions (32,000) on a tidal wave of oil from the Salt Creek field. Tall buildings grew on the prairie where tar paper shacks stood only the day before. (Casper's population today, 33,731.) Speculators spent fortunes on a night of fun, confident they would recoup it the next day. Drillers, roughnecks, truck drivers and speculators flooded the town with money and the country's largest and gaudiest collection of painted ladies was there to gather it up.

Bill Henning came to Casper in those days on a freight train, slept the first night behind a signboard near the tracks. When he died a few years ago he left two fortunes, a hotel, a vault full of securities and one of the most magnificent mansions in the Rocky Mountain Empire. Bill imported the brick from England and moved into the house directly from the shack he had lived in up to that time.

Henning was no isolated example of success. Patrick J. Sullivan came to Wyoming, an Irish immigrant in search of a job. He landed at Rawlins, went to work herding sheep and a few years later commanded a fortune and a seat in the United States senate.

John B. Kendrick rode into the state behind a herd of long-horns from Texas, saw opportunity and rose to a fortune and a senatorship. Similar stories are abundant. Successful men of the state most often got theirs the hard way. That perhaps accounts for the difficulty in discerning between rich man and ranch hand. Both dress alike—in blue jeans and cowboy hat. Don't look down your nose at the man in overalls in Wyoming. He might own the bank. Wyoming doesn't stand much on ostentation, formality or social position.

Old Joe Back, Will Rogerish packer and hunting guide before he turned to art a few years ago, was hired to take an eastern moneybanks out from Dubois to hunt moose one fall. He gave the eastern nabob a lesson in western courtesy.

It happened when the hunter became discomfited in rugged country by something for which he blamed Joe. He expressed his displeasure by bawling out the guide much as he would a personal servant. Joe cussed right back with a vocabulary that always moved the stubbornest mules.

The big shot wasn't used to being spoken to in that fashion. He screamed that he could buy out Joe's outfit a hundred times over. Joe's retort was classic:

"If you ain't satisfied with the way this here spread's being run," he said, "you take some of that money of yours, go to any garage in these here mountains, buy yourself a new car and drive back to Dubois." They became fast friends.

16

The easterner's underestimation of Joe's character is no more exaggerated than the popular misconception of Wyoming's weather. Wyomingites mutter imprecations on city editors when they read weather stories which begin "An arctic blast swept out of Wyoming Tuesday and brought Colorado its first real taste of winter." They complain that Wyoming receives no credit whatsoever when cool breezes out of Wyoming bring blessed relief to Colorado in summer, thus enabling the Columbine state to live up to the claim of being the "climate capital of the world."

Wyoming is much maligned, too, by stories about its wind. Sure the wind does blow over much of the state's flat prairies. But weather records show that Lander has the least wind of any place in the nation, and Sheridan runs it a close second.

But what about those awful winters? Well, there are cold snaps. But they last only a few days. Then the sun shines. Wyoming has an average of about 250 days when the sun shines each year. Temperatures drop to a minus 30 for short periods in some areas during December, January and February. In summer the mercury seldom climbs above 90 and, even if it does, you usually can sleep under a blanket at night anywhere in the state.

Climate varies in sections of Wyoming. Valleys such as the Big Horn basin in north-central Wyoming are veritable "banana belts" of balmy winters, prolific farming and variety of growth.

Grass is the greatest factor in Wyoming history. Before the white man it brought the Indians in pursuit of the buffalo herds that fattened on the blue grass, wheat grasses, fescues and redtops —150 varieties in all. In turn came the cattle herds and cowpunchers and the sheep and their herders. Towns sprang up where enterprising individuals had built saloons and trading posts to serve the cross country trade on freight and cattle trails.

No one knows definitely who first saw Wyoming. Some French trappers came into the state as early as the 1740's, and one of them timidly named the three Teton mountains the Pilot Knobs. A far more imaginative lot of Frenchmen came along later, however, and dubbed the spectacular upthrusts *Les Trois Tetons*. Bluntly translated the terms mean "the three teats." The name took and remained to identify the Grand Tetons, the most beautiful mountain range on the continent, sometimes referred to as the American Alps.

John Colter left the Lewis and Clark expedition on its way

back from the Pacific, and became the first tourist to visit Yellowstone park. His stories about Wyoming's steam-heated natural wonder won it the appellation "Colter's Hell." In time came a grand cavalcade of adventurers and fortune seekers—Jim Bridger, Kit Carson, John Hunton, Buffalo Bill Cody, Calamity Jane, Wild Bill Hickok, cavalrymen, cowmen, sheepmen, gunmen, gamblers, miners, railroad builders, rustlers, and vigilantes.

Wyoming saw strife. Hardly had the shooting died down in the Indian wars when bitter feuds broke out over range and water rights. In the infamous Johnson county invasion only 62 years ago, troops had to be called in to rescue a handful of big cattlemen and some imported Texas gunslicks who had opened hostilities with so-called rustlers and settlers.

There were hangings and dry-gulch jobs in which good men and bad were disposed of. Whole bands of sheep were "rimrocked"— run over cliffs and killed by range jealous cowmen. Wyoming has settled down to more peaceful pursuits now. The carbine and the six-shooter have been put away and attention is focused on development of irrigation, electric power, oil fields, and sorely needed industry.

It is an odd comment on human nature that better than half the state's population came from somewhere else, and most of them have been trying ever since to make Wyoming over into something resembling the place from which they migrated. Only recently a former Chicagoan who had fled the congestion of the Windy City to find tranquility in one of Wyoming's peaceful communities, was leading a Chamber of Commerce fight to "attract big local industries."

There are, however, space-loving, outdoor-minded Wyoming-ites unalterably opposed to raising a crop of smokestacks. They don't want their clear horizons clouded with factory smoke and a smog pall.

Wyoming has one big industry that is dustless, smokeless and profitable—the tourists. It has many other assets—the greatest wild game herds in the nation; so many trout that Coloradans go there to fish; practically a monopoly on the earth's geysers; largest mineral hot springs anywhere; biggest and oldest rodeo; some of the finest schools and public assistance institutions in the U. S., and a loyalty to its own kith and kin that is unsurpassed. It has enough oil to float the American navy (85 million barrels last year with a value of $187½ million), and from it an income to the state ($2 million a year) sufficient to maintain an educational plant second to none.

Yellowstone National park is not only the biggest in the country (2 million tourists a year), it was the first national park. Devil's Tower, monolithic rock shaft that juts 600 feet from its base which in turn rises 600 feet above the Belle Fourche river, was the first national monument.

Wyoming was in the forefront in the matter of equal rights, too. The women who shared adventure and hardship of the frontier with their men were granted equal rights by the territorial legislature in 1869, first in the nation. In 1870 women served on juries in Laramie and in that same year the rip-roaring mining town of South Pass named Mrs. Esther M. Morris the first skirted juctice of the peace in the world.

In 1925 Nellie Tayloe Ross became the nation's first woman governor. In recent years she has led women from all states to Washington and high position by blazing a trail to the directorship of the national mint.

Needless to say, I love Wyoming. I love it because it is a man's world where every girl's a queen; where the latch string's always out but you don't ask a stranger's last name; where a spade's still a spade, the men are men and the women are glad of it and only a newcomer or a darned fool will predict the weather.

There is a land of skies so clear and blue that miles shrink to walking distance and you can reach out and pluck yourself a star 'most any night; an unspoiled, contented land of belly-deep grass, care-free folks, bottomless lakes, thundering mountain streams, dry creek beds with startling names like "Crazy Woman" and "Poison Spider," virgin forests and breathtaking purple vistas scented with sagebrush and evergreen and pulsating with the music of the meadowlark.

I love it for its majestic mountains; the bawl and bleat of mighty herds that form a symphony of loneliness with the cry of the coyote; for its wild horse herds, its bucking broncs and its flinty cowpokes. I love its vivid springs, its sun-splashed summers, radiant autumns and positive winters; it's oldtimers, the imagined creak of a covered wagon, a redskin's yell, the bark of a .45.

I love it for the friends I have there, for its two-inch steaks and for its colossal modesty which prompted the blushing slogan, "Wonderful Wyoming."

Wyoming doesn't brag. It doesn't have to. Bob Steiling, manager of the Newcastle Chamber of Commerce puts it this way:

"We're not like those Texans. We don't want the biggest of anything—only the best."

Hurrah for Santa Fe!

Maybe you're like most of us and don't have the moola to finance a trip abroad. And you'd like to enjoy something different from the usual tourist gimmick. You'd like to "get out of this world" and away from the humdrum, run-of-the-week montony.

Well, brother, you don't have far to go. Just pack your outdoor things—nothing stuffy—throw the kids in the car and drive down to romantic old Santa Fe. I say drive because an automobile is indispensable there. You'll find just a little more than a million things you'll want to see and do in and outside the fabulous New Mexico city. (Of course you *could* rent a car there from my old pal Paul Ragle.)

But why Santa Fe? I've kicked that question around considerably in the last few years and have at last decided that Santa Fe is my favorite resort area. If, for instance, someone from back east had only one vacation in his life to spend, and he wanted to visit the most interesting, exciting spot in America—I'd send him to Santa Fe.

Santa Fe has managed to absorb great population growth without losing one bit of its original, centuries-old atmosphere. The flavor remains. No easterners have come to Santa Fe to change the place into something resembling the miserable spot from which they escaped. Santa Fe is still the end of the trail, the beautiful, harmonious, friendly spot it always was. You don't hear talk there as you do in Denver, that we have made great progress in "easternizing the city."

Who the hell wants to easternize any part of the west? Who wants any part of the west to look exactly like the congested, standardized, un-individualized, tired and shop-worn east? If we like the east, we can always go there for a visit. And the east will continue to visit the west so long as it remains different—and that's why I love Santa Fe. It's different.

The missus and I were guests recently on a Chamber of Commerce tour of resorts at Santa Fe, arranged by my old buddy Hugh Gray. At the opening dinner at La Posada Duran, there were approximately 75 ladies—each dressed in a gorgeous squaw dress. The little woman, an expert in such matters, commented that she had not seen any two dresses alike in the entire crowd. That's the fashion there—Santa Fe's own fashion. Thank goodness there's one spot left in the west where the "style" dictates of effete France and the puny east do not dominate the thinking of women.

Possibly you think of these Santa Fe women as backward hogan-keepers vegetating in the social unenlightenment of the vanishing frontier. Mostly they are artists, the nationally prominent, shop-keepers, students, writers—and dress designers. And they looked radiantly beautiful in their striking costumery. No cheap calico, either. Some of these dresses cost far more than the average "formal" worn by the unimaginative, follow-the-sheep copy cats who undaringly bow east.

Needless to say, I like Santa Fe. I like its vast panoramic history, its friendly folks, its hospitality and its bold individuality.

The Death of the CY

It seems that at least somebody could have made a speech. But as it was, no one said a thing. There was no ceremony, no celebration, no hollering in the streets—nothing. They just went ahead and tore down the old red barn that had stood there for years by Highway 220, dug up the grazing land with bulldozers, ripped out the fences, poured a lot of concrete. And thus did Casper, Wyo., overrun the CY ranch on a little corner of which Judge Joseph M. Carey had founded the town in 1888.

There wasn't much there when Judge Carey trailed 15,000 head of cattle into the Platte valley the autumn of 1876. But in 1885 the Chicago & North Western railroad pushed its lines into the area and Judge Carey foresaw the makings of a sizable settlement. So he staked out a corner of the cow pasture for a townsite and by

June that year when the railroad came, about 100 persons had settled there.

Casper served as the terminus of the branch line until 1905 when the line was extended to Lander. In 1889 Casper's population numbered several hundred. There were eight saloons on main street and cowpunchers from the CY were among the best paying customers. For a while there was considerable hurrah and shooting, then Casper's more sedate city fathers passed an ordinance prohibiting the discharging of firearms in the city limits.

But that didn't prevent a subsequent mayor from beating an opponent to the draw on the city's streets a few years later, and the ordinance designed to keep women from cussing and drinking and smoking cigars didn't work too well.

Casper grew. It needed space for a city hall and a park. Judge Carey supplied it—free. The city began spreading toward the ranch along the old CY cattle trail which ultimately became known as CY avenue.

Like Denver, Casper had a water problem. The city bought a fancy fire fighting outfit and, for some time, the bright red equipment would charge to all fires and stand proudly while the blaze was extinguished by a volunteer brigade.

Then one day Casper was rocked to learn that it was the center of a gigantic oil boom. Overnight the shack town became a teeming metropolis of 30,000 oil stock promoters, drillers, truckers, tankies, roughnecks.

About that time a night club entertainer from Denver blew into town, sent his entire wardrobe to the cleaners to impress his manager and was so shocked by the bill he stayed and opened a cleaning establishment of his own. His name was Harry Yessness, and an old pal of mine even if he is worth a million now. Harry used to sell *Denver Posts* on Champa and Arapahoe streets. But from his clothing business which he entered later, he made enough money to buy the old CY ranch and not long ago subdivided it to allow growing Casper to let out its belt.

I was just a little sad the other day when Casper swept over the whole ranch, past the old barn and beyond the original homestead site of Judge Carey. I'd like to have made a speech.

Truth or Subsequences

If you've ever been down in the southern realm of the Land of Enchantment you no doubt remember the pleasant little, sun-splashed town of Hot Springs, N. M. I dropped rein there for a couple of days about five years ago and later composed a quite laudatory piece about the place.

Life in Hot Springs consisted mainly of just breathing in and out—not too rapidly, just fast enough to sustain a slow pulse. It was nice.

Nature had endowed the desert community generously with a seemingly inexhaustible hot spring that has a special appeal to rheumatic oldsters and the arthritic. This spring was, indeed, a wonderful tourist attraction. The spring, plus the fact that the sun shines warmly on winter days, made the place a mecca for creaking greybeards and their ladies.

According to the tourist folders, the bureau of reclamation had teamed up with nature and the citizens of the community to create "the world's largest body of impounded water" in a giant reservoir back of Elephant Butte dam on the Rio Grande river. Of course the recreation development program is a strong argument used by the bureau when all else fails to convince the natives that they ought to approve construction of this or that dam.

Well! On the way home from our recent vacation in Mexico, me and the missus decided to stop over in Hot Springs and spend a day loafing on the shores of this lake. First off I should note that I'd forgotten what had happened there.

The place has been renamed Truth or Subsequences or something like that, and only a little suburban town on the outskirts of Cash or Consequences retains the name of Hot Springs. Something about the personality of the town had changed, too. People were still friendly enough, but now they seemed to be more conscious of the fact that they were out to make a fast buck off the tourist traffic. Oh well, we would camp out.

We drove over to the lake. I never saw so many "no camping" signs. In fact there are few places on the map where there are more "no" signs than in this wonderful "recreation" area built by the taxpayers' money.

We couldn't drive up one road because there were some reclamation bureau homes up there and the people who live in them

23

don't like taxpayers poking around their neighborhood. We couldn't camp here and we couldn't camp there. We could, however, buy sandwiches and things like that in a little privately owned store over in the state park which New Mexico has built on the shores of the lake.

And they did have a place they called a campground where for 25 cents a night you couldn't put up a tent on the grass. You could conceivably sleep on the graveled parking if you parked your car on the grass. So we didn't stay there. We just took our cash and headed north with it and Truth or Subsequences paid the consequences.

Ah, Yellowstone

So far as scenery is concerned from the driver's point of view, the only difference I can see between Yellowstone Park and East Colfax Avenue is a little more variety in license plates on the cars that are always in front. Every hamlet in the country is represented in the park.

It was so crowded on my recent visit that a ban on all Texans was being considered for next year unless some agreement can be reached. Rangers estimated that if motorists from the Lone Star state were kept out, they could squeeze in each day at least 2,000 additional automobiles of ordinary length.

One Texan I saw was driving a custom job so long he had three horns. The first one warned that he was going to pass. The second was situated midway of the body and warned that he was still going by. And the one on the back honked "Earned in Texas from an oil well."

A roadside cleanup crew reported privately, however, that tourists were spending less money this year. There is less cleansing tissue in the ditches and the ratio of beer cans to bonded liquor bottles is running 500 to one.

Official statistics showed a drop in the number of tourists from last year, but at Old Faithful naturalists were trying to figure how to make the geyser erupt every thirty minutes instead of each hour so more people could see it and get the heck to going.

I tried to see some of my old friends up there—Bob Robinson,

Scotties Bowman and Chapman, Lee Coleman and a few others—
but planned my trip wrong. I was always in the outside lane of
traffic and couldn't get across the highway after finding a place to
park.

The first day of driving was good. I came in South gate and got
to Lake junction. But there traffic had stalled and the explanation
was that someone had stopped at Canyon (fifty miles up) to feed
a bear. A man and his wife got separated on opposite sides of the
highway at West Thumb, but they've managed to keep in touch
by air mail all summer.

Rumor has it that the park superintendent will ask for a record
appropriation this next fiscal year. He wants to annex Montana
and use it as a parking area and campground.

But honestly (it's about time, isn't it?) I've never seen Yellowstone in finer condition. Public facilities were clean, considering
the awful volume of traffic, roadsides were spic and span, roads
much improved over previous years and the crowding was being
taken good naturedly by park hands and visitors alike.

The only thing that is needed right now is a uniform and sternly
enforced bedtime hour in the campgrounds. The tents are so close
together that campers have less privacy than a roadside moose and
unless one gets into the sack before the snoring starts, he may as
well give up for the night.

Alpha and Omega

The New Mexico sun was belittling the best efforts of atomic
scientists at Los Alamos as we drove from ancient Taos and headed
southwest toward the brooding Jemez mountains. Old Sol was
putting on its best show.

For a long time it hung almost directly over the A-bomb capital
in dazzling brilliance. Then, just before it plunged out of sight to
refuel, it spread a golden canopy over the blue-purple distances,
touched fiery radiance to some fleecy white clouds and beamed
great spokes of light above the dimming valleys.

As we drove into the gathering quiet of evening, long fingers of
shadow wrote a promise of tomorrow and pointed insistently to
the direction from whence the sun would return. Lights behind

brown adobe walls winked on in the low places. Blessed cool routed the heat of day. And a comforting peace and calm of an age-old civilization settled upon the scrub-scented land.

The rapidly descending road led past contented villages, tiny streams and over deep arroyos. Truly, this was a land of enchantment. Spread below us and faintly visible in the dim light of a hesitant moon was the broad Espanola valley where men have lived in a state of advanced culture more than a thousand years. Here are some of America's oldest traces of continuous civilization.

The Pueblos San Juan, Santa Clara, San Ildefonso, Nambe and Taos are in the general area. A few miles from Espanola village is Chimayo, home of a proud people noted for their excellent blanket weaving.

Eastward, toward Truchas peak in the Sangre de Cristo range, are mud-walled villages that have changed but little since the first Spaniards settled there long before the eastern seaboard was populated.

Truchas, mountain retreat of narrow streets, hand-carved doorways and thick adobe walls against the winter cold; Las Trampas, relic of Spanish colonial days where harvesting is still done by hand; bloody Santa Cruz, scene of rebellions and treasury for rare books, old paintings and church ornaments. El Sanctuario, two miles south of Chimayo, is a sacred shrine credited with healing powers. Up the Chama valley and through Navajo canyon, the road leads to Tierra Amarilla, a study in antiquity.

Because of an erroneous belief that much of the country is closed to visitors because of the secret A-bomb development in the area, tourist travel is dropping off in the Espanola valley. The result has been noticeable. Store buildings are vacant and a hotel is for sale or lease.

This should not be. The area is open to travelers—open and begging for visitors. The only area they may not visit lies west where the sun went down—over there at Los Alamos where men are fashioning weapons capable of destroying civilization. Here in the Land of Enchantment are truly Alpha and Omega.

26

I Like a Uke, Myself

We couldn't get a room at the Jerome hotel when we arrived in Aspen. So we threw in with Elliott Roosevelt and some other commoners and stayed at Guido's. We sat so close together I could have reached over and touched him. I'd have like to touch him for about a half million.

It was my first experience in Walter Paepcke's summer haven for overheated musicians. I just picked the last of the cotton out of my ears only yesterday. If you can imagine Toscanini in rolled up blue jeans leading the Boston Pops, the chorus of the Metropolitan Opera company, Spike Jones' music slayers and Tex Beneke's aggregation in as many different tunes and all at the same time—you've got my impression of Aspen.

Aspen is the queerest mountain town I ever saw. They dug all the silver out of the hills around there and then took off with it. Paepcke brought it back in a bank book.

Noted as a ski-jumpin' joint by winter, it is, nevertheless, a piccolo player's paradise by summer. The annual music festival there attracts young musicians from all over the world. Each brings his or her instrument and all try to practice at the same time. Some of them seem to be utterly inexhaustible. They blow, puff and tootle, saw strings or sing songs seemingly around the clock. There's a music stand in every room in town and a boy or girl at every window in the rejuvenated village's ancient buildings.

If some of the old-timers could see what's above them on Aspen's streets they'd turn over in their graves. Young, skinny girls in horn-rim spectacles and baggy overalls; young fellows in slacks or shorts, lugging fiddles and wearing esthetic expressions. They give the old mining camp the appearance of a college campus.

Then, too, there are the rugged, barrel-chested, bare-headed Norsky types who stand around like toothpaste advertisements and look like they just wished it would blizzard so they could hit the slopes with their boards. They look healthy in a practiced sort of way and you can just tell they do 100 pushups before breakfast.

Into this collegiate collection of arched eyebrows are stirred culture-minded cosmopolites from Denver, generously plunging into the spirit of the whole thing driving Jeeps and Cadillacs, wearing masters' degrees and fraternity pins and hoping somebody will recognize that the tune they are whistling is Beethoven's first movement.

Thing I liked most about Aspen was Guido Meyer's hotcakes. He made them for American airmen in Switzerland before he came to this country just after the war. They loved his hotcakes, too. He loved the airmen. Then he moved to Aspen, met for the first time a Swiss maid named Trudi who grew up ten miles from where he lived in Switzerland, married her, opened a new restaurant and lodge and got his first taste of American competition which he doesn't like as much as the air force boys.

Name of a Name!

Fellow up in Big Piney, Wyo., wants to know if "Lady Wonder," the talking horse, had anything to do with naming Denver's streets. If not, sez he, somebody must have pulled the names out of a hat at a Halloween party and stuck them up at random.

Research shows that one Bill McGaa had much to do with naming the streets. For this and other contributions, the city fathers named a street after McGaa. They later regretted the action and rubbed out his name.

McGaa had been a stellar character of exceeding community pride with an unquenchable thirst for (among other things) civic improvements. Indeed, so fierce were this thirst and pride that McGaa embarked on frequent projects to paint the town red.

McGaa was considerably put out when the town dads hauled down his name on McGaa street and changed it to Holladay in honor of the Overland stage company man. So McGaa moved to Laporte, Colo. His community interest in Denver was unflagging, however. McGaa continued his painting project in the city and made frequent excursions here to complete the job.

On one of these, McGaa was taken to a cell in city jail to sober up. Next morning he was found dead.

Nevertheless, Holladay street went on to bigger things. Commercialized sin became big business on the street. Merchants dealing in more legitimate wares in desperation had the name changed to Market street, thus hoping to confound and discourage dealers in wickedness.

It didn't work. The fleshpots stayed. So did the name Market street. But the good and righteous folk on the north end of the thoroughfare rose up in great indignation and seceded. They changed the name of their end to Walnut.

And all that helped to make for just one of the many minor confusions forever cast upon succeeding generations of Denverites by the street namers.

History records that pioneer settlers at first wanted to use the national capital's system of letters and numerals. It worked for a time, but soon the city was a confusion of arithmetic with four First streets; three Fourth streets; two Gilpin streets; two Denver streets; two Fairview avenues; three Fifth streets and numerous pairs of duplication.

McGaa gave the town some colorful names. Wewatta supposedly was chosen in honor of an Indian squaw who won considerable favor with McGaa.

For one particularly busy street, McGaa came up with the name Wazee. Nobody ever bothered to find out what it meant. Wapoola street was named after Trader John S. Smith's squaw but an unpoetic city council changed it later on to Court place. A neighboring artery had been named in honor of Capt. J. T. Parkinson, an estimable citizen. But the council changed that to Cleveland place.

Tremont came about its name because of a desertion. William Clancey, after whom the street originally was named, left Denver so the council rubbed out Clancey's name, too.

The Saga of Newcastle

JENNIE ELLIS' HEALTH SHOP

HRB

Frankly speaking, my first impression of Newcastle, Wyo., was that they shouldn't have done it. That was one night back in the early 1920's. Clay Chambers of Douglas (my old home town), Wyo., and I were passing through en route to Hot Springs, S. D., in a brand new model T Ford.

We were going to visit a friend in Hot Springs. On his request, and for that reason and no other—honest—we stopped to pick up two small flasks of Red Lodge, Mont., spring tonic which was extremely difficult to purchase in those days unless you knew the right people. Jennie Ellis, about whom more will be said in this department at a subsequent date, was one of those people.

Well, while we were inside haggling with Jennie over the price of the stuff, somebody stole a tire off our model T. After that, neither of us ever gave a whoop about staying in Newcastle.

Right to this day I always sneak through the place as though expecting unpleasantries with the sheriff.

Once, a couple of years ago, however, I did pause there long enough to jot down a few harsh words about the condition of Newcastle's streets. Later on, my observations were published and

30

brought down the wrath of the entire community. At the time, just the same, the streets were as corrugated as a night marshal's knuckles in a boom town on Saturday.

But oil, sudden wealth, and a spectacular rash of civic pride have changed all that. The streets have been modernized, other municipal improvements made—and a new sheriff has been elected.

Newcastle, built on coal, has been washed to the forefront of Wyoming cities on a tidal wave of oil. It boasts a gaudy past and a promising future. It is famous for its Republican politicians, a determined minority of Democrats, a junketing mayor, bald-headed Chamber of Commerce manager, the Newcastle *News Letter-Journal* and Jennie Ellis.

Newcastle, situated in the northeast corner of the state, was born officially the year the old century died. It probably could be said that it nursed in infancy at the tipple of the Cambria coal mines seven miles up the canyon from Newcastle.

J. H. Hemingway, superintendent of the coal camp, named the town after his birthplace in England. But it remained for an individual named Deloss Tubbs of Custer, S. D., to inject real life into the arteries of the little frontier community.

Before Newcastle had a chance to gain any prominence whatsoever, Tubbs decided to build a town of his own on the railroad that was then being surveyed west from Edgemont, S. D. So he put up a store and a bar. That was enough to start anything in those days. Tubbs built on the east bank of Salt creek on the Belle Fourche and Custer trail.

Another bar followed, railroad outfits flocked to the new town, and in three months it boasted three saloons, two dance halls, two eating houses, a milkman, and a Chinese laundry.

A city ordinance was passed with considerable formality and great show of enforcement, making it mandatory for anyone passing that way to "set 'em up for the bunch."

The town ran wide open, all stops pulled, day and night, until a newspaper, the *Stockdale Journal,* set up and published in its second edition that the railroad was to run through Newcastle.

Within forty-eight hours, the whole of "Tubbs Town" was on the move—dance halls, saloons, general stores and all—toward Newcastle. Thus did "Tubbs Town" become the first to carry coals to Newcastle.

A Tale of Two Cities

A gayer and more fantastic safari never hit a western trail than the one we began to tell about last week in our column on Newcastle, Wyo. That hilarious spectacle lit out of Tubb Town, Wyo., on a September day back in 1889 like something ablaze. It resembled a mixture of a Chinese fire drill, war refugee column and a barroom brawl that had outgrown its quarters.

In it was Tubb Town in its entirety, bent on blending its culture with that of the foundling community of Newcastle which had bloomed suddenly on a coal mine and railroad construction boom.

The motley column included Tubb Town's general store, an enterprise founded by the foresighted Deloss Tubbs; the community's two-week-old newspaper, the *Stockade Journal;* a collection of frontier saloon-keepers together with their liquor stock and disorderely patrons; the dancehalls; Chinese laundry and all the disorganized municipality's citizens of varied worth.

Not to be overlooked was a contingent of approximately forty "dancehall girls," most notable among them being Big Maude, Old Humpy and Jimmy The Tough. It was Jimmy The Tough who won undying fame for, among other things, horsemanship by once accepting a bet from a cowpuncher that she couldn't ride his cayuse.

Clad only in a chemise—that's what they used to call women's underwear—Jimmy raced out of one of the town's bistros before a delighted audience of wide-eyed and somewhat inebriated cowboys, and leaped into the saddle. With miraculous mastery of the cowboy's horse, Jimmy loped up and down the street, took a little side junket into the woods, and returned to receive the plaudits of her admirers.

Tubb Town burst upon Newcastle like Russian cossacks on a vodka tear. Then and there they established as common practice the custom of galloping up and down the main street on horseback, hollering and filling the air with six-shooter lead.

Newcastle was wild and woolly. From the mines at nearby Cambria flowed payroll dollars that kept the roulet wheels oiled and the three-card monte games going full blast. Railroad construction men from the camp on Goose creek pumped life aplenty into the arteries of the thriving hurrah village.

A month after the wedding of Newcastle and Tubb Town, the marriage was made official by incorporation. Nov. 12 a city election was held, Frank W. Mondell became the first mayor and launched what was to become one of Wyoming's most memorable political careers.

Either Newcastle's gunmen were notoriously poor shots or were just plain having fun, for history records that actual wounds were as scarce as social workers at the time. Nevertheless, the practice of gun-toting was frowned upon by the city fathers, and the time-honored routine of shooting up the town was held in even lower favor.

So the first act of the new city government was to ban such entertainment. Jim Swisher was hired as marshal. The first night he was on duty, the sleep of the city's government heads was shattered by an ear-splitting yell and a volley of shots fired by none other than the mayor's own friend, Hunter Bowen.

Bowen paid a $50 fine. Some women established a Sunday school which was supplied with beer-keg seats, the boys quit using their guns on the streets (with some exceptions), and Newcastle set about attaining respectability. This precipitated a sharp drop in population. Some citizens left of their own volition. An equal number departed by invitation.

Don't Feed the Animals

It was a dramatic little scene there in the ranger's office at Canyon, in Yellowstone National Park. A New Yorker who walked like a soprano and talked like he was directing the Boston Pops orchestra, was complaining about the bad conduct of one of the government's bears.

This cute little fellow—he just knew he must have been somebody's pet, he could tell by the way he came up to get cookies—was standing outside the tourist cabin when the man from New York got up that morning.

There were some biscuits left over from breakfast, so the man from New York took them out to the cute little bear. Now this particular little bear wasn't fat, so the sign about not feeding the bears surely didn't apply in his case.

Therefore, and with commendable caution aforethought—he put on a pair of kid gloves just in case—the kindly tourist tossed some cookies and biscuits to the cute little bear who didn't seem to be afraid at all. In fact, he came real close to the nice man from New York.

But when the cookies were all gone, the bear demonstrated a regretful lack of appreciation and manners in general. It wasn't so much what the bear did overtly that bothered the man from back east. It was what he did behind his back that annoyed him.

Just as the nice man turned to go back into the cabin, the bear wounded the man's dignity. In fact, he was unable to sit on it for several days.

And that's what happens to kind tourists who believe that the "Don't Feed the Bears" signs are put up for dietary protection of the bears.

Honest Injun, visitor, them there b'ar are not pets. They're wilder'n Comanches on a Saturday night jag off the reservation. Give 'em a chance and they'll eat your hand off right up to the elbow.

Another dangerous critter that appears deceptively docile is the buffalo. You may call him a bison if you want to. But if he demolishes your bumper, tears off your fenders and, even possibly, knocks you higher than tomorrow's meat prices, you'll call him things we can't print here.

Mostly you'll find buffalo in Yellowstone Park and Custer State Park in South Dakota. They have the big herds, but others are scattered over the Rocky Mountain Empire.

And, for heaven's sake, don't enrage a moose. Up around the Jackson Hole-Grand Teton country, you will see plenty of them. View them from a safe distance. Remember, none of the aforegoing animals like closeup photographs. They might give you an autograph that won't rub off.

Just for safety's sake, too, it's always best to look and make sure that the fence you're climbing isn't the one around the bull pasture. Even though most bulls nowadays look like oversize office desks, some of them still will put you and your picnic basket right up a tree.

There are a few varmints, too, that you must watch out for.

Wood ticks are small brown bugs widely prevalent in livestock and wildlife country. It is possible that a bite from an infected tick will cause serious illness. They become increasingly scarce as the summer wears on, and they're not too difficult to find on the body. If one digs in, put turpentine on him or hold a match close enough to warm him up, and he'll back out. Don't pull him off and leave his head buried.

Snakes? Our breed of snakes, like our wolves, are found mostly in cocktail lounges and night clubs. At high altitude there are none at all. Only rattlers are dangerous. Whisky, darn it, is not a snake bite antidote. It makes it worse. Anti-venom kits can be rented at almost any drugstore at a nominal cost. If you're out in the open country, carry one. The filling station man can tell you if you're in rattler country.

Welcome, tourist, to the vacation paradise!

T-Days A-comin!

Our boots-and-saddle governor, Dan Thornton, declared in a political speech recently that Colorado is destined soon to become a state of 5 million souls. That's a lot of souls.

But the significant part of that statement escaped most people as neatly as a Denver county jail prisoner.

Dan had not long ago been down Texas way, from whence he came to the Columbine state a decade ago. Undoubtedly he visited with a lot of old Texas cronies while there. And maybe he got a piece of information he hasn't cut all of us in on yet.

Now it is well known that no governor wants to come by an undeserved reputation for loose talk except, maybe, in such matters as political promises, taxes and appropriations, which can always be laughed off later on. So it is safe to assume that Dan knows what he is talking about.

But so far, it is only possible to speculate on what he meant by the forecast of great population growth for us.

To anybody with anything approaching 20-20 vision, it has been clearly apparent in recent years that Texans have been coming into Colorado like rich refugees fleeing a conquering tax collector.

They've bought homes, ranches, businesses, oil wells, leases, farms, interests and banks and have staked a wide claim on the gold and climate of both the eastern and western slopes.

At one time the invasion became so pronounced that a Walsenburg beauty shop operator staked up a big sign in front of her paint and curl business declaring "Texans Welcome!"

Could Thornton mean that Colorado's new population millions will come from Texas? Could it mean that Dallas and Fort Worth will be drained? That Amarillo will pull stakes and move to the land of the Rockies?

If so, Dan should up and tell us about it right now so we could get ready for the changeover. Some drastic revamping will have to take place.

The Colorado flag may as well get set for the addition of the Lone Star. There'll have to be a new song—*"The Eyes of Texarado Are Upon You."*

And school kids will have to learn all about Sam Houston and the Alamo with fresh emphasis on the historic importance of the two.

Anybody with less than $10 million automatically will be in the peon class. However, there will be general prosperity, an oil well in every backyard and a millionaire uncle in every family.

Football teams won't dare use anything except the "T" formation without running the risk of being jailed for treason.

Colorado products will bear the stamp for all the world to see: "Made in Colorado by Texans."

The most popular undergarment sold in stores to the younger set will, of course, be the "T" shirt.

Nobody seeking political office will ever get elected unless he can boast some family connection with the Houstons, the King ranch, Davy Crockett, the Texas & Pacific railroad or the Texas Rangers.

The Rio Grande railroad will be known as the Dallas & Rio Grande Waco and there will be only one oil company allowed corner franchises in our big cities.

Hang onto your Confederate money, son. The Mason-Dixon line is moving nawth, suh.

The Ghost's Gold

The kid named Chester (Friday) Rogers jerked to a stop in half-stride, his feet paralyzed by fright. A soggy beam of light from his carbide lamp stabbed the blackness of the old cave and wavered as his hand shook. The bobbing shadows of dripping stalactites danced crazily on the cavern wall.

What horrified Friday was the thing on the damp floor.

He had penetrated miles deep into the myriad corridors that honeycombed the mountain up Clear Creek canyon. He had chalked his way in so he could find his way out. Now he wanted to run.

Suddenly, and as unexpectedly as death itself, the beam of light had fallen on the grotesque figure of an ancient and withered man sprawled incongruously on the floor of a subterranean room. Friday wished he hadn't played hooky that particular Friday—a practice which won him the nickname he carried to the grave not so very long ago.

The old man clawed at the beam of light as though it were a living thing. It seared his eyeballs. He squirmed in torture. Then suddenly he broke into a confusing gibberish.

"Don't let anybody get my gold!" he screamed. Then he leaped to his feet and with insane yells raced down one of the black corridors that led from the room.

After a moment, Friday followed—cautiously. His feet again came to a stop, this time at the brink of a bottomless pit that sliced across the floor of the cave. There was only silence below, beyond and all around.

Back in the big cavern Friday took stock of what had happened. In the big room were some scattered cooking utensils and tattered bedding. Apparently the ancient one had lived here many months —if not years.

Friday's light slowly circled the room, came to a halt on a narrow ledge. Back of a protecting rock nestled a row of small bulging sacks.

The boy's fingers groped along the shelf, caught at one of the sacks and pulled it down. It hit the floor with a heavy thud. The string came off and out spilled a king's ransom in gold nuggets.

Friday did a championship sprint toward the mouth of the cave. He stumbled and fell. He floundered into blind turns, lost his way several times but finally gained the shaft opening and half ran, half rolled down the mountainside toward his home in Golden.

Well, nobody believed his story. And Chester Rogers became the butt of many a joke. He returned to the cave eventually with a friend. But nowhere could he find the three corners in the cave where one shaft led off to the rich cache.

Some folks said Friday just spun the yarn to get drinks at the bar. Some said he had taken one too many drinks and had imagined the whole thing.

But Carl Hall Hungness, who lives at 915 Illinois Street in Golden, recalled the 1890 incident not long ago, and undertook to locate the caves and the "lost cache of the mountain ghost."

He and a friend explored the mountainside and found the cave. For hours they poked through the seemingly endless caverns and passageways, but to no avail.

The mysterious caveman and his lost fortune in nuggets had vanished as completely as had Friday Rogers who had crossed the Great Divide, no doubt in continued search of the fabulous find.

But Hungness says any fortune seekers who care to brave a few rattlesnakes and fight off swarms of bats, can find adventure—and maybe sudden riches in the old caves now easily accessible by way of the new Clear Creek canyon road.

The caves are just west of Golden, around the first bend in the highway, past the first tunnel and just beyond the trickle of water from the mountainside.

Last one in this Sunday just doesn't hanker for hidden treasure.

Over the Pass

The sleepy peaks of the Sangre de Cristo mountain range, off in the distance to the west of us, were nodding in their fleecy white blankets. Snugly bundled, cozy and comfy in their Colorado cradle, they were ready for a long winter night's dream of spring.

Without warning, they suddenly blushed clear to their foothills. The brash February sun had leaned impulsively across the broad Pacific and had boldly kissed them a fond goodnight.

Behind us a lazy drift of smoke marked the spot where Trinidad lay buried in the shadows. Above us towered the crags of Fisher's peak, its ramparts catching the last rays of the sinking sun and reflecting them in broad golden spokes into the canyon gloom.

A chill breeze scurried about on its nocturnal rounds among the junipers and *pinon* trees, rousing the slumbering ghosts of the old Santa Fe trail. Presently the dim canyon was alive with moving figures. Some walked alone carrying long rifles. Others trudged beside straining ox teams that struggled laboriously upward over the faint trail, pulling big, creaking wagons behind them.

Raton pass—broad and bloody imprint on the frontier—was putting on its show for the imaginative who love the romance of the old west enough to spend an hour there at sundown.

For me it was a repeat performance, an encore, so to speak, for I had stopped there many times to get the feel of the place. I had almost developed a speaking acquaintance with some of the shades of the past, it seemed. They were buckskinned figures, some of them; some exhausted, some fired with a feverish hunger for gold and quick riches, some bent on revenge, some out for adventure, but all writing a colorful chapter in the history of this spirited land of tall peaks, big men, broad prairies and happy cities.

To me, Raton pass has long been a tonic for a tired soul—a retreat from the congestion of the city, a restorative revitalizer that soothes while it rekindles the flame of life.

Always, after an hour's stop there, I look forward almost with pioneer enthusiasm to the remaining trip to Las Vegas that invariably completes the restoration.

The junket is never monotonous—not one inch of it. Raton, the city, never fails to surprise me for some reason or other. Springer and Wagon Mound, and the other cowtowns along the way, always are inviting, always colorful. The great lava flows never fail to intrigue, and the purple distances never disappoint.

There's usually something new and modern to be found, too. At Raton, for instance, the Crystal cocktail lounge and cafe, sports the only glass dance floor to my knowledge in these parts.

Not many years ago I was writing some articles boosting development of western industries based on domestic natural resources. Glass dance floors were suggested as a potential market for our silica sands.

Proprietor Charles Marchiondo is justly proud of his innovation. A rainbow of lights beneath the dancers' feet lends a new and fascinating touch to tripping the light fantastic.

39

Modern eating establishments and inviting automobile courts characterize Raton's highway entrance from the south. They never fail to cause someone in the crowd to comment:

"My, hasn't Raton grown since they opened La Mesa race track."

But Raton's growth wasn't entirely attained to the tune of drumming horses' hooves. They say Raton's climate is excellent for sufferers of respiratory diseases. It is the center of a large stock country, and its coal deposits are blood brothers of the big veins that make up an industry in neighboring Colorado.

'Vegas Was Wide Open

They haven't had a good necktie party down Las Vegas way since they tore down the windmill in the old plaza and dismantled the cover over the Gallinas creek bridge.

Time was when a man could go to town there 'most any Saturday night and see a first-class grade A hanging with a shooting affray thrown in to offset the amusement tax.

When a gent became too obstreperous a few of the boys would cull him out, take him down to either the windmill or the bridge and put a lot of good, clean New Mexico atmosphere between his boots and the ground.

Yea, verily, Las Vegas was a good, wholesome, hell-roaring town that bristled with six-guns, barrooms, bawdy houses, boardwalks and booby traps.

There you could get a shot or get shot at with equal ease. It was no trick to get into trouble at all. Almost anybody would accommodate the fuss addict.

It got so bad there at one time that a big notice had to be posted. It let it be known to one and all that the forces of decency and law and order were taking over and soon would bring culture, taxes, restrictions, taxes, good government, taxes, regulations, taxes, peace and quiet. The notice that put an end to the good old days said:

"Notice to thieves, thugs, fakirs and bunko steerers among whom are J. J. Harlin, alias 'Off Wheeler,' Sawdust Charlie, William Hedges, Billy the Kid, Billy Mullin, Little Jack the Cutter,

Pock-marked Kid and about twenty others: If found within the limits of this city after 10 p. m. this night, you will be invited to attend a grand necktie party, the expense of which will be borne by 100 substantial citizens."

When they ran out the thieves, the politicians took over as they had everywhere, and now, instead of hangings and shootings, they have elections.

Much of the old-time atmosphere continues to surround Las Vegas with an aura of romance that tends spectacularly to set it apart from other cities of the Rocky Mountain Empire. In fact, the historic old spot stands out in the company of western towns like a loaded hip pocket at a church bazaar.

It affords my own particular brand of relaxation, contentment and peace. I like its ramshackle, antique mansions that cling to the wind-scooped soil like tottering, grey-headed old men in the sun; I like its low, thick-walled adobe houses, its massive, imperturbable churches, peaceful people, barren hills and plains and its unperishing spirit.

When it's dry there, it's drier than the blistered plains of Hades. But there's always a moist, cool spot downtown, and the owner of it is "Uncle" Earl Augerot, whose greatest complaint in life is that he and his son wear the same size shirts.

Earl used to live in Denver, but he moved out when it got crowded as they started to build homes along Colorado boulevard. He likes Las Vegas. He opines, though, that many good characters no longer exist.

When he names them, he leaves no doubt that Las Vegas was most richly endowed with nicknames. Here are a few:

Caribou Brown, Dirty Face Mike, Hoodoo Brown, Scar-face Charlie, Pawnee Bill, Kickapoo George, Jack-knife Jack, Flyspeck Sam, Mysterious Dave and Hatchetface Kid. Then there were such lovely kids as the Durango Kid, Pancake Billy, Wink the Barber, Doubleout Sam, Minnie the Duck, Flapjack Bill, Buckskin Joe, Cold-deck George, Pegleg Dick, Ted River Tom, Hog Jones, Long Lon, Soapy Smith, Stuttering Tom, Tommy the Poet and, of course, Billy the Kid.

They made up the worst gang of cutthroats, rascals and bandits ever to infest that part of the west.

But they made Las Vegas a fine town; they left it, many of them via the long rope route.

41

When Yellowstone Is White

This should be right around the "season of the second pipe" up in frosty old Yellowstone National Park. In case you don't know it, the "season of the second pipe" is pretty far advanced into the winter.

It's that time of year when hardy park rangers add another length of stovepipe on top of their snowshoe cabins. The reason for this regular formality is simple enough:

The snowshoe cabins are overnight shelters for the men who patrol the park's fortunes in game against poachers. And the stovepipes guide the patrolling rangers to the exact spot where they start shoveling snow to get down to the cabin entrance.

That, neighbor, is a pile of snow!

But the average trail-toughened, year-around park ranger in Yellowstone or any other of our national parks, is usually a sizable pile of man. So, dig out he does—and with gusto, too, because there's dry firewood, warm beds and solid food inside that cabin.

There are some good yarns of the trail in Yellowstone. Many a man has shivered out a chill afternoon in a tree because some outraged moose has elected to lay siege to him.

Grouchy grizzlies just coming out of hibernation in the spring are not exactly the most congenial trailside companions, either. And a bull elk can give a man on skis a bad time for hours on end. Both are plentiful in the dense forests and open meadows of Yellowstone.

As if these hazards and hardships weren't enough, the hardworking ranger sometimes finds himself subjected to the hilariously funny practical jokes of his own buddies.

Can't recall the fellow's name right now, but one ranger conversely dubbed "Tiny" once toted a cannon ball all the way from the Lake ranger station to the Canyon ranger station and didn't even know it.

He arrived at Canyon in a state of near exhaustion after his nearly forty-mile hike on skis. He complained of not feeling well, spoke of his failing strength and went to bed early.

Next morning he found the cannon ball in his pack sack, so on the homeward trip he carried the thing back with him so he could stash it in the pack sack of the buddy who had tricked him.

George Bagley once spent a hectic night stranded in the middle of Yellowstone lake—on skis! Because of the warm springs on the lake bottom, the ice usually goes off in one day. It honeycombs and—swoosh—it's gone.

Before Bagley became an official, he was patrolling across the lake one day when the temperature soared unexpectedly. The ice dropped, but fortunately Bagley, who was crossing the lake on skis, was on an island. His buddies rescued him.

At the outset of winter, the rangers used to "buddy up" for their winter stations. Remote Snake river station at the south entrance, and Bechler river station on the Idaho side in the southwest corner of the park, were the two least choice spots.

A hundred miles of snow-blanketed trail lay between them and the headquarters at Mammoth. And reports were required once a month.

Before the rule permitted rangers to keep their wives with them during the winter months, there were many tales of "cabin fever" among the buddies.

Because one of the two buddies one day came in and hung his cap on the nail reserved for the other, his cabin mate spent the entire winter in monastic silence.

Any bachelor can see the logic of letting the rangers have their wives with them during the long months of isolation.

They're so busy battling with their better halves that the company of their working partners is welcome, indeed!

Rough-ridin' Rawlins

Anything even remotely resembling it in Denver would be termed an attention-all-cars riot of page one proportions. In Texas it would result in calling out the ranger force. In the effete east it probably would be cause to bring out the militia.

But up in rough-and-ready Holden's Hole, Wyo., it was considered just plain boot-bustin', three-dimensional frontier fun. It was the type of fun enjoyed by the descendants of rugged pioneers of the beans-and-bacon variety that tamed the west.

I'm talking about the annual town-wrecking that goes on under the guise of a celebration each year during the big Antelope Derby in that plains metropolis frequently referred to in timetables and highway maps as Rawlins, Wyo.

I personally prefer the name Holden's Hole because of the Holden boys—Paul, Chuck, Eddie and Dick—whose guest I was during the recent antelope chase. And speaking of the Holdens, don't miss the chance to feast the glimmers on Paul's petite wife, Teri. She'd make Venus hunt a hogan.

Well, call it whatever you want to. That Union Pacific town knows how to put on a blowout. In fact, my old friend, Roscoe Ates, the stuttering western movie star, just about got his "head blowed off" during the fracas.

Somebody fired a .45 too near his head and he got powder burns. It was during one of the quieter moments of the occasion and somebody wanted to stir things up some.

Another couple of yahoos—Mark Jackson and Leo Schinkel— who hail from the Elk Mountain region, shot a hole in the ceiling of Paul Holden's Teton bar with a shotgun. Then they woke up the dead with a combination trumpet and banjo show that would have done justice to any Broadway vodvil.

Everybody in town had to grow whiskers. Even the antelope I got had 'em. The day after the show ended nobody knew anybody else. Introductions were going on all over the place.

After it was all over the silence by comparison sounded like a double-header freight running through the city hall. The big shindig proved wilder than the one when they strung up Big Nose George down in front of the Senate saloon and skinned enough of him to make a pair of shoes and a coin purse.

But don't get the impression that Rawlins is a backwoods, stiff-neck city. It just plays that way for its own fun and the amusement of the visitors who are, I must admit, sometimes a bit surprised at the antics that go on.

Rawlins is an up-and-coming city of excellent—far better than average—municipal facilities. Its city hall, courthouse and new school, just under construction, are tops in Wyoming for beauty and utility.

Its mayor, Sam Tully, is typical of the community-mindedness of Rawlins' citizens. Twice elected, Tully is a brakeman for the railroad. It is not unusual at all to see him hurry into the city hall on his way home from work still wearing his overalls.

A few days ago he laid off work to personally investigate the

44

death of a Rawlins child who had been struck by a city truck. Part of the investigation included a test run of the truck by his honor in person.

When the plumbing gets plugged (as it did when the whiskers came off) you can expect that a call to the city hall will bring the mayor on the run to take a closeup gander at the trouble.

He maintains a year-'round employment agency free of charge for Rawlins kids, believes they are better off earning a few dimes in the summer mowing lawns, putting up hay and doing odd chores than they would be idle.

To one and all in Rawlins, I'd like to say thank you for one of the grandest week-long entertainments I have ever had.

Up in Dubois, Wyo., Everybody's a Friend

You ask the telephone operator for a number up here, and if you're used to the ways of the big city you might be surprised by the result.

That will be Mrs. Al Boland on the switchboard, and she's likely to say: "Won't do any good to ring there. They went hunting. But if you hurry, you might catch them at the grocery store. They were going to get some crackers."

Now, Mrs. Boland had not been snooping. In a town of 500 it would not be unlikely that Mrs. Boland knows everything that goes on. Anyhow, the Smiths probably telephoned Mrs. Boland and had asked her to tell callers they would not be at home. That's the way things are up here. Everybody knows everybody else and what everybody else is doing.

That's how come the postmaster, Les Luedtke formerly of Lusk, Wyo., got himself thrown bodily a few nights ago into the chill waters of the Big Wind river.

Everybody knew Les was getting married. So in a spirit of high good comradeship they charivaried him and "throwed old Les in the crick, by golly." They would have thrown his bride, Anne Sundstrom, in with him but they couldn't catch up with her.

Dubois was named after some forgotten Frenchman who trekked through the country years ago. It is perhaps more familiar to Hollywood screen figures and big business executives from the east than it is to the average citizen in Cheyenne. It is a mecca for tourists and big game hunters who follow Francis Titterington's pack strings into the high country this time of year in search of Big Horn mountain sheep, elk, moose and other prized animals of the fading frontier.

Dubois has no doctor, no hospital, no mortician, and it is said they had to shoot three men to start a cemetery. They do have a nurse. She is Mrs. V. Warnock. But even she finds it tough going to keep in throats to paint.

And they do have churches. In fact one of them a few years ago needed a roof and couldn't afford one. So one of the local bar owners opened his place to a public dance. Slot machines went into action. Roulet wheels came into play. The proceeds went to the church and the roof was put on.

Now and then some old-timer passes quietly over the Big Divide and the little town mourns. Most recent of these was Mrs. George Hayes who refused to the very last to blemish the town's record by having a town doctor come out and take care of her.

Another was Tony Burlingham, the first white child born in the upper Wind river valley where nestles the little town of Dubois. He had suffered a broken leg a year ago when he was 66. A horse fell with him. He never recovered fully. Too bad, folk said. He was right in the prime of life.

"Daddy of 'em All"

"But we can't have a crop show. We don't raise anything up in Cheyenne except hell!"

"Well, then, let's raise hell and make a show out of it. Let's call it Cheyenne Frontier Days!"

So they did, they continued to, and they still do. That's Cheyenne Frontier Days—The Daddy of 'em All—and the brief story of its conception on a train between Greeley and Cheyenne one summer afternoon back in 1897.

The conversationalists were Warren Richardson, chairman of the first Frontier Days committee, and Col. E. A. Slack, editor of the Cheyenne *Daily Sun Leader*.

The two had just witnessed the "Potato Day" show, now the

46

"Spud Rodeo" at Greeley. Colonel Slack was chagrined. If Cheyenne had any show at all, Greeley might have been said to be stealing it. But Cheyenne didn't, and the fact was a burr under the colonel's editorial blanket.

So now "hell raising," as such, has become a big business, bronc busting an industry, and Cheyenne a world-famous city because of it.

Colonel Slack went to work on the idea in the next edition of his newspaper with the result that the following year all hell did bust loose one September noon. Train and factory whistles blew for a half-hour. Residents grabbed shooting irons of all descriptions and blazed away.

At 1 p. m. the first of the big shows got under way at the fairgrounds. What a show that was:

Spraddle-legged broncs were eared down right out in the arena. Booted and spurred compunchers clambered aboard, raked the animal from stem to stern, and rode him until either the rider was scattered to the winds or the horse was plumb gentled.

Sometimes there would be three or four bucking at the same time. They'd plow through the crowds. Knock over women and children and upset buggies.

Sales of beer and hard liquor far exceeded whatever soft drink output there was that day at the grounds.

A group of cowpunchers decided the show needed some Indian dancers, so they took them off the "blinds" of a Union Pacific passenger train where they were customarily allowed to ride free. The scared tribesmen put on a real dance—Cheyenne's first.

Racing proved popular. Next year a dog race was a featured attraction and would have proved a big success had not all the dogs in town been attracted by the baying and barking. They joined in the race, fought over the rabbit's skinny carcass, bit women and kids and outraged the judges.

Then a huge wedding ceremony was arranged for the show. Beauties from Colorado and Wyoming were chosen from many towns by newspaper contests. They were to serve as bridesmaids for whoever should volunteer for the one-way trip to the (h) altar.

Miss Cora Baer and Dr. C. M. Mathews of Denver became that couple.

The wedding was a huge success. The grandstand collapsed, piling the beauteous bridesmaids into a wild scramble of roses and wedding lace.

Soon presidents began to attend the big show. Among these was Teddy Roosevelt. Teddy was spotted in the stands by cow-punchers who brought out a big bay horse. The old-time Rough Rider mounted the animal, and with frocktails waving in the breeze, raced around the entire track while waddies yelled themselves hoarse.

Not long ago they *didn't* holler when Gov. Thomas E. Dewey of New York showed up and declined to don the customary ten-gallon hat given to dignitaries.

But they'll be hollerin' at presidents for years to come, I hope. I intend to holler with 'em one day, at least, this year.

I'll let you know, T. Joe, and you, too, Sheriff Tuck, so's you can look out for me.

"High on the Hawg"

Colorado is young. On its Diamond Jubilee the Centennial state is chipper as a yak-weary husband witnessing the wedding of his domiciled mother-in-law to the town bully.

Colorado is big. To be exact it boasts 104,247 square miles of land area. Actually, it's bigger than Texas. If its 1,143 mountain peaks (anything under 10,000 feet doesn't rate as a mountain) were ironed out flat, Colorado would overrun New Mexico and Wyoming and would crowd California into the Hawaiian island group.

Colorado is wealthy. It has more coal than any other state in the nation, can produce enough oil from its shale deposits to keep the world going longer than the Democrats will be in office and boasts enough water to irrigate Texas. In fact if Colorado were to corral all its water resources, most of the states around it would dry up and blow away.

The Pacific ocean might even dry up in the Los Angeles area and the famous bridges of San Francisco would become nothing more than tourist novelties.

Colorado eats high on the hawg. It raises enough beef to make the starving Armenians a race of gluttons; enough leather to shoe the Russians where it would do the most good and enough wool to make suits, sweaters and long underwear for a whole race of Paul Bunyans. Its beets produce enough sugar to sweeten Joe Stalin and it raises enough wheat to inundate the steppes of the Soviet.

Colorado keeps the rest of the nation going. It consumes one and one-half gallons of Kentucky liquor a year per capita, guzzles fifteen and one-half gallons of beer on the same basis (it produces the finest beer in the nation) ; imports its governors from Texas and its newspapermen from Oregon and Wyoming; buys its grapefruit from California and Texas and grows the biggest, sweetest cantaloupes in the world. In the latter connection it isn't even necessary to mention that its high-altitude celery and other sunkissed crops including its McClure (that's Irish, neighbor) potatoes, are the finest raised anywhere east of the Himalayas.

Colorado is a wonderful place in which to live. It has its share of preachers who will take a drink and its bartenders who go to church. It has 824 churches of Christian denomination, 1,128 bars, fifty-two beer-and-wine-only establishments, 185 club liquor licenses, 602 package liquor stores, 303 drugstores where thirst quenchers can be bought, boasts 2,451 of the best schools in the country, 130 hospitals, 149 banks containing $1,500,000,000 of the depositors' money, not counting what the bankers are holding back, and a happy population of only 1,325,089.

Colorado is the land of sunshine and sunshiny smiles. It has more days of sunshine each year than rainstorms in California; pretty girls, fast horses, speedy dogs, fewer pickpockets, the friendliest people, bigger spendthrifts, the fightin'est and marrin'est men, more wild game, fewer ills and complaints, the healthiest citizens and the best-cleaned-out taxpayers and the most and biggest trout in the nation.

Colorado is a place you'd like to visit this jubilee year. It's got it's ten-gallon hat in one hand and the other extended in a handshake. It's been training its rainbows and cutthroats to grab your fly and been prodding its bucking horses to do their utmost for you at its rodeos. It even hired some western-garbed gals to show you through the Colorado statehouse, and it's laid down the welcome mat in front of Pike's peak.

From Cripple Creek to California street; from Steamboat Springs, Craig, Glenwood Springs, Grand Junction and Fruita to Alamosa, Canon City, Colorado Springs and the steel city, not to mention some farther-east cities, Colorado welcomes you. Come once to see and a citizen you'll be.

I'll Take Chugwater

Now I am not one who could complain validly of ever finding the high school history class tiring. With me it was exactly the opposite. I usually left the history room each day completely refreshed. A nap always does that for me.

That daily period of somnambulism, however, perhaps explains any number of glaring gaps in my general knowledge. And it is no doubt responsible for my complete ignorance until recently about the origin of the fascinating name of Chugwater, Wyo.

Each of the many times I have driven through there to or from Cheyenne, I have wondered about it. Once I almost turned back to make inquiry. Finally curiosity overcame me and one day not long ago I asked an old-timer there how Chugwater got its name. He told me the story:

It seems that years before the white man came to settle the cliff country around Chugwater, a Mandan Indian chief, Wecash, was killed during the hunt by a wounded bull buffalo. When his son, Ahwiprie, assumed leadership of the tribe, he changed the method of bagging this particular game.

Under his direction the great beasts would be herded to just the proper position, then stampeded over the cliff. Their bodies were described as striking the rocky ground below with a "chugging" sound.

The Indians called the spot "Place by the Water Where the Buffalo Chug." With typical efficiency the white man condensed that to Chugwater.

Not all names of places so accurately retain their true origin, and some are outright misnomers. Laramie, Wyo., and a host of geographical features around it, are named after Jacques La Ramie, a French Canadian who came to the area to hunt and trap, and Dubois, Wyo., was named after an explorer who never even came near the place. He camped many miles away.

Incidentally, there was some talk recently about changing Dubois' name to something else.

Shoshoni, Wyo., actually should be Shoshone. The latter is the proper spelling of the Indian tribe from which the name stemmed.

Probably the most red-faced of all the early figures who ever tagged a place by name, however, was the explorer, Lewis, of the Lewis and Clark expedition.

Lewis, so the story goes, was anxious to give to some area the name of a lady friend of whom he reportedly was enamored and who remained in the east while he tramped through the wilderness.

Accordingly, when he reached the area of what was to become Lewistown, Mont., he proclaimed with a flourish that the basin country there and a certain mountain range should be named "Judith basin" and "Judith mountain."

To his great embarrassment he learned upon returning to his lady love that her name actually was "Julia" and not "Judith," the name which still sticks in Montana.

At least the Rocky Mountain Empire seems to possess more originality when it comes to names than do the eastern states. Elsewhere there are no less than five New Yorks, twenty-eight

Washingtons, thirty-one Franklins, twenty-five Clevelands and even twelve (you should excuse the expression) Moscows.

We also have two Utopias, twenty-two Eurekas, eighteen Arcadias, fifteen Hopes and fourteen Eldorados.

Me? I'll take Chugwater.

The Big Horn Country

All day the blazing sun had seared the flat stretches of plains country that swept westward from the base of the towering Big Horn mountains in northern Wyoming. Shimmering heat waves danced above the prairie like the wraiths of departed savages tortured in the purgatory that sprawled at our feet.

It was cool where we stood. But as we looked across the vast expanses we could see here and there the mirages of cool water that took the form of great blue lakes, illusory mirrors of the cloudless sky.

To the north could be seen the mud-like black cliffs of a butte that arose abruptly from the prairie around it. To the west was a tinge of burnt umber streaked with red. It afforded pleasant relief from the monotonous brown of the late summer dryness.

Slowly, almost as if reluctant to relinquish its hold on the scene, the sun dipped toward the horizon 100 or more miles to the west in the Yellowstone Park country.

As it dipped ever lower to tip the high purple mountains with gold crests, it hurled giant spokes of flame across the heavens as though to mark its trail for the morrow.

Lengthening shadows crept eastward across the flatlands bringing precious cool and quiet to close the day.

Soon the night began to form in the depths, lighted only by the sun's flaming reflection that hung in the west like molten clouds. Lingering patches of fire-tipped mountain peaks remained like beacons of hope in the gathering gloom.

But night claimed the earth eventually with an unpretentious gesture, and replaced the sun's glory with tiny campfires in the coolness above. The moon, sure the sun had gone, rose slowly to heights of majesty in the firmament and flooded the scene with soft, borrowed brilliance.

Thus ended one day in one of Wyoming's least publicized but highly deserving beauty spots—the Big Horns.

All but omitted from the travel pages, brushed off even in Wyoming, the Big Horns some day, I am sure, are destined to become one of the nation's great play places.

It has history but few roads—romance and beauty but remains primitive.

Across its southern section, or perhaps you'd call it the middle, a good highway connects Buffalo, Tensleep and Worland. To the north a highway that leaves Sheridan on the east, divides half way across the high country. One leg runs north to Kane and Lovell, the other goes through beautiful Shell canyon and on down to Greybull.

The southern leg runs through historic country—country rich with romance of the old west. Here one of the greatest wars ever fought between cattlemen and sheepmen claimed the lives of gun-totin', masked riders, saw thousands of sheep "rimrocked"—run in great herds over high cliffs to their death.

In this region, all up and down the great hogback, are vast primitive areas accessible only by pack train over difficult terrain.

Travel up the highways of the Big Horns affords breathtaking views of great panoramas, glimpses of sudden death in the yawning canyons edged by roadway, and an opportunity to listen to the music of tumbling mountain torrents.

Wars, ticker tape machines, traffic, no-parking signs—all the complications of modern life seem far distant when viewed from the cool of the Big Horns.

They become the shimmering wraiths that dance in the distance when the sun ball sears the earth.

ABOUT PEOPLE

A Wild Goose Guy

Singin' Sam Agins is one smart fella. Right now he's down among the sunshine and saguaro, the dust, rattlesnakes and tourists of old Tucson, Ariz., strumming his guitar and giving with those western ballads for which he is famous. And I'll bet that right as this is being written and, as it is being read, Singin' Sam is smiling. I've never seen him without a smile.

Somehow smiles and crutches don't seem to go together. But they do with Singin' Sam. They've been part and parcel of Sam's makeup ever since he was old enough to get around, which was a little late in life because Sam never could walk on his own two legs.

Sam was born a cripple which doesn't seem to be the right thing to say about him. It's not exactly that Sam is "crippled." He would be the last to admit that. It was just that his legs from the hips down never seemed to amount to much. They didn't grow like the rest of him. So Sam has had to get around on crutches all his life.

He does even this, as he does all things, just a little bit different, and a little bit better than the other fellow. Sam actually lifts himself on those crutches and, with 17-inch biceps that are hard as a credit company's heart, he swings along without so much as a hitch. His shoulders are the envy of every footballer or cowpuncher, and his arms on a prize fighter would scare an opponent out of the ring.

But Sam's not a fighter. He's a singer as his name implies, and he has a yen for the soft life which means that he traipses to Jackson Hole in the summer and down to Arizona when the snow comes to the Tetons, although he claims Denver as home. It seems that ice is a mighty treacherous thing to a man who walks on crutches the way Sam does. So he goes where the snow doesn't.

Oldtime western ballads are Sam's favorite music. He doesn't exactly know how many he has in his repertoire, but one time, on request, he sang five hours without repeating a single song.

Western ballads, unlike the stuff you hear on the juke boxes, are genuine cowboy songs. They were born in the bunkhouse, composed on the spur of the moment by some untuneful bronco buster, but are somehow mighty expressive. Typical of the modern ballad that adheres to the same type music as the old ones is *I Want to Go Where the Wild Goose Goes*. Sam does it up smartly.

But his favorite is *Ten Thousand Goddam Cattle*. In it a cowboy moans despair over his sweetie pulling out on him, and neglecting to tell him as she left just what in the heck she did with his French postcards. The off-beat turn in the ballad is another distinguishing aspect of the true western ballad, which is something sadly lacking in the nasal nostalgia groaned out by today's run-of-the-juke-box.

But being different pays off if it's done right. This year Sam's going to sing before the nation's colleges to aid studies of ballad writing which is enjoying a new national interest. But northern colleges will have to wait for spring weather. Singin' Sam's a wild goose sort of guy and he won't be back until the weather's cleared.

T-Joe's Busy Season

Of course he works at his self-chosen assignment the year around. But this is the busiest season for Wyoming's grand citizen T-Joe Cahill. The man whose slogan is "Do a good deed today, you may not be here tomorrow," is up to his broad-brimmed hat trying to make Christmas bright and cheery for his adopted wards—the children of St. Joseph's orphanage at Torrington, Wyo.

It's pretty much a one-man job with T-Joe, a job he cut out for himself many years ago for no accountable reason except that the bigness of his heart simply demanded that he do something to help others. And T-Joe works at his undertaking with vigor that increases with each passing year because he really believes he should "do a good deed today." T-Joe was 77 Aug. 7, 1954.

Joe solicits funds from his friends, numbered in legions, and this year has the gift of Old Cowboy Ed Wright's book, *The Representative*, to help him. Wright, whose heart is big as T-Joe's, donated the book to the orphanage. It gets the proceeds.

But this didn't start out to be a solicitation for funds. I intended it to be a yarn about T-Joe and his old buddy, Stub Bruner, Elks club secretary at Cheyenne. Pure fabrication, the yarn nevertheless illustrates a point.

It seems that T-Joe had been "name dropping" around the Elks club. Every time someone would mention the name of some nationally or internationally known person, T-Joe would up and declare "Why, shucks, I've known him for years."

This practice got on Stub's nerves to the point where he decided to challenge the venerable T-Joe. First time he got the chance he looked Joe coldly in the eye and said:

"Joe, I will bet you 100 Wyoming dollars that you do not know Bob Howsam of the Denver Bears."

"Called," exclaimed T-Joe. "I've known him since he was a kid."

That's how the trip to Denver got started and that's how Stub lost $100. Undismayed and anxious to recover his century note, Stub offered another bet—$200 that T-Joe couldn't walk up and claim acquaintance with President Eisenhower. "Ike?" T-Joe chuckled. "Known him since World War I." They went to Washington. Ike was delighted to see T-Joe. And that's how Stub lost $200.

In desperation Stub next bet $300 T-Joe didn't know Senator Joe McCarthy. "Well," Joe admitted hesitantly, "I do know him."

But McCarthy was in Buffalo, N. Y., making a speech. They went there and found him under heavy guard. Joe explained to Stub that it would be difficult to see McCarthy. But would it satisfy Stub if T-Joe just appeared briefly with the senator as he spoke from the hotel balcony? Stub agreed. An hour later two men walked out on the balcony.

Stub didn't have his glasses and couldn't identify McCarthy. He turned to a man and inquired: "Is that Joe McCarthy up there?" The man took a look and replied:

"Well I don't know who that other fellow is, but that big one up there is T-Joe Cahill from Cheyenne."

Big, Tough and 76

I'm gnawing my fingernails the other day wondering what to write about this week when who should blow into the office on a blast of garlic and loud conversation but Big Chief Bill Hot Wells Lone West. Chief Bill, who wears the same size shirt as a moose and hails from just about everywhere, claims to be almost everything the average male American would like to be except 76 years old.

Now don't get me wrong about the age. At 76 (I'm proud of my age, he says) Bill possesses the heartiness of a Kodiak bear and the vitality of a Mallet locomotive. I'm sure that were he of a mind to do it, he could pick up a full grown steer and eat it like corn on the cob. In fact I'm not sure he hasn't done it. He's done just about everything else.

He says he's been a movie star, bit player, muscle man, all-American tackle under Pop Warner, Olympic weight tosser, prize fighter, pal of Jim Thorpe, promoter of anything and everything, author, lecturer, physical culturist, manufacturer and, on top of all that, is three-quarter Indian and one-quarter Irish, boasts that he is a cousin of Will Rogers and wears a size 12 shoe. Whew!

Bill's been working out lately in the lecturer's ring before service clubs. He's made 42 programs in Denver in two months and hasn't run out of conversation yet. One of his favorite stunts is to pick out the biggest man in the audience, glare at him and dare him to come up on the speaker's stand. Then he invites the man to take a roundhouse swing at his midriff which looks like an inflated tractor tire and is just about as hard. The result is always the same. The puncher goes back to his luncheon seat shaking and blowing on his injured knuckles.

Bill's hard as a picnic egg. And he's big. He measures 6 feet 4, tips the beam at 240 pounds and, unlike most men that size, gets around like a ballet dancer. He cooks a favorite dish called Chero-kee chicken, loves garlic, talks like a machine gun and is ticklish.

To that latter affliction he attributes his success as a football lines-man with Carlyle during the Indian school's heyday.

Anything else about Bill? Well he claims that Thomas Edison, Henry Ford, Amos Alonzo Stagg, President Roosevelt and most movie stars either were or are pals of his and that once he exchanged lumps with Jack Dempsey.

Right now he's finishing four books—*Hollywood Then Hell*, *First American Heritage*, *Jim Thorpe's Finest Hour* and *Texas the Magnificent* which he figures will sell a million copies in the Lone Star state just on the name alone.

In movies (his chest measures 50 inches) he usually took the role of the mean, ornery character with bulging biceps such as the head jailer in *Cleopatra* and the vicious villain in *Princess and the Pirate,* to mention only a few.

But Bill's not through yet. He wants to go back at 78, two years from now, and play one quarter with the University of California football team, and he'd like to get married. He also wants to build a big university for Indians. But he wonders if he shouldn't wait till he gets settled down before taking a wife. A fellow's not stabilized, he reckons, until he's had his fling.

Just Act Normal

When you go to visit the W. B. Ludwigs, you just take your shoes off and make yourself at home. I don't know whether that would be the proper thing to do at their home in Laramie, Wyo., but it certainly is at their weekend ranch in Colorado.

There you can obey that impulse. If you want to mope around the place alone, cork off for an hour or two in the shade of a pine tree, seek out the refreshment stand or make yourself a sandwich, you just haul off and do it. Nobody gives a hoot or asks any questions.

The Ludwigs love the west so much they aren't satisfied with living in only one western state. So they bought a second home two years ago out in the rolling foothills not far from historic Virginia Dale.

There probably were some buildings already there, but the work the Ludwigs did in two years is amazing. They did it all by themselves, too. They fixed up an attractive little house and added a handsome patio and rambling stone fireplace, gouged out a swimming pool, erected a garage with an upstairs den, then fashioned an inviting little shed for outdoor gatherings.

Mrs. Ludwig boasts and apologizes at the same time for the interior decorating.

"We did it ourselves," she says, pointing to a wall covered with paper of cowboyish design. "We selected our own colors—Doc and I. If he wanted brown, we just used some brown. If I wanted a dash of chartreuse, I just went ahead and put it there. The result may floor you, but it looks nice to us."

Doc got the nickname from his former practice of chiropody. He got tired of massaging other people's feet, however, and concentrated on faces. He and his wife now operate a photo studio in Laramie with considerable success.

A few weekends ago, the Ludwigs were hosts at a joint get-together for the Colorado and Wyoming Westerners, a sort of packrat organization of western lore lovers who would crawl on their hands and knees through broken glass to capture the tiniest relic of the ghostish yesteryear.

A whole flock of Colorado Westerners showed up. They milled around the place, met and were impressed with Bill Carlisle, the reformed lone bandit who also was a guest, then they tromped through the house and worshipped at the Virginia Dale shrine of trail days, and lined up for chow.

The meal was a kitchen triumph and consisted of good old, solid western food—mainly beans and beef. (Oh, yes. There was a corner of the shed devoted to a pastime called "bellying up to the bar.") Anyway, everyone had a good time. But as soon as the meal was served, the Colorado Westerners did a very unwesternish thing.

With one or two exceptions, they separated from the Wyomingites and formed a little railbird gathering of their own. There, in the friendly company of themselves, they munched happily on the hospitality of the Ludwigs. Now this, I protest, is an encroachment on custom reserved exclusively for newspapermen who are guests at cocktail parties given by big business executives to promote better press relations.

The Speedy Salesman

HRB

A couple of ranchers were moaning about business conditions the other day. One of them squinted at me to study the effect of his words, then solemnly summed up the situation as being pretty dire with this observation:

"Why only last week," he said "an automobile salesman from Casper drove out to my place to show me one of the new models. He was the first car salesman I'd seen outside the city limits since Lee Doud left the country almost 25 years ago."

Lee Doud! Now there was a car salesman—perhaps the most colorful this western region ever produced. Denver folk know Lee as a real estate man and a builder of homes. But I knew him as a super-showman of the automobile business and I'll never forget the ride I took with him in 1928 from Casper to Douglas (my old home town), Wyo.

He was driving a Willys-Knight. The road was the finest. It was gravel-surfaced—modern as heck. We made that 52 miles in less than 50 minutes. That, brother, was better than 60 miles per hour all the way!

Lee sold Whippets and Willys-Knights. When one of the cars came out with "three-wheel suspension," he demonstrated it by driving his own car around town at all times with only one front wheel.

Four-wheel brakes were the sensation of the industry. Lee set up a $500 piece of plate glass across the end of his used car lot.

When a customer came in for a demonstration, he got one. Lee would wind up his demonstrator and go flying at the plate glass, accelerator wide open. He'd bring the car to a stop inches from an expensive crash.

He didn't fiddle around with want ads. He bought whole pages of advertising. One of these announced one day that a Whippet would go anywhere. To prove it, Lee drove one up the courthouse steps, another up the statehouse steps in Cheyenne, and he put another one on top of Independence Rock, monolithic "register of the Red Desert." It was a Herculean task and probably never repeated.

One afternoon the Casper *Tribune-Herald* carried a full page ad that asked only one question: "How far can a Whippet go in 24 hours?"

Readers got their answer next afternoon. Lee had driven, around the clock through Wyoming to tally 1,077 miles.

Lee loved speed but he was a safe driver. He bragged up the power of his Whippets—thirty dynamic horses—and he used big ads to caution drivers against taking chances. He held every speed record in the territory and his test runs always were accomplished with great fanfare. He got more press notices and attention in Wyoming than the Indianapolis Speedway. Denver to Casper (300 miles) in 4 hours and 44 minutes was one of his records, Lee claims.

His last big race was against a Star roadster from Casper to Rawlins and back, 240 miles. It was the only time he ever was coaxed into making a bet but he wagered $500 with newspapermen putting up the lion's share.

Lee didn't learn until after he had won the race at an average of 55 miles per hour, that the other driver was a professional race driver from Denver, wheeling a souped-up special and backed by Denver gamblers.

Sold Again

A. L. Doud, the nonagenarian Denver attorney who died in 1945, was a sagacious gent who abhorred snap decisions. When his nephew, Lee W. Doud, was orphaned as a small boy, Attorney

Doud waited until Lee became 21 before taking out adoption papers.

"I guess he just wanted to make certain that I turned out all right," Lee explains.

That Lee "turned out all right" is a matter of record. He has succeeded at everything he ever undertook, even to beating the pants off a professional race car driver back in the 1920's when Lee was the 60-mile-an-hour speed king of Wyoming.

If you read last Sunday's Range-Ridin' piece you already know that Lee was a spectacular automobile salesman at the time when four-wheel brakes were an innovation. I hadn't seen him since that exciting era, and I was anxious to know if he used the same flamboyant methods in his present occupation of selling homes here in Denver.

He was upstairs reading when I called on him recently at his handsomely modern home at 3845 Everett St. in suburban Wheat Ridge. Lee bounded down the steps two at a time, hand outstretched. He had changed surprisingly little in 25 years. He was a bit heavier and somewhat greyer. But the old fireball enthusiasm burned undiminished.

By way of conversation I observed that his house was brand new. "Sure," he beamed. "A car salesman always gets a new model each year."

He shoved an expensive hat onto his head as though mopping perspiration off his brow, and said "Let's go for a ride." My last ride with Lee was to a Kiwanis club meeting 50 miles from Casper, Wyo., where Lee sold Whippets. (Those were automobiles, son.) We made the distance at the breakneck speed of 60-per, with me hanging on to everything in the car.

Fortunately Lee's foot has grown lighter on the accelerator since that time. We drove along a winding row of houses set attractively on streets named by the master salesman. There were Sunset lane and Twilight and Skyline drives. Each of the approximately 125 homes built and sold by Doud is different from its neighbor in some respect, a selling point on which he prides himself.

"I like to build homes for young families," Lee said. "My system is to visualize a family. Then I build something to fit that family's needs and individuality. And before I get it finished, that family materializes out of somewhere and buys it."

65

Lee was disclosing the very thing I had come to ask about—the secret of his selling ability. Later I put the question to him straightforward. "Put yourself in the buyer's place," he said. "That's the secret of good selling. Think of his problems and his limitations.

"Now I still sell insurance, too. For instance, Red, how old are you? How much have you saved?" I blushed and he went on. "How much can you save, then, in the years that remain." He talked softly, confidentially. I got out my pen ready to sign. He smiled. "Oh, I'm not selling you anything. Just showing you how."

It's Called Crow Soup

Folks around the Badlands and Pine Ridge Indian reservation wonder to this day why Dude Rounds didn't just up and murder his old pal, George Porch, especially after the cow sale. But according to Will H. Spindler, our Wounded Knee, S. D., correspondent, the two old cowpunchers died in recent years, still the best of friends.

In the famous cow deal, Dude had ridden up to George's place one night just at milking time. George was squatting on a battered bucket and patiently juicing a placid ranch cow. The bucket was brimming full. Dude struck what he thought was a hard bargain with George, bought the cow and went home whistling about getting a real milk-producer.

A week later he came back howling mad. He couldn't get more than a half bucket if he had squeezed her with a barn door.

"Yuh just milk her too often, Dude," George soothed him. "I only milked her every two days."

Then there was the time they took the cattle train together to Omaha. Dude was always full of pranks on these annual trips. He loved to kid the waitresses.

The first night in Omaha, George and Dude headed for a steak house. Dude confided that he was "ravenous hungry."

When the waitress came over to their table, Dude pulled his old "deaf and dumb trick." He wiggled his fingers and the waitress looked at him with kindness and pity shining in her eyes.

Then she leaned down to George and said, "What does the poor fellow want?"

George pretended to relay Dude's message and said "He wants a bowl of soup and some crackers. Me, I'll have one of them T-bones."

The waitress hurried back with the soup. Dude chuckled and said, "Don't let on a thing to her until we're all through eating." Then he waved at the waitress, ready to put in his order for a steak.

Dude and George went through the finger-wagging routine again. George looked up at the waitress, smiled and said, "He wants some more of that soup and some more crackers." Dude glowered. But he downed the soup and muttered under his breath.

George beckoned the waitress a third time and said, "My friend here says that is the best durned soup he ever had. He wants another bowl, this time a bigger one and lots of crackers."

Dude's face went livid. He choked. He sputtered crackers. The waitress took one look and lit out for the kitchen. Dude leaped up in hot pursuit and grabbed George's steak that was just ready for serving, then, in a voice that could be heard clear out to the stockyards, announced:

"I'm eating this here steak, myself. It's my friend that wants soup. And dang him, he'll eat three bowls of it or I'll wash his hair with it."

Folks around the Badlands country say that when George would tell the story he'd always remark:

"Shucks, I wasn't hungry for steak nohow."

Just Call Me Irish

Faith and it would seem that it is the very map of Old Erin itself that is gracing the cover of today's *Empire* magazine. In truth, however, it is the magnanimous mug of none other than County Denver's own Bernard J. Duffy, the Lord bless his ancestors.

Mister Duffy, in case you're a stranger in the town, is the friendly Champa pubman who parlayed a million-dollar Irish smile into a grog dispensing business that grosses a quarter million a year. While this is enough to leave Mister Duffy a tidy sum, the most of it goes into the pockets of the various governments. (A plague take the tax collectors.)

Now comes St. Patrick's Day, glory be to the occasion, and Mister Duffy's elbow gymnasium will resound with songs of the Auld Sod and reflect the glories of the Emerald Isle. Not a record on the juke box that day but will sing the praises of the Shamrock land.

At all times, Mister Duffy's fleet-footed waitresses are a'wearin' o' the green in their special uniforms. His menus are printed with green ink and feature such items as Italian spaghetti, Dublin style, and imported Irish whisky with a lilt of the pipes in each drink. In fact, it is said that Mister Duffy is the town's foremost professional Irishman.

But the morning and the night, too, of St. Patrick's Day, Duffy's joint will fairly glitter with Irish splendor. There'll be green beer, green shamrocks from over the sea, green potato chips, green ice cream, green carnations and green lights. And back of the counter, resplendent in green top hat and suit, Mister Duffy, himself, will be raking in the long green. For St. Patrick's Day business is better for the Champa street son of Dublin than any other holiday.

In all other respects, however, Mister Duffy will be his own personable self. With much declamation, hand pumping and back slapping, he will welcome each customer like a long lost cousin who has just inherited tax-exempt land. For each and every newcomer he will admonish a waitress to "Knock yourself out, honey. This is a *real* friend of mine!"

Duffy boasts that "All the Irishmen in County Denver will be here for the festivities. And all who are not Irish will be here to see what the Irish are doing." He could have added, too, that all will be a'wearin' o' the green because St. Patrick's Day has come to be everyone's day.

Originally it was a religious feast day honoring Ireland's patron saint who Christianized the country and chased out the snakes about 435 A. D. Now it is a day of celebrating for the Irish and all kindred spirits who share Erin's fierce passion for independence, its love for Irish tenors, good fellowship and ready wit. There is a universality about the day simply because all that it symbolizes is basic in the hearts of men everywhere. It accounts, too, for the

fact that the Irish are never thought of as a "minority group."
And, indeed, they are not.

In any crowd, anywhere, it usually takes only one good Irishman to make up a majority.

Why Ed Missed Supper

What old Honest Ed Wright did to Mrs. Murphy's outhouse
was purely unintentional. But pulling down her clothesline with
her old man's overalls on it was entirely calculated. Ed owns up
to that much readily. What irks him is that Mrs. Murphy blabbed
the story all over the country on her bobwire party line telephone.

You see, Mrs. Murphy was the wife of the section foreman and
they lived beside the track near Arvada, Wyo., not far from where
Crazy Horse creek empties into Powder river.

Ed was riding for a big spread in the region and, like all the
other cowpunchers, used to circle miles out of his way just to enjoy
the fine water hauled in to the section house by the railroad. The
fact that Mrs. Murphy had two attractive daughters had nothing
to do with it of course.

On this particular day Ed was riding hard to cross Crazy Horse
creek before a threatened storm broke. Big black clouds hovered
over the foothills out of which the creek flowed. And that meant
flash flood.

Anybody who ever put any stock in the old cowboy yell about
Powder river—"A mile wide and an inch deep"—had never seen
it after Crazy Horse creek had dumped the runoff of a hailstorm
into it. Then it flowed with dead cows, old tree trunks, sagebrush
and mud.

Just before he reached the creek crossing, the storm hit. Ed
took shelter under a cottonwood tree and waited. As usual the
creek swelled into a river of flood proportions. It was getting
late when the storm subsided, and Ed, thinking of a warm supper
at the ranch, elected to ford the stream on horseback.

He slipped out of his clothes, wrapped them in his slicker and
tied the bundle to his saddle.

His half-broke bronc didn't take to the water too willingly. But
Ed booted him in the belly and in he jumped. Rider and horse

went under in the roiling flood crested with about two inches of cold hailstones big as a bridle concha.

Ed slipped off, grabbed the horse's tail and, together, they swam ashore. Both shook—Ed with the cold and the horse to get rid of the excess moisture.

The bronc apparently had never seen a naked cowboy before. At the first sight of Ed's blue skin he snorted, threw up his tail and lit out. Barefooted, Ed chased the danged animal over the cactus-grown prairie until he hit the fence and headed for the railroad section house.

Cornered at the house, the cayuse stopped and trembled. Ed talked nice and held out his hand. The bronc leaped away, lashed out with his heels and splintered Mrs. Murphy's privvy. From inside the thing came Mrs. Murphy's angry voice: "What's going on out there?'

"It's just me—Ed Wright," the troubled 'puncher hollered.

"Then git!" Just then Ed spied the two daughters running out the back door to their mother's aid. That was when Ed spotted old man Murphy's overalls on the clothesline. He grabbed a wire, jerked over the pole at the other end and hauled the garments toward him back of the privvy. As he covered himself he muttered darkly:

"And I'll bet they've already et at the ranch house, too."

Jennie Was a Lady

HRB

Although most of its more colorful citizens departed the community by request (as we hinted last week), Newcastle, Wyo., was never without its fair share of characters. Perhaps the most notable of these among the fairer sex, at least, was one Jennie (Crazy Horse) Ellis, town bootlegger-philanthropist.

No one seems to know how Jennie earned the soubriquet of "Crazy Horse." Jennie was seldom seen outside her own precincts, and was not known to be overly boisterous.

She was simply one of those who chafed under the bonds of conventions and whose soul sought rougher lines of expression than were afforded in the drawingroom.

I met Jennie years ago, but I am indebted to the Newcastle *News Letter-Journal* for most of the details on this fabulous frontier woman.

While most girls of her age were learning how to pour tea and wear a bustle with grace, Jennie mastered gunnery and horsemanship. She could outride and outshoot most men of her acquaintance.

For many years she ran a ranch and sawmill near Newcastle and became famous as the female bachelor of the Black Hills country. Now and then Jennie would roll into town on a lumber wagon. She would unload and, like any good lumberjack, would

71

proceed to heist a few toasts to the congeniality of the neighborhood in which she did business.

Many's the time Jennie has left town riding hell bent for leather on the running gear of her lumber wagon, drawn behind four galloping horses. Jennie frequently brought in a load of lumber and left town loaded, according to the editors of the *News Letter*.

Jennie came west from Iowa with the railroad construction crews. She freighted with ox teams, hauled logs and ties to the construction camps and took her place among the men like any other good hand.

She ate at the camp mess, slept beside the other laborers at night. and neither asked nor gave favor. Jennie was treated like a lady. In fact the quick fist and hard knuckles of the woman won for her perhaps considerably more respect than would have been accorded some others of her sex under the same circumstances. Men left Jennie strictly alone.

She homesteaded in the area in 1903, and hewed the logs from which she built her own cabin. She never married, although she was not without allure. Contrary to the mental image which an account of her feats creates, Jennie Ellis was a small-statured woman with a demure, almost wistful face of considerable beauty.

She could be as gentle in one extreme as she could be rough in another. She was the community's best friend of stray cats and dogs and downtrodden men.

Jennie moved into Newcastle when prohibition turned the flowing oasis into a barren desert. Jennie could see no reason why men should monopolize the lucrative bootlegging business.

She never operated a "red light" place. Jennie insisted that women and alcohol never mixed. But she sold the best quality goods her money could buy, and she maintained her place with great good order.

She did pay a couple of fines to the federal government, but stayed in business to the very end.

She insisted she had no need for the companionship or protection of a man, but many, nevertheless, were beneficiaries of her charity. Ones who patronized her place to excess were sobered up and sent home if they were married men. Not one of her customers ever parted with any money that wasn't spent for—well, legitimate purchases. And Jennie's only romance ended when the male partner tried to tell Jennie how to run her business.

When Jennie died there was no dearth of mourners. She never had a constant lover, but her friends were legion.

Schoolmarm and a King

What would you do if you were 40 miles out on the windswept Wyoming prairie in 20-below zero weather, driving a seldom-used country side road, and the gas line on your automobile suddenly broke in two? Suppose you had no friction tape and there was only one way to keep from freezing. That was to fix the line somehow and drive on.

Pauline Peyton, as resourceful a little Wyoming gal as ever judged a beef, did the only thing she could think to do. She delved into her purse as any woman would, and came up with repair material. She chewed up a wad of gum that would have stuck two fence posts together, molded a blob of it over the break, wrapped her hanky around it and drove into town.

Pauline grew up in the Wyoming school of initiative where they used to think nothing of giving a 12-year-old boy a .30-30 rifle, some bacon and beans and loading him on a freight wagon to drive 60 miles into town for groceries. In such environment you just naturally get used to taking care of yourself under any circumstances.

Pert, pretty and perspicacious, Pauline is now the journalism teacher in the old Converse county high school where she graduated and where I spent several years as a sophomore. Pauline and I were in the same class in a manner of speaking. She headed it and I brought up the other end.

Her father was Al Peyton, the two-gun ex-sheriff from Douglas (my old home town), Wyo.

Being stuck out on a patch of frozen Wyoming prairie is only a minor experience so far as Pauline is concerned. Once she had to chase a family of skunks from under a country school house where she was teaching, and on another occasion went hunting clams at midnight with the king of Siam.

She was a Wac major at the time, and had some sort of diplomatic assignment that took her to a lot of unusual places, among them the king of Siam's mansion. His royal highness was throwing a state party for high army brass, and he apparently took a shine to our Polly. Anyway, when the festivities wore on him along in the later hours, he invited our Wyoming schoolmarm to go clam hunting on the beach.

She went, and afterward reported that the king is a really nice fellow. One time she went to a dinner where they served birds nests and monkey brains. She said she got to thinking about the good beef out on the Wyoming ranges and became so homesick— and hungry—she could have eaten a steer raw.

Like everybody else who lives at Douglas, Polly thinks there is no other place on earth. And she's seen a lot of the world, too. But someday, when the diplomatic war gets real tough, I suggest the government call Polly to the front. She'll think of something to effect world peace and I'll bet she will make it stick like gum on a gas line.

Dorothea at the Amador

A traveling salesman with a pretty grim-looking wife in tow shows up occasionally at the Amador hotel in Las Cruces, N. M., and says to Martin A. Campbell, co-owner: "You tell her, will you, Martin. She doesn't believe me."

Without waiting to be filled in further on the nature of the beef, Martin goes into his routine. He knows the situation. It's happened many times. And it will happen again.

Friend wife has found a copy of a telegram among her spouse's things which reads something like this: "Would like to have Dorothea and bath for Friday night. If Dorothea taken, how about Lupe?"

Of course, the telegram is addressed to the Amador which, in Spanish, has something to do with love. Friend wife has put two and two together and has a sum of six or eight.

Martin explains: Rooms in the hotel, in keeping with old Spanish custom, have names instead of numbers. The names usually are those of senoritas. By this time, however, the wife isn't even paying any attention. Her eyes are darting about the lobby as though seeking some avenue of escape.

It *is* a bit startling. To one side of the lobby is an Apache cigar

74

store Indian. Beside the stairway is the lacquered nude figure of an Indian prince reclining on his stomach. Inside glass cases are the delicately tinted busts of Fifteenth century Spanish maids. There are stuffed rattlesnakes, tom toms, war bonnets, old pistols and rifles, the handcuffs that once held Billy the Kid, the odds and ends of centuries of history.

The balcony is alight with multi-hued serapes, Indian blankets and rugs. And in the middle of the whole thing is a collection of animal heads. There are two Murillo paintings and a valuable Madonna by Tomasso Martinez of Seville. Nearby are ancient grandfather clocks and a giant bronze incense burner from China. You could go on for the duration of this column and still have only a partial itemization of the strange collection in the lobby of the Amador.

Informality is the word at the Amador. You lug your own baggage and if the manager is out, just register, help yourself to a room and go to bed. People have come to stay overnight and have lived there twenty years. A key? Nobody locks his door.

Don Martin Amador, freighter, founded the place just 100 years ago this year. At the time he was rich. His wagon trains plied from New Orleans to the west coast, from Denver to Juarez and on to Chihuahua, over the Santa Fe trail from St. Louis.

The Amador was the center of culture and of justice, too. The back rooms that now serve as diningrooms were once courtroom and jail. Billy the Kid was once an unwilling guest there. Martin Campbell was born there after the conversion.

But Martin wishes the hotel weren't so attractive to writing folk. It's had so much publicity, visitors don't believe there can possibly be a vacancy in such a popular hostelry.

"Tourists come to see the hotel. But where do they stay?" Martin complains. "At the tourist courts, of course."

Next time you're down that way, stop in and see Martin and tell him you're a friend of mine. But for heaven's sake rent a room. I've never stayed there overnight myself.

Cow Country Doc

It was forty-six miles out from Lusk, Wyo., across sage-grown flats, dry washes and steep-walled badlands. All this by spring wagon, too. But the emergency was considerable. Otherwise the weathered old cowman never would have called for the doctor in the first place.

Now a lifetime in cow country as medical practitioner, sagebrush philosopher and all-around Scattergood Baines had prepared Dr. Walter E. Reckling of Lusk for almost anything. Thus it was not at all surprising to Reckling that he should be called upon to minister to the infirmities of four aging Hereford bulls.

Doc arrived at the ranch, dusty, a bit worn from travel but accommodating as always. He diagnosed the trouble and prescribed an infallible remedy. The ranchman was bubbling over with gratitude. He paid the medical bill almost enthusiastically, walked back to the spring wagon and was bidding Doc a warm farewell when an afterthought occurred to him. "You treat human bein's, too, don't you, Doc?"

Reckling admitted to the charge, whereupon the owner of the bulls exclaimed: "Well, come into the house a minute, Doc, and take a look at the old lady. She's been ailin' nigh onto three years!"

Doc insists it's all in the day's work. Once the owner of a fine quarter horse over in nearby Nebraska called on him to do some veterinary surgery. The animal had cut himself on a barbed-wire fence. After long but futile argument over making such a long trip, Doc gave in, locked up the office and drove to the horse owner's place and sewed up the equine.

It wasn't long afterward that the horse owner's son suffered acute appendicitis and was rushed to Reckling's hospital in Lusk for emergency surgery.

Just as Reckling was preparing himself for the operating room, the father and horse owner grabbed him by the arm and in his most earnest voice said solemnly:

"Doc, do as good a job on the boy as you did on that gelding, will yuh?"

Sometimes impatience overrules gratitude. Like in childbirth, for instance. Several years ago before telephones became common household conveniences in the cattle country, Doc was summoned by a relative of the parents-to-be to deliver a baby miles out in the acres.

On the way out, while crossing a swollen stream, the wagon overturned, spilling Doc in the drink. Doc first rescued his bag of tools and pills, then hauled out the driver.

Going up the other side, the wagon overturned again.

The two already aggravated agents of mercy righted the vehicle and resumed the trip.

At the ranch gate they met the restive father-in-the-making, pacing a three-wire fence and cussing like a man possessed. When he spotted the wagon he raced to it, waved his arms and expostulated:

"What in the name of great smoking heck kept you so long, Doc?"

Wyoming Safari

Every time I make a trip up home to Wyoming I come back to the office chock full of enthusiasm and loaded down like a pack string with things to write about. Almost invariably, however, I find that space limits me to one or two small items. But this time let's talk about the whole trip:

Weren't many people on the streets in Cheyenne on account of the wind. But up at Casper where folks are used to it, the streets were packed and the oil city seemed to be as busy as a pocket gopher in a *pinon* patch. They're building clear out toward the Texaco refinery up there and many improvements have been made. But Casper is still my nomination as the best place in the Rocky Mountain Empire in which to build a new, and really *big* motel. They just don't have any big or elaborate ones there.

Speaking of the wind: Everybody in Wyoming was cussing about the awful spring this year. January hung on through April and May didn't count for anything. March roared in like a lion early in June and gave every indication of hanging around until midsummer. The grass on the ranges was never greener but nobody was celebrating. It's not easy for a stockman to get excited about green grass at today's livestock prices.

At Douglas my good old dad, the Burlington agent, was loading out 50-cent wool that was bringing up to $1.25 not very long ago. At that rate, it takes 75 per cent more wool to pay off the bank and there's no market for that much wool.

Saw Ted Ryan at Douglas, the man who taught me how to read. He was the circulation agent for *The Denver Post* about thirty years if I remember correctly, and that's the paper that served as my primer. Ted, who raised five nice girls, becoming mother and father to them after his wife died, doesn't look any older than he did when I was a kid. And he still is the town's best dancer.

Learned of a new twist on the automobile business. Wyoming car dealers are bragging up their better used machines nowadays with the assertion that "it's never been driven on Denver streets."

The Sagebrush Inn at Shoshoni now advertises that it sells food only. "No liquor." Cowboys thereabouts complain that the place is strictly out for the tourist trade.

Saw Charley Miller and Billy Omenson at Thermopolis. Both were formerly of Douglas. Billy's totally bald head doesn't even show a scar where George Arnold once mashed out a hot cigar at the end of a decidedly unprofitable poker game in the old College Inn.

Of course, everybody in Thermopolis is a booster for the town. But Cecil Harris, late-comer from Canon City, Colo., is among the more rabid. He is running the Shirley hotel there and doing everything he can to help out the Emery and the Carter hotels.

Cecil excitedly explained all the points of interest to my little biscuit-maker, Silva, and asked "Isn't that wonderful?"

"Yes, I know," she said. "You see I grew up right near here, at Worland."

Sam Sees Trouble Ahead for Humanity

At Lyman, Neb., the soles of Sam Gilbreath's feet are as hard as a shrew's heart. They are tougher than four cops ganging up on a lone drunk. Summer and winter, indoors and out, Sam hasn't worn shoes in five years.

Sam lives in a little cottage here in this pleasant North Platte valley farm community. In the unfolding of his seventy-three years he has evolved some interesting philosophies and has acquired not a few talents.

Among the latter is an awe inspiring ability to handle a cud with such degree of expertness that I would wager my gold tooth against a 1927 edition of Whiz Bang that he could spit through a keyhole at ten paces and never splatter the doorknob.

My introduction to Sam's marksmanship occurred with unexpected and rather disconcerting suddenness. I had made my way through a yard piled high with an amazing collection of nondescript articles ranging from old boxes to tires, and had knocked on the cabin door.

The door swung open. A tall and well muscled gent loomed large in the doorway. His tan face listed slightly to one side under the impressive weight of a king-size cargo of cut plug. Without warning the man's phisog screwed itself into a spitting stance and, with a quick jerk, professionally squirted a stream of tobacco juice over my shoulder.

"Come in," Sam invited cordially. "Come in and sit down."

I peered at his feet to see if they really were unshod as I had been told they would be. They were as bare as they were the day Sam was born, but they had begun to show some signs of weather-checking.

I stared in unconcealed admiration. All my life I had harbored a secret yen to walk life's pathway unencumbered by the No. 10's which chafe my corns and nick my pocketbook. Here was a man who dared to defy convention and to live as he damned well pleased.

Then I became a bit embarrassed as I realized he was conscious that I mentally was giving him a hotfoot. He broke the strained silence, and in a pleasant voice inquired:

"I suppose you would like to know why I don't wear shoes? Well, I have no feeling in my feet. It all began when I got sinus trouble. When I wear shoes they hurt me. When I go barefooted I feel good."

I wondered how he got by in the winter. But Sam said it didn't bother him and there are any number here who really testify that Sam creates no excitement when he goes shopping although the snow may literally be ankle deep.

Sam believes the human race is heading for trouble. We're living too fast. There are no morals left. And women are to blame for much of the world's woes. They no longer respect marriage vows—they get divorces easily and too many of them become tramps. There is not enough family and community life. A man living in the city isn't well enough acquainted with his neighbors. He doesn't know them.

Sam avers, and I agree up to a point, that people would be better off if they didn't wear shoes at all. They would stay home more.

Oh, I forgot to tell you what Sam does for a living.

He is the village shoemaker!

Crisis on the Range

Comes now and then a refreshing little yarn that revitalizes one's faith in humanity. For this particular one, I am indebted to old friends Keith Rider, editor and publisher of the famed Douglas (Wyo.) *Budget,* and my old schoolmate, Heinie Reese, sheepman of some renown.

It seems that last fall, according to Rider, a natural gas rancher known to one and all as T. Lee Reno bought some cows from a short grass rancher name of Rhea (Peep Eyes) Tillard. Now Tillard has a farflung reputation for honesty and fair dealing that prevails from the National Western Stock Show northward to Crazy Woman creek and even beyond.

When delivery time came, Tillard's riders duly tailed the cows over to the Reno place, arriving well after sundown. Next day, Reno rode through the herd and discovered that one of the cows had only one eye. This is a source of surprise to Reno whose contract with Peep Eyes called for all stock to be in first class condition.

Thus a few days later, he approached Peep Eyes on the streets of Douglas and forthwith accused him of false dealing by handing over a one-eyed cow in the night in violation of contract terms.

Ordinarily that is shooting talk in Douglas. But Peep Eyes only shrugged and calmly assured Reno that he would make good on the contract.

Months passed and nothing was done to rectify the wrong, Rider reported in *The Budget.* T. Lee Reno was much concerned by this time. As Rider wrote in his newspaper, "He begins to wonder if some people can be trusted as far as they can be heard in a crowded barroom."

Cause of Reno's perturbation was the nearness of calving time for the one-eyed cow and a foreboding that something dreadful was about to happen.

Reno calculated the cow's reactions. He feared she might look around on her blind side after labor and, seeing no calf there, might suffer ill psychological effects in view of what she had just been through. She might even get to brooding on the whole thing and suspicion that her affection had been trifled with. This could conceivably cause her to question whether all bulls had honorable intentions toward her and lead her to shun them. This would preclude her from ever bearing another calf.

Reno lost sleep over this and finally wrote Tillard a stern letter demanding the matter be cleared up.

As of last report, serenity had settled over the rangeland once again. Reno is sleeping contentedly, Peep Eyes has eased his conscience and vindicated his good name, and the cow has her calf.

Tillard replied to Reno's letter as follows:

"Enclosed you will find one glass eye for the cow that was short one eye. I hope this will complete our deal. Yours truly, Peep Eyes."

When Tony Got Mad

Among the many familiar boyhood figures I miss in this so-called modern era is the oldtime, barnstorming, ugly-mug, tough-as-leather carnival wrestler. He went from town to town with the carnies, taking on all comers and usually doing quite well for himself.

One favorite trick to boom business was to insult the masculinity of the local yokels until some dim wit would become enraged and crawl into the ring with the visiting grappler to be all but torn asunder and scattered piecemeal among the clamoring crowds.

While this usually packed the tent with customers at 25 cents a head, it also had its disadvantages. Now and then a bruising victory went to the hometown hero—but not often.

We went for these red-blooded demonstrations with great gusto when I was a kid up at Douglas (my old home town), Wyo. We had a local champion who could whip any five carnival wrestlers. We knew it but most of the itinerant arm breakers did not.

Our champ was Tony Wrobleske, the town marshal, later a detective on the Casper, Wyo., police force. Tony stood about 6 foot 3 inches, was handsomely muscled and could have beat a mule to death with his bare hands. During World War I, Tony had met and decked each and every contender for the heavyweight championship of the Atlantic fleet.

Trouble was, Tony always insisted upon arrival of each succeeding carnival that he would not wrestle "this time." He had to police the carnival and couldn't be bothered. But one night an especially abusive master of invective pranced onto the platform in front of the athletic show and began to harangue the crowd. He had no takers. No one cared to wrestle this giant who strutted back and forth showing his hairy chest, shaking his fist and hurling insults.

"Why I never saw such yellow sissies," he bellowed. "I ought to stay right here and look out for you people. I could run this place."

Tony was in the crowd, all eyes on him. He smiled mild amusement. Actually he was boiling mad. The hairy-chested one continued:

"And you women out there. Who protects you? Anybody? What would you do if the Indians attacked this town? What if some drunk went berserk? You got any cops here?"

Tony landed on the platform, his shirt already off. He wanted to fight then and there. But order prevailed, trunks were donned and then began the most glorious donnybrook ever to shake the old prairie.

Our Tony banged the visitor's head on the mat. He used him to break off a ring post. He hurled the invading muscleman out of the ring, chased him outside the tent and back in the other side, dragged him into the ring again and made him apologize to the crowd. You think Tony wasn't our hero?

On Taking Up a Collection

Some people go in for milder fields of "collection" like stamps or milk bottle caps. There's a man in Gillette, Wyo., who says he owns 100,000 buttons.

Others are bolder. They filch hotel silverware and linen. Some have a stampeding yen for lobby spittoons and clutter their rumpus rooms with the splotched brass of a bygone era. I know folks who would run through fire to rescue (and keep, of course) an old fashioned, gilded picture frame.

Me? I save characters.

In nearly twenty years of low-level, strictly non-lace-curtain newspapering, I've assembled enough characters to stock Barnum & Bailey's and have sufficient numbers left over to fill a deuce of laughing academies.

Take "Wireless Willie the Walking Wonder," for instance. It seems that right after World War I, some people in a hospital "wired" him for radio. Willie is constantly receiving disturbing communications from the White House to the effect that the President is plotting his demise.

Willie drops in occasionally just for reassurance that the press is constantly behind him and will protect him against any violence from Washington.

There used to be a "Diogenes" McFarlane. Old "Di" hasn't been around our newsroom for seven years. He used to drop in occasionally carrying a barn lantern and a gunnysack, search around the office for an honest man, and then depart—disappointed.

There's "Harry Short Beer," one of the truly great contemporary musicians. Short Beer can name the works of virtually all the old masters. He can recognize them by ear, tell the story behind each opera and concert. Trouble is, Harry can't play a note. He only hums through his teeth.

Harry hangs out at Ronnie's Revitalization, Recreation and Rest haven in downtown Denver. Ronnie, himself, is something of a character. He went three years on the old dry and dusty trail, working as a bartender. He swore off drink because it made him highly susceptible to head and chest colds.

It was 29 below zero—coldest night of the year—when Ronnie collapsed and fell off the wagon to be run over by the team AND the wagon. Celebrating the occasion, Ronnie ran around the downtown area in a summer suitcoat visiting friends.

It was the only time that year he didn't have the sniffles.

Another friend of mine swore off thirteen years ago just after his wife divorced him for over-indulgence. Once each month for thirteen years he has written his wife, telling her that he's quit drinking and asking to be taken back.

She never has learned about it. She faithfully returns all his letters and each Christmas mails back an unopened Christmas package which Jimmy takes sorrowfully to Larimer street for division among the ragamuffins.

Then there's a fellow who punches cows with a typewriter. . . .

Desert Business Woman

You can spin on your heel in the middle of the road at Farson, Wyo., and see the whole town in one turn. But you could search house by house in much larger towns and not find a more interesting woman than Farson's Marj Pinnock.

Some western gals are noted for their curves. Marj Pinnock is better known for her angles—four of them to be exact.

Marj is sort of kingpin out here at Farson which is indicated on the map as a tiny pinpoint of green in that kaleidoscopic phantasmagoria known as the Red desert. The desert itself fills a gaping space in southwestern Wyoming with awesome emptyness.

Temperatures at Farson soar to furnace intensities in summer months, and drop in winter to 5 to 10 degrees below those of Big Piney, Wyo., which usually is listed in weather reports as "coldest spot in the nation."

Reclamation has brought vegetation to many acres around Farson, but beyond the perimeters of this green island is bleak, unbountiful desert. Out here the men are still men, the jack rabbits tall and rangy, the water holes mostly alkali, and the women unusual.

If you're city bred and favor drugstores and steam heat, Farson and the barren terrain around it might cause you to wonder why any woman would stay here longer than it takes to gas up and hit for the next town.

But it requires all types to make a world and, thank goodness, there still are women of Marj's courage, rawhide will and frontier spirit.

She stands about bridle high to a short Indian pony on soggy ground, has reddish brown hair and an eye for business. She was born here at Farson, spent a brief high school period in Denver, then returned to her native acres to wrest a pretty good thing from the salt sage and cactus spaces.

She and her husband, Rowe, worked hard together. Then two years ago he was killed in a hunting accident. But Marj, far from giving up, expanded her field of operations.

In fact Marj Pinnock is now the area's foremost businesswoman since Becky Thomas. Becky made history by charging 10 cents a head to water horses at Blair's stockade near Killpecker creek and the Chalk Bluffs back in 1866. Becky catered to a crusty crew of mule skinners, cowboys, miners, trappers and adventurers.

So does our Marj, but in a different way. Marj runs a neat, clean roadside cafe at Farson. She is also the town's only beautician. Besides that, she serves as "for-free" barber to all comers— cowboys, sheepherders, reclamation crewmen and town citizens. These are three of her four angles. The fourth is the ranch she ramrods in her spare time.

When there are extra moments, she roams the hills looking for mine prospects. She already has her sights on some uranium indications, has staked a gold claim and is doing a great job of raising her son, Gary, 7, and daughter, Virginia, 4.

What do desert women do? What pasttimes do they enjoy? They spend most of their time living with a capital L.

Canterbury Tale

One of the most exciting things that has appeared at Buffalo, Wyo., since the U. S. cavalry ruined a heck of a good cattle war is Grace Canterbury.

Perhaps it is not appropriate to say that Grace just happened. It took a few years and some remarkable circumstances to produce the Grace of today.

But there she is, anyway, making skillful and effective use of some unconventional weapons scorned by others, to cut herself a generous slice of the hotel business in one of Wyoming's most beautiful cities.

Grace's highly unorthodox weapons in the hotel competition are a coffee pot, genial conversation, informality and good service.

The guests there are like one big, happy but not too-well-acquainted family. Grace, a restless hyperthyroid type, works constantly for the type of informality that marks the Mansion House hotel.

During the evenings, gregarious Grace is all over the place, introducing folk, chatting about the rundown condition of American politics, sewing buttons on salesmen's coats and shirts and, generally, making everyone "feel at home."

Occasionally some retiring customer will shout down the broad, winding staircase from upstairs: "Hey, Grace, how's about a couple extra towels?" "Can we borrow your radio?" Grace always acquiesces good-naturedly with a spontaniety that makes the customer feel he has done the manager a favor.

All guests retire in high spirits with good-nights shouted up and down the old, dignified hallways that have been rejuvenated by some modern color schemes.

First thing in the morning, Grace tries to spot the sleepier-eyed risers. These she hails into the kitchen with an invitation to "help yourself to the coffee." Sly woman! Few refuse this little extra gesture of hospitality.

It was about 12:45 a. m., three weeks ago, that I discovered Grace after a long, moonlight drive over the Big Horn mountains from Worland. Frankly, I had made the mistake of getting into the wrong hotel, and was about to give up and head for Kaycee when I spotted the old mansion trying to conceal its age wrinkles behind a sympathetic screen of cottonwoods.

Grace was out of bed and pronouncing salutations and welcomes in a jiffy. Three minutes later I had Grace's blessings, her alarm clock and was standing in the middle of a modern hotel room on the second floor.

First thing next morning she gave me a good morning at the foot of the stairs, got out her coffee pot and won herself another booster.

Grace was born in Buffalo, married, moved away, had some children, then broke up with her husband.

"I came back to Buffalo, settled down and married the kid I was in love with when I was in grade school," she imparted over the java. "Should have done it in the first place, maybe. Anyway, we're hitting it off together in a fine way. He's working and I loaf around the hotel with a broom in one hand and a dustcloth in the other."

The word "loaf" is contained in Grace Canterbury's vocabulary only as a gag expression. Tormented since childhood by a relentless drive that seldom lets her sleep, Grace explains that one of the great enjoyments she gets out of life is seeing others enjoy their rest!

That's really Grace's big secret weapon in the hotel business. More hotel operators could use a good case of thyroid!

"A Man Who . . ."

The time has come to deflate Colorado's insufferable ego over having a cowboy governor. Long before Dan Thornton threw his cinch on the governor's chair and made the Columbine state pipe-and-hat-conscious, Wyoming boasted a cowpunching chief executive who would make Dan look like Dean Acheson.

Wyoming's much maligned cowboy-statesman of another era was none other than Nels Smith, Newcastle rancher and breeder of fine bulls. Nels towered to a majestic altitude of six feet three or four inches in his high-heeled boots, and he tipped the beam at just a tot under the weight of a yearling heifer.

I haven't seen Nels in recent years, but at the time he sat in the gubernatorial saddle at Cheyenne more than a decade ago, he was a splendid figure. Gray at the temples, outdoorsy, hearty in a genuine western sort of way, Nels was a man's man. He looked exactly the way one would expect the governor of Wyoming to look.

Nels' great weaknesses were his inability to deliver the dynamic speeches written for him by high-powered lawyer-advisers, and an unfortunate facility for mangling the English language. At times, he murdered it.

The first chink in Nels' political armor became apparent when he was called upon to deliver an important address over which his writers had apparently worked hard. They had included some pungent polysyllabic words. When Nels tried to masticate them, he had the appearance of choking on his chewing tobacco.

Born to saddle leather and bunkhouse conversation, Nels just wasn't cut out to be an orator. When he read a speech, he read it as though it were one long sentence. He didn't even slow down to a trot when he came to a period.

Nels' advisers attributed this to an eye condition. Accordingly, they began typing his speeches in the big, bold-face type used by the weather bureau on postcard storm warnings.

The result was a voluminous manuscript, the sight of which struck panic in Nels' audiences.

Occasional stage directions were inserted in parentheses in the verbal broadsides. These had surprise results, too.

One night Nels struck a dramatic pose in front of his listeners, painstakingly thundered through an exceptionally devastating sentence, and droned on: "Pause for applause."

That brought down the house. It may also have helped win the election, too. For Nels became governor.

He was much in demand. Asked to express his views on the then controversial student union building at the state university at Laramie, Nels went over and left no doubt about where he stood on the matter.

"I am unanimously for it," he told the students.

Later on, this story about Nels went the rounds of the state:

He was invited to a dinner by a prominent Cheyenne woman who was entertaining a society-type guest from New York city. At dinner they chatted amiably, Nels talking mostly about his prize bulls on the ranch at Newcastle.

Then the conversation shifted to big game hunting under the gentle nudging of the hostess. Nels was a mighty hunter and each year bagged his limit. He always got a big horn sheep and this interested the New York visitor tremendously.

"I understand their meat is simply delectable," she said.

Nels fixed her with a reproachful eye and reprovingly said "Aw, no, ma'am. It's really purty good eatin'."

Maybe Next Year

Everybody can't be a winner at a state fair, and I thought old Jim O'Leary was quite philosophical about losing. He accepted defeat with becoming good grace.

Just the same, he was disappointed. He had worked hard and long on his entry, and had applied considerable skill. But competition at the Wyoming state fair this year was keener than it usually was.

"It was just too blamed tough for me," old Jim said resignedly. "Maybe next year . . ."

Jim had been saying that for years in just about everything he had ever done. "Maybe next year . . ."

Now when you're 75 and a few months older, it takes a world of confidence in the future to look forward always to a break next year. But Jim was never without confidence in the future.

He was full of it when he came to Douglas (my old home town), Wyo., thirty-five years ago. Jim and seven brothers and six sisters had grown up in Clark county, Iowa. After they came west, the more venturesome members of the family homesteaded on nine sections of Dry creek flats, thirty-two miles north of Douglas.

The area was more popularly known as "Starvation Flats." It was barren land, unproductive of anything save jackrabbits and prairie dogs, except when there were heavy summer rains.

Each year when the rains failed to come, Jim would say "Maybe next year . . ."

He became a philosopher quite naturally. Philosophy is not exactly a solid substitute for riches and success but it does dull the pain of doing without.

But withal, Jim knew when to withdraw. When he learned it was more profitable to lease the land to grazing, he put away his cooking utensils, closed up his homestead shack and moved into town.

He became a familiar and loved figure on Douglas streets. He fancied himself always as a working man. Therefore his dress was always the same: blue shirt, bib overalls and a narrow-brimmed hat trimmed down to suit his particular taste in chapeaux.

Keen Irish wit glows in his soft eyes which try to conceal their tenderness beneath a heavy overhanging of scraggly eyebrows. An unruly mop of hair always has pushed itself out in front just beneath the hat band. The hair has stayed with Jim through his seventy-five years.

Perhaps that's because he has been a lifelong bachelor. Jim's proud of it too. "I've always been self-supporting," he says.

Then in March, 1946, an automobile hit old Jim, a devout Catholic, just as he was on his way to vespers one afternoon. He was hospitalized in Casper and later in Denver.

Old Jim liked Denver. "It's a nice town," he said. "But it's too far from Douglas ever to amount to anything."

The accident left Jim next to helpless.

"I get mighty low at times," he says. "Other fellows my age are up and getting ahead. And here I am, getting around on a cane. But I can properly be thankful that I'm able to get around at all. When I think of some others I feel sorry for them.

"Just the same, I'd like to be able to catch a day or two of work harvesting or doing something like I used to do all the time. I like to be getting ahead all the time, Bobby—just can't be still and not doing anything.

"I was just a little bit disappointed when I didn't win something at the fair, too. But, oh, well. Maybe next year . . ."

It seemed that this year a few exhibits entered by some women, just naturally topped Jim's pretty assortment of crocheted and embroidered pillow cases.

"Maybe next year . . ."

Honest Ed Shows Up

Anybody who thinks I am the biggest liar in Colorado ought to talk to Ed Wright. Now I don't mean that Ed is a bigger liar than

I am or that he is a prevaricator at all. It just so happens that Ed was there in person when a few of the tall tales I tell actually happened.

He is a mortal verity that materialized out of the past, a few weeks ago, to testify before one and all that most of the lies I tell are truths.

Ed Wright, in my opinion, was the greatest rodeo clown ever to exchange unpleasantries with a brahma bull. It was he, prior to the 1920's, who conceived and first employed most of the clown stunts used nowadays by the daredevil funsters of the broken bones circuit.

Ed had several acts no longer used. One of these was preceded by great fanfare from the announcer. Attention was directed to one of the bucking chutes.

When the gate swung wide, out charged Ed determinedly sitting a wild-eyed bucking bronc—riding backwards! One hand held a giant umbrella. The other clutched the sursingle and packed an oversize suitcase. On the first jump the umbrella would turn wrong-side-out. Then the suitcase would fly open and out would flutter about a dozen excitedly cackling chickens.

I've seen him ride out as "pickup man" apparently intent on helping a cowboy clear the back of a bucking bronc, then leap on behind the bucking contestant and ride the horse with him— double.

Ed was a "fightin' type" cowboy. He roughed the arena as clown, got his share of broken bones, competed with the best of them in all events, won many honors, and would battle anybody— big or little—who cared to be entertained. He loved and thrived on bare-knuckle conflict. I've seen him fight three men at one time—and win. (You should see his nose.)

He would do anything—take any dare. One time in front of the grandstands at Cheyenne Frontier Days, he was acting out a stunt arranged with the Sioux Indians. But instead of merely removing his overalls as per agreement, the war-whooping tribesmen gleefully stripped Ed naked as a jaybird.

The undaunted fun master just grabbed two of the most immediately available headdresses from the noggins of the redskins, clamped one fore and the other aft, and raced off to the shelter of the bucking chutes.

Ed came west as a kid from God-knows-where back east, grew up in Wyoming and became a cowpuncher for some of the big outfits.

One time up in Fremont county he lost all his money in a poker game. He allowed as how he had been jobbed, hauled out his six-shooter and quickly recouped his losses.

The other players had him arrested. The judge listened to the case, stared hard at the complainants then fined each of them for running a crooked gambling game. Wright went free with the court's blessings.

After Ed disappeared from the rodeo circuit he settled down in California and more or less vanished so far as old pals were concerned.

Then this corner told of the famous sideshow we once operated together. That was "Reptilena," remember? Ed read it and not long ago turned up at Centennial race track with a stable of thoroughbreds, testified to my veracity for the benefit of friends, and proved his own.

"This horse, 'Dog Tag,' is going to win something," he confided.

Dog Tag came in all righty, paid $19.80 for a deuce, and I natch, disbelieved old Honest Ed Wright.

Leave 'em Smiling

When Asa Weatherwax died almost twenty years ago, the home-town newspapers took customary notice of his passing. They observed that he had led a good life, had been in business in Cheyenne, Wyo., for a number of years, and that he was survived by his wife and daughter.

Asa's obituary consisted of routine stuff. It named the place and date of birth, education, affiliations, cause, time and place of death, and listed the method of disposal of the body. In Asa's case this was cremation.

Omitted without even casual reference was the fact that Asa Weatherwax's exit was marked by an easy and extremely enviable good grace heightened by a display of rare good humor.

In fact, the skinny little warrior who feared neither man nor death managed to work in a hearty chuckle over preparations for his own crossing of the Jordan.

He had been in ill health a long time. A lung disorder made necessary a difficult operation which had to be done in three stages.

First, the surgeons carved a hole in Asa's chest big enough to contain a handball. The ribs were sawed away and discarded permanently.

The next step was to cut his shoulder bone, bend the shoulder forward and lock it in that position long enough to permit a covering of skin to be grown over the opening. Then the shoulder would gradually be replaced in its normal position.

Asa never got beyond the first stage.

He spent his remaining years with that infernal hole in his chest, and used to entertain friends by allowing them to pull aside the rubber and gauze covering and gaze at his respiratory innards.

I knew Asa well and visited him as often as I could. He was refreshing company and high, good fun. Conversation was difficult with him. He'd have to close his mouth and suck hard through his nostrils to get his breath. That interrupted his flow of talk. But it never deterred Asa from arguing volubly for the candidacy of Alf Landon for president.

One day the infection returned to the ailing man's lung. It festered. The doctor told Asa he was dying. Asa said that it was all right with him. But could the doc do anything to speed the thing along? Asa was tired of waiting.

Between lapses into coma, Asa managed to have telegrams dispatched to his loved ones. These messages brought his ex-wife, his then present wife, and a daughter, an unforgettable red head.

No time was wasted on sentimentality. Asa was dying and there were things to do. He gave orders to produce an undertaker's catalog.

With palsied hand he made a wavering circle around the coffin of his choice, chose the site of his own cremation, then shakily signed his name to a check to pay all expenses.

Right after that he showed improvement, got better and soon was sitting up. He sent his family home with genuine expressions of regret.

Later on he confided that he wished everything had worked out all right—that he had died as he expected he would. Then:

"That darned coffin, Bob. Looks like I'm going to have to get the thing brought here to the hospital and put it under my bed for a hope chest."

A few weeks after that, Asa went to sleep one night and never awakened.

He was not on hand, as he hoped to be, to meet death face to face.

"When I do," he used to say, "I'll make a Republican out of Saint Peter or I'll go someplace else."

Fast on the Drawers

The South Dakota gun fighter, Wild Bill Hickok, had been appearing on the stage at Cheyenne with Buffalo Bill Cody when Doc Howard, fresh out of of the cavalry, was dispensing shots and water at Murrin's saloon.

It was Hickok's pleasure to drop in at Murrin's for a nightcap before turning in. One night he showed up early, remarked that he didn't feel so well, took a small drink and retired.

Next morning he failed to put in an appearance at his usual hour, and Doc became alarmed. He poured a stiff drink, carried it next door to Bill's rooming house, and ventured upstairs.

For some reason the gambling gunslick, who trusted no one, had gone to bed without locking his door. Doc turned the knob and let himself in. What he saw caused his heart to leap into his throat.

"Bill!" he gasped. "Are you all right? What's the matter?"

Hickok's lanky frame was sprawled on the bed. But what surprised Doc was the man's unorthodox position. Instead of lying lengthwise in conventional manner, Hickok was draped ungracefully across the foot of the bed, his feet almost touching the floor.

Doc was about to turn and race into the street with news that Hickok had died in his sleep or had been murdered, when the gambler stirred, roused and grinned:

"Nothin's the matter, Doc," he drawled. "I always sleep this way. Yuh see, if I have an argument with anybody and they come on me unexpectedly, I can pull my pants and boots on all together."

Doc (J. W.) Howard, the old Indian fighter and early settler, knew them all. He wrote interestingly, if briefly, about them in his private memoirs which he left to his son, Sam Howard of Denver, retired police officer, when he passed over the Great Divide here in 1938.

Of Calamity Jane he said: "She was not the boisterous character she was represented to be. She accompanied the government trains in male attire, but always acted like a lady.

"The last time I saw her, she was all slicked up clean as a whistle. I said, 'Gee, Calamity, you sure look swell. There ain't no flies on you.'

"To this flattery Calamity replied:

" 'Nope, they left their tracks and flew'."

Before Doc moved to Colorado he was jailed once for "rustling," typical treatment for homesteaders in those days.

One day he tired of prairie winds, bundled his wife and their belongings into a wagon and lit out for Denver. He sold his horses, except for one team, at the Joseph Holmes corral on Larimer street, then went to work as a "skinner" for the West End Cable company, forerunner of the Denver Tramway corporation.

Later on, he quit the tramway company and joined the Mount Rose company's colony on the western slope.

The Colorado Co-operative was putting through a 20-mile irrigation ditch, and times were tough. The colonists, Doc wrote, lived mostly on beans and sowbelly. But there was fun at the schoolhouse on Saturday night when the women folk would scrape their larders clean and put on a feed and dance.

Doc became mayor of Pinon, and because he was a "jack of all trades," was dubbed "the woodpecker general."

Prosperity and contentment reigned with completion of the ditch. The *Altruian* began publication; gardens were in "fine shape," everybody was happy and in good health. Each colony member had forty acres of land. Doc said:

" 'We called this little site Nucla."

Doc Said a Mouthful

The scene: western Kansas. Outside was blowing one of western Kansas' famous dust storms.

Three spectators sat in the lobby of a hotel, watching the storm rip up the real estate and fling it into the next county. One of the three was Doc Walter Reckling from up Lusk, Wyo., way. Doc is an old friend, favorite cracker barrel philosopher and observer, as well as a frequent contributor to this department.

I said Doc was sitting. The truth is that he was standing near the stove trying to keep warm. One of the three was an old lady, a guest at the hotel only because she was marooned by the storm. She kept mincing back and forth to the windows and complaining about the dust, the storm and the general unpleasantness of her immediate status quo.

Party of the third part was an oldtimer, grizzled by the wear and tear of many seasons and similar dust storms.

As he sat there, rocking back and forth in an old chair that squeaked dismally, he chewed tobacco with a vengeance. Now and then, Doc relates, he'd aim a full mouth of tobacco juice at a big, tall brass gaboon that teetered under each shot and stood a full six feet from the chair.

Doc says he watched the old boy hit the target with a splattering "kerplunk" again and again, each time bringing deeper disgust to the face of the old lady.

"If I hadn't been there," Doc recalls, "I am sure she would have murdered the old gent with what she must have felt would be justifiable homicide."

After a particularly bad shot from oldtimer, she exclaimed, "Does it blow like this all the time out in this country?"

The oldtimer shot Doc a look that signified he would handle the query on the basis of seniority.

"Lady," he began patiently. "It ain't so bad. It don't allus blow like this here." He punctuated his remarks with another long shot at the brass.

"It just blows like this for a couple days, then it blows like hell."

Doc cited the incident in applause for the self-same tobacco chewers who were patted on the back in this space a few weeks ago. Doc calls them deeply human figures, "lovable in tolerance if messy in sanitation."

He confessed—and to heck with the college of surgeons, too—to having once been tempted to try chewing tobacco. He quit when he saw spots in front of his eyes and his skin turned a beautiful apple green.

His dad chewed tobacco. One of his favorite pasttimes was to watch a couple of Blackstone disciples wrangle over legal cases in the county courthouse, because both were veteran tobacco chewers and the one that made the most spectacular shot at a spittoon in the middle of the courtroom usually won the case.

Folks in the courtroom followed each drive to the brass like spectators at a tennis match.

Doc's pop wore a beard. Part of it was always getting streaked by the backspray of his expectorating, and the sides were stained from overflow. He used to always say, "Why try 'em in court? Let 'em fight it out back of the courthouse," which they always did anyhow.

So Doc came about his admiration for a man who can spit a hole-in-one, by quite natural persuasion. "And," he says, "if the women want to take it up to show the men they, too, can play— LET 'EM, by gum!

"With the home fires about to burn again because of television, what could be more homelike than maw and paw sittin' by the screen just like they used to do by the stove, a'chewin' and a'spittin' to beat heck?"

The Undefeated Champ

After watching him bust both the hopes and the bones of some of the nation's top bronc stompers, *Denver Post* Reporter Al Hayes once wrote that "Midnight" must surely be the reincarnation of Bucephalus.

That fancy-named hoss was the murderous steed that the king of Thrace sent to Philip of Macedon. Bucephalus was "broke out" by the stripling Alexander who said none but a king should ever ride him. None other ever bestrode him.

"But among our buckaroos," Hayes lamented, "there are no Alexanders."

Perhaps no other horse in history ever had so much publicity— not even the blue-blooded princes of the Bluegrass country. Midnight was a range-country fable.

Rodeo press agents called him the "King of the Outlaws." What the cowboys called him out in back of the corrals couldn't be printed.

When he died in November, 1936, at the age of 20 on the green pastures of Verne Elliott's rodeo ranch near Johnston, Colo., Lev Chapin, another *Post* writer, typed out a touching memorial to the great bucker—and it was printed on page one, an obituary space reserved only for the great.

"Midnight was a bucker and the best in the business," he wrote, "not because he was mean or a man killer as some horses are, but because he understood that it was all a game and that he should play it with every ounce of energy and every drop of courage he could command.

"If there are animals, like men, who engage in sports for the thrill of a clean victory, Midnight was one of them."

Midnight was not the kind of horse that turned and attacked a downed rider. He knew the rules of the game and he obeyed them. When his rider was off, he knew the contest was over.

Once in Nebraska, he threw a rider so hard the 'puncher was knocked cold. Midnight turned and walked toward him while the audience tensed.

The mighty terror of the rodeo arena merely bent his head, sniffed at the rider as much as to say "Sorry, cowboy," then ambled off to the corral.

Foaled on Jim McNab's Cottonwood ranch near McLeod, Alberta, Canada, Midnight just decided all at once to become a bucker, it seemed. He piled McNab and all his riders in turn. He was part thoroughbred, part Morgan and part Percheron.

In his time, he threw such men as Earl Thode, Pete Knight, Paddy Ryan, Doff Aber, Eddie Woods and a host of others. He bucked for London rodeo fans and thrilled spectators from coast to coast.

Woods, the Emmett, Ida., hero of the crutch-manufacturers' favorite sport, said Midnight's secret was an ability to whip the front of the saddle upwards a full eighteen inches whereas most other bucking horses were considered tough to jerk the saddle only six inches.

His peculiar breeding gave him a right unhandy ability to kick higher and with greater strength than any horse alive.

Tough as he was, however, I believe Casey Tibbs, the Fort Pierre, S. D., world champion, could possibly ride Midnight.

99

Verne Elliott goes along part way with that opinion. He puts it this way: "Casey could put up a pretty good ride on him."

Bronc stompers ride a different style these days—a style, I might add, that the old-timers shunned as "tenderfoot." It's a free and easy, fast moving change of balance—a lightness in the saddle and a system of spurring the horse at the most opportune point of his takeoff for the sky.

Old-timers clamped themselves down in the saddle and beat the heck out of a bucker with both hat and spurs. What's more they were squalling while riding.

But the Midnight-Casey Tibbs ruckus like the John L. Sullivan-Joe Louis fight can only remain a matter of conjecture.

Only Midnight, however, died undefeated.

Otto's Steamboat Ride

Now, you take old "Steamboat." *There* was a bucking horse.

'Punchers used to allow as how he could kick the watch out of a rider's pocket with his hind foot if he had a mind to. He could stand on three legs and, without turning his head, scratch back of his ear like a dog.

He was the animal kingdom's nearest approach to jet propulsion. He shook like the San Francisco earthquake, and when he'd "come undone" it was with all parts flying. Any man who could ride him could break a Kansas cyclone for a roping mount.

"Steamboat" was the terror of the rodeo arena around the turn of the century. He humbled the best of them.

The big, rangy beast hailed from Chugwater, Wyo., and ruled the rodeo rack back in the days of such bronc stompers as Sam Scoville, Harry Brennan, Hugh Clark, Guy Holt, Thad Sowder and Clayton Danks. All were champions at one time or another.

T-Joe Cahill, the daddy of the "Daddy of 'em All," had seen him on the rampage at a private showing and had been impressed. Steamboat had scattered Bud Gillespie, best rider on the Bosler ranch, to the four corners of the place.

T-Joe arranged to have the horse put in the bucking string for Frontier Days. The first day he took part in the show, he jolted three would-be riders into the dirt so hard their Stetsons still were vibrating the next afternoon.

Steamboat's fame reached the Potomac. He already was a fable wherever he had appeared—in Denver and Colorado Springs, at rodeos throughout the Dakotas, Nebraska and Montana.

When President Teddy Roosevelt visited the big show at Cheyenne, he asked to see this hoof storm in action. Teddy appreciated the violence of infuriated horseflesh because he sat a pretty tight storm deck himself.

Rannies and spectators alike spoke of Steamboat's feats with exclamation marks in their voices. Later on they were to accord similar respect to a green young cowpoke from Sybille, Wyo., who met Steamboat back to back, so to speak, at the Cheyenne show.

He was Otto Plaga, a newcomer to the rodeo circuit.

Otto took a leave from the prairie dog towns of his range habitat and began to appear as a contestant in hurrah rodeos at small towns. Then he hit the big time.

By some arrangement that is not quite clear, the gangly-legged agreed to ride the equine earthquake in an exhibition for the president.

Oldtimers say it was the greatest ride of all time. Judges looked on in awe. They suspended the rules. Otto, who didn't believe any horse could be that tough, raked the animal with his rowels.

Steamboat exploded! His ears went back, his head down. The back arched with unsprung power and his nostrils flared with flame. 'Punchers on foot sought points of safety.

The big beast pounded the earth in a rage. He used his full bag of tricks. The rider was flung into the air. He came back down—on the horse's rump back of the saddle. Then he heaved himself forward with the next jump, forked the saddle and found the stirrups.

Steamboat twisted in midair to kick at the sun. The "green 'un" from Sybille hit the dirt.

Otto got up with tears in his eyes. He thought he was forever disgraced. He was crying openly when he retrieved his hat.

Then, from audience and contestants alike, came the greatest cheer that had ever acclaimed a rodeo rider. And Otto later showed he merited it.

Sybille's pride went on to the world championship.

McFaddlefoot the Diviner

If my old grandad's soul had contained so much as a mite of larceny, he could have made a million.

He knew how to engineer a divining rod.

I was about 8 years old when he introduced me to the wonders of this strange scientific device. It was a simple gadget—a forked branch cut from a willow.

By turning his hands outward at the extreme ends of the two little limbs and pointing the fork toward the ground, he could walk back and forth over any given area and "locate" a water well. It never failed. Grandpa found water for a great many people although he consumed little of the stuff himself. My grandpa thought water was fit for nothing except bathing.

His divining rod proved to be a great source of wonderment to me for many years. It remained that way until I met the peer of all divining rod operators. Just for fun let's call him J. Humphries McFaddlefoot—it seems to describe him to a T.

McFaddlefoot's divining rod was a vast scientific improvement over the crude willow switch used by grandpa. It was a device that had many wires, radio tubes and switches on it.

By expert use of it, McFaddlefoot assured one and all, the operator could locate oil wells. The thing never missed except when there were climatic, atmospheric or solar interferences.

Of course McFaddlefoot had no control over those elements although to behold the man one would gather a rather general impression that he could sway the universe if so minded.

Mac was an impressive cuss in a short, squdgy sort of way. He stood about 5 feet 4 inches tall, and looked like the original Mr. Five-by-Five.

He drove into town in a Cadillac one day, parked the machine where it would attract the greatest notice, then sat back in his hotel room to receive a host of telegrams and telephone calls. All of these, incidentally, arrived just as his room was filled with people who wanted him to use his divining rod to find an oil well near town or on their own particular property.

The telegrams testified abundantly that McFaddlefoot was in tremendous demand. Indeed, he was in certain sections of the country.

Sheriffs almost everywhere were constantly seeking McFaddle-foot.

Anyway, it was not long until McFaddlefoot permitted himself to be persuaded to make several "exhaustive scientific measurements of underground strata."

He took his divining rod which he called a "doodlebug," and paced back and forth over many acres in the vicinity of Douglas (my old home town), Wyo.

Then one day McFaddlefoot waxed extremely serious and mysterious. He locked himself in his room and refused to see any visitors. Meanwhile a hotel attendant was rushing back and forth between his room and the Cadillac out front, carrying impressive maps and papers.

Before long, however, he disclosed his amazing discovery to a small group of confidants. Oddly enough, they were the only people in town who had any money.

McFaddlefoot had probed the bowels of the earth and had come up with a peculiar formation which contained oodles of oil. He took his followers into the field to prove it.

At just the right spot in a field not distant from town, Mac's doodlebug lighted up like a Christmas tree and gave with a noisy clamor. Before long McFaddlefoot and associates had a Star rig on the place.

There's a short piece of oil pipe sticking above the ground to this day to mark the place. But McFaddlefoot is nowhere to be found.

These Rugged Pioneers

The United States government would have to get out one of its biggest maps to find Muddy Gap, Wyo. A gimpy cowboy with a pocket full of rocks could stand in the middle of the road here and break dern near every window in town. That's how big the place is.

Seventy-five-mile-an-hour tourists from three corners of the Equality state drive past here every day during the summer season. Each and every one of them is reminded by well-placed signs that before him there traveled through this western strip of prairie dog towns a hardy breed of pioneers who wrote history with Winchesters and Colts and beans and bacon and barren living.

"That's a thing of the past," each one says to himself. "Too bad that people like that aren't still living."

The next thought is invariable: "What in the heck do these people out in this God-forsaken country do? What a place to make a home!"

The more patient and curious-minded will find out if they stop for an hour in Muddy Gap. (What a name for a town!)

I stopped there a few days ago and had one of the grandest experiences in many a highway mile. I met the Hoths. Pioneering, believe you me, brother, is not over and done with.

The Hoths, Jack and Mattie, operate a wayside eating place and bar here. It's not one of those fancy spots where the customers slump in plush booths. Here the guest stands to drink and sits on a hard stool to eat. And the food is good and western.

If the visitor is a sociable sort of cuss, Mattie will haul out her rock collection. It's something that would baffle professor guys, so it's easy to see that it would fascinate greenhorns like you and me.

That rock collection is the answer to what people do with their leisure moments out here in the big, bald badlands.

When time wears on Mattie, she hoofs it out into the hills and picks up rocks. She says it's more fun than going through the biggest museum in the country. What she finds is hers. It doesn't belong to some scientific society and doesn't bear a sign that says "Hands off."

Mattie's collection includes the petrified head of an ancient reptilian critter that she picked up one day when they used to live near Craig, Colo. It's about the size of a small dinner plate and is obviously from a prehistoric tar pit where many behemoths perished ages ago. The thing makes you wonder whether the scientific guys are really on their toes when they say fossilized remains are limited to just a few old bones.

Her collection also boasts an enormous eye that she believes once belonged to a deep sea fish. It's a dead ringer for a fish's eye. Then there's a gizzard—as real as life but all stone. It has every indication of reality.

But thus far most geologists have just given Mattie the ha-ha, principally because no real geologist has ever seen her collection. She's written letters to them but has seldom had an answer.

Mattie has a collection of quartzized fish with scales and all, and jade and petrified wood galore. She has a good story to go with each piece of her collection.

But the best story she tells, and usually it comes after the conversation is near its end, is the one about the night she had the toothache.

She groaned and tossed in bed.

It is eighty-four miles from Muddy Gap to Lander, Wyo., seventy-six miles to Casper and forty-six to Rawlins.

What in the dickens are you going to do about a bad tooth that far from town?

Jack had the answer. He simply got out a pair of pliers and pulled the mischievous molar.

What became of the pioneers? Just stop in Muddy Gap or any other wayside spot in Wyoming if you're interested. And if you have a toothache, Jack will take care of it. He's pulled three of his own, too.

Preacher on Horseback

When Roy H. Porter hung up his saddle and crossed the Great Divide up in Lusk, Wyo., a few weeks ago, the family had a special request for his funeral service. They wanted someone to sing *Headin' for the Last Roundup*.

Now Roy was a right rank hand in his day, as the cowboys say. He spent most of his sixty-two years riding knot-headed cayuses and tailing wiry dogies across the endless prairies of the Equality state. His leg had that natural saddle turn and his face bore the marks of weather.

Headin' for the Last Roundup was a natural for his funeral.

Well, about the time Roy was in his prime, a young, onery cuss over in Douglas (my old home town), Wyo., was just fitting his legs to saddle leather and was making quite a name for himself as an athlete, too.

He was Glen Perry, a husky, broad shouldered gent built close to the ground and gifted with more muscle than the Budweiser brewery team.

Perry used to love to shoot flies off the bunkhouse ceiling with a .45. He couldn't wait for Saturday night so he could "git with it" in town. He used to jump at the barn dances, played piano, sang, and generally had a jack under one corner of hell and a block in hand ready to put under it.

He will be remembered in Nebraska as an all-state back from Chadron Normal and one of the state's greatest broken field runners. But he is remembered in Lusk, Wyo., for what he did at Roy H. Porter's funeral.

It seems that somewhere in the twenty-five years that elapsed between the time I knew Perry as a gun-slinging cowpoke and the present, something happened to him. Perry, as he puts it, "got straightened out with the Lord." He's plumb sincere about it, too.

After several years of picking drunks out of Los Angeles gutters and helping them back on their feet, Perry returned to Wyoming a self-ordained preacher of the Gospel.

His old friends stared at him in amazement. They thought he was pulling a typical Perry prank.

He wasn't. Perry's musical talent was transferred from rough cowboy parodies to the songs they sing in church. His fingers became accustomed to a portable organ he carried around with him in his house trailer.

He was still a cowpuncher at heart, however, and it was on horseback that he began carrying the Gospel to sinners of the range country. Perry's church was the rolling plains, its spires the towering ramparts of Wyoming mountains. Perry preached softly in bunkhouses to two or three punchers at a time, rode with them on the roundup and prayed over the chuckwagon suppers.

Once he accepted a challenge to fight a cow waddie to prove to him that religion is not "sissy stuff." This went on for several years and the trail finally led to Lusk.

There Undertaker George Earl Peet was in a quandary. The only authorized preacher not on vacation had flatly refused to allow anything so impious as a cowboy song to be rendered during any service he conducted.

Peet called Rapid City, Casper and other towns without any luck whatsoever. It was the first time in his experience that he had ever "run short of preachers."

Then somebody happened to think of Glen Perry, the Cowboy Evangelist.

Perry hesitatingly accepted the commission to say words over Roy's body. It was his first funeral.

In rangeland phrases that were understood by the rangeland folk who came to bury Roy, Perry spoke his piece. Roy had been a mighty good hand in his day, a God-fearing hand who took his work seriously and never dodged his responsibility to other folks. Perry said so.

Then, guitar in hand, Perry opened his shirt collar, slipped down his bandana, and in a voice that brought real tears to the weathered cheeks of the ranch folks present, sang *Headin' for the Last Roundup*.

Dick Jewell's Downfall

It was a thrill-hungry, slap-happy, cockeyed era that Dick Jewell walked into when he stepped out of uniform just after World War I. It was that unforgettable era of bathtub gin, home brew, speakeasies, jazz music, flappers and balloon pants.

The country had gone topsy-turvy overnight. People stood in the streets by the thousands and watched human flies scale tall buildings and gaped at marathon flag-pole sitters by the dozens. Any building without a flag-pole sitter was considered only partially equipped.

It seemed natural that Dick should get himself all het up about pulling a few stunts like that himself. He learned years ago that he possessed amazing strength despite his 146 pounds. And he had a sense of balance and timing.

Dick hit the tanbark trail. He followed circuses a while. Then he struck out for himself.

He'd book an appearance in some small town, put on his show and draw the folks in from the country to spend their money in the stores which paid him handsomely for doing their advertising.

From El Paso, Tex., to Podunk, Mont., from San Francisco to New York, Dick worked the little villages and occasionally a big city with his stunts. He thought nothing of hurtling a motorcycle smack through a burning wall. For less than it would take to buy

him a wooden kimono he'd step off the rear bumper of an automobile going sixty miles an hour, or he'd drive one car headlong
into another.

One of his favorites was the "slide of death." One of these he
put on at El Paso. He tied a rope to one corner of the top of the
Cortez hotel, stretched it across San Jacinto plaza, then slid down
the thing hanging to a leather strap by his teeth.

When things got dull, Dick would take a job wing walking
one of those flying crates that used to frighten old men and horses.
He'd board a plane by rope ladder from a speeding automobile.
Then he'd crawl out on the wing of one plane and jump over to
another. He did these little things to satisfy a thrill-hungry world.

He had feats of strength, too. He'd pull a fire truck with his
teeth. He'd let two strong men bend an iron bar which he held
in his mouth. As a follow-upper he'd get the village blacksmith to
break a 200-pound cake of concrete on his chest.

Dick is one of a vanishing breed. Before he retired he'd sign
away his life for a gag, then bet you'd worked on the wrong hunch.
He'd risk his neck on the flip of a coin. And he'd furnish the coin,
too.

One time at El Paso he walked out on the cornice of a tall building to attach a rope for his "slide of death." A Tarzan-like human
who was watching passed out in a cold faint.

Throughout this career of neck-risking Dick Jewell never incurred anything more serious than a few bumps and a small assortment of scratches.

Then one day back in 1942 he decided to quit the stunt racket
and take up safer and saner pursuits. He had just turned 41 and,
thinking life began at 40, he undertook for the first time to prolong it.

I saw Dick a few days ago here in Denver. He walked into the
place sad-eyed. Said he had gotten himself a small job not long
before that on Coulter's Lake dude ranch near Rifle.

But he didn't know whether he would go back. It didn't seem
to be a safe occupation. He went on to relate that he had been
leading a colt a few weeks ago from horseback when the colt reared
and jerked him out of the saddle.

"So I got me a little banged up and I don't like it," he says.
"Maybe I'll go back to stunting."

Then he picked up his crutches and eased himself out the door.

Sober Smith's Roan

I was taking my ease in Tony Ferretti's Athletic, Social and Up-lift for the Sagging Society one afternoon of recent date when who should walk into the place but Sober Smith from the 2-Lazy-2 out-fit just west of Orin Junction.

Sober's tongue was hanging out like a grass widow's personality. It shone with heat and reflected thirst. It looked like last winter's flannels just before being rid of alkali. It was the first time I had ever seen Sober hankering for a drink.

"Gimme a double shot of yogurt with Hadacall on the side," he mumbled.

Then, looking at me with bloodshot eyes ,he said: "D'ja ever hear of the Bitter Roan?

"S'durndest critter that ever grew ears," he stated in a matter-of fact manner. "Just now got in from tryin' to break 'im."

Then he gulped his Hadacall.

"Couldn't understand what caused all the rukus out't the ranch when they mentioned this hammer-headed barn buster 'cept that he was just plain bronco.

"Seemed nobody had ever rid 'im.

"Well, you know me, Red. Never was a four-footed critter that I couldn't ride one way or t'other. So when the spring roundup of hosses took place, I just culled 'im out, sacked 'im in the corral for a couple of days, then busted 'im and put a hackamore on 'im.

"Gimme another Hadacall, bartender.

"We got a couple of the boys together, pulled 'im in and I put my kack on 'im. He threw a hump in his back that would'a stopped a high-altitude airy-plane.

"F'got to tell ya, we'd shod this rennie just the day after we brought 'im in cause I reckoned as how, after countin' his ribs, that he'd make a good work hoss.

"S'funny, he took to shoein' like a newspaperman takes to yogurt. No trouble a'tall.

"Gimme just one more yogurt with this, willya?

"So I mounted up, figurin' kinda like that he would take to leather just as easy.

"Well, ya know me, Red. I never was known as a hand to walk back from any ride. I take 'em and break 'em.

"So I mounted up."

109

He rubbed his mouth with the back of his hand.

"This thing gave one leap and we wuz there in the corral. We hit the dirt in Laramie county. First dig I give 'im with the spurs, I blunted both rowels. Next time, I bent both shanks.

"Well, I knew it wouldn't make no difference then. I just tried to ride 'im. Sure, I raked 'im. He was just in off winter range and was fuzzy. The hair flew so thick I couldn't see the sun.

"Gimme another yogurt, willya? Boy, am I ever disgusted. I wouldn't go back to thet ranch if they gimme the place.

"Thet critter bucked clean across Wyoming and on into Fort Collins. I wuz not so scared of bein' bucked off as I was of being starved to death.

"Yuh know I cain't go without food for more'n two days.

"Well, anyhow, I got 'im broke. But d'ya think I'm goin' to ride 'im back to the ranch? Not on yer life, Red. Me? And have them there rannies out t' 2-Lazy-2 spread kid th' life outa me?"

Well, I couldn't see just why Sober felt the way he did until after three more Hadacalls. He explained:

"I'm so durned sick and tired of hearin' them tall stories about fellers breakin' horses, I just cain't no more stand their gol-durned comp'ny."

The Lemon Peel Kid

I've often wondered whatever became of George Supplee, the baron of LaPrele creek in the fat cow and fine folks country of central Wyoming. George remains in my memory like a schoolboy's first pair of long pants. The last I heard of him he had moved to a spot near Wheatland.

It seems he finally succumbed to the wiles of the opposite sex and got himself married off. I recall that for years on end, George resisted the marital hogtie like a bronc fights a hackamore. He put up a beautiful and touching fight, perfecting the art of living alone to the point where he could turn out the best tasting ranch biscuits I've ever herded into my gastronomic corral.

George was a tophand cowpuncher, too. He taught me how not to thumb a horse's neck until after you are able to crawl under him without being kicked to Providence.

He also demonstrated in forceful fashion why a rider should never permit an untrained horse to sidewheel and get a lariat under a flank.

George's life of single bliss was led in a log ranchhouse beside the dirt road that led from Douglas (my old home town), Wyo., to Cold Springs. It was more like a bunkhouse in appearance. It was long, low to the ground and had a shed-roof porch that ran the length of it.

Because of an unusual gift of gab and a sense of humor that somehow is distinguished from city cleverness because of a certain dryness, George had frequent visitors among the ranch owners and their sunup-to-sundown hands.

Among these was a newcomer to the area—a Kansan who went to work on the Bill Hinton ranch a few miles distant, with an uncontrollable hankering to become a cowpuncher.

His real name is lost to mind just now, but I do recall that he was a study in contrast with the average man of those precincts. He wore—of all things—bib overalls, with stripes, too! Atop his head drooped a slouchy straw hat. He wore low-heeled shoes— farm shoes.

Primary requisite to becoming a waddie, in this Kansan's opinion, was the knack of curling a brownie (rolling a cigaret, to you). So George patiently rolled them for him, demonstrated with grimaces and gesture just how the magic was accomplished.

"Yuh've got to be careful, though," George warned, "yuh've got to light 'em plumb out on the tip if yore Durham's powdered, 'cause when it's that way the stuff's just like gunpowder."

With that George finished a cigaret and the tenderfoot stuck it between his lips.

"Now yuh light it," said George.

He did and the thing promptly blew up in his face, set fire to the straw hat and peremptorily terminated his interest in rolling cigarets.

"Durn it," George exploded, "I told yuh not to light that so fur back."

What he didn't tell him was that the cigaret was loaded with enough powder from a .30-30 to kill a bull elk.

And speaking of bulls: George asked the flatlander one day how he traveled between his and the Hinton ranch. Hinton's man replied: "Across the cow pasture."

111

"Cow pasture?" Supplee explained. "That there's the bull pasture and it's full of killers. Here, when yuh go home, now take this lemon peel. Keep it ready, and if ary of them bulls charges yuh, just stand yore ground and when he gets close enough, squeeze juice in his eye. There's nothing like lemon juice to keep a bull from chargin' yuh."

Thereafter the Hinton hand was known as Lemon Peel. He was never without one. And he was never menaced by a bull, surprisingly or not.

The Amiable Amicks

Now, I stoutly disavow any reputation for ever having been an all around, catch-as-catch-can heck raiser. But I do admit to a modest participation at one time in the hollering and innocent fun making that usually goes on at rodeo time.

I enjoyed getting with the boys wherever the boys got together, which was usually where we all wished we hadn't the next day. (If you don't catch that the first time, read it again.)

We would swap gab, tell lies to each other, brag on our pasts and let out a yip or two before the night was over. Aside from that, we never did anything brash enough to get in trouble.

As time passed, however, and the other fellows seemed to be getting older and showing their age more all the time, I began to concentrate seriously on the vital things of life such as the resilience of my backbone, state of my liver and the lining of my stomach. I hollered less and less and pretty soon became almost inaudible at rodeos and state fairs. On visits to the state fair up at Douglas (my old home town), Wyo., I commenced to withdraw from the mob and seek peace and sleep when evening came on.

That's how I started staying at the Bellwood tourist court at Glendo, 25 miles south of Douglas, and that's how I got acquainted with Roy and Betty Amick, the proprietors.

Each day of the fair I would drive back and forth between Glendo and Douglas. Now that sounds like quite a price in distance to pay for quiet. But it takes less time to drive it than it does to get to work each morning here in Denver in spite of the fact I can look out my back bedroom and see *The Denver Post* building only three miles away.

Roy and Betty became priceless friends of mine. There's always something new and interesting at the Amick's motel. Last time I was there it was a litter of pups presented to the Amicks by one of the many stray dogs that have taken up with the couple over the years.

Roy putters, collects rare rocks, makes fascinating furniture out of pine and quakers, writes western stories and is a sort of local Scattergood Baines and Will Rogers. Betty just smiles, tolerates Roy and, with him, keeps the Bellwood spick and span.

The first time I registered at the motel, Roy fixed me with a look like he had just caught me checking out with the towels. It seems that a couple years before, some jasper had telephoned a reservation from Lusk for "Red Fenwick and party of twenty" for the duration of the fair. Roy reserved the rooms, stuffed cotton in his ears and waited for the onslaught. Nothing happened. Nobody showed up. I assured Roy there had been an awful mistake. Somebody had used my name unfairly.

Roy was nice about it. He said it was okay and I went to bed. Far into the night I lay there thinking: *When was the last time I was in Lusk?*

SOME PERSONAL SLANTS

The Sun Worshiper

I used to have an Indian friend who made a yearly ritual of welcoming spring weather by going out to a sand draw on the first warm day, taking off his clothes and soaking up the sunshine. He'd sprawl there for hours just reveling in the warmth, dreaming dreams and adding years to his life.

If I could find him I'd go with him this year. I'd like to go out to some sunny ditch, strip and lie there on my back looking up at fleecy white puffs in the sky for a whole day. I'd like to get miles away from traffic lights, automobiles, telephones, traffic cops and traffic snarls, greasy spoon restaurants, surly public officials and forlorn city dwellers for a while at least. I'd leave my typewriter, too.

It may sound rather odd, but I have to confess at this point that I've many times toyed with the idea that it would be pleasant to take a job for a year, at least, just herding sheep on some remote range miles from the city.

My dissatisfaction with cities goes back to childhood. I distinctly remember one time when my father brought me to Denver on a shopping trip. We rode in a cab from the Denver Union station to an uptown hotel and, on the way, I was impressed more with the expressions on people's faces than I was by the big buildings and other city sights supposed to impress youngsters from the sticks.

So many people seemed to have a hang-dog look, a sort of beaten, hemmed-in, tired expression of hopelessness on their faces. That's been my impression of the city ever since—a spot where slaves work to make a living, wishing all the while they could find again

117

the peace, calm, and deeply abiding sense of happiness and security they knew as country kids; wishing that they had never left the jerkwater town in the first place.

Oh, cities are nice in many ways. They have parks and big amusement places, but I've always insisted there's a big difference between amusement and sheer happiness and contentment. And only a country Jake who has known both can appreciate the difference. The difference becomes more distinct and acute the older one grows.

Cities have big buildings, too, and great hospitals and accomplished physicians and a great many police. But there's also the missions, the dirtiest type of poverty, the most abject depravity, the skid row, stinking alleys and too many little boys and girls who grow up in them. And our big cities have too many sick people who can't afford either the doctors or the hospitals.

Cities have splendid churches. too, far fancier structures than the little jerkwater towns, but far too many people go to them because it gives them an opportunity to show off their Sunday best or to impress their boss who goes to the same church or to meet somebody socially who might help them in business.

Of course, it's the same God in the city and small town churches. But somehow I think God is a little closer to the small town church. And now that I think back on it, my old Indian friend's favorite day for sunning himself in a draw far from the city was Sunday. Perhaps there was more to his ritual than just enjoying the sun.

A Hick at Heart

There used to be an old saying that you can take the boy out of the country but you can't take the country out of the boy and I guess that's me all over. Oh, city living is dandy. But there's something about the crossroads that's appealing as a cider keg in a spring house on a hot day.

Now we do have a lot of extras in the big city. We have more and bigger things including people and taxes, and we have a commodity called efficiency that's almost unheard of out in the sticks. It's an unsmiling thing but it's absolutely necessary because it takes us from two to three times as long to get things done in the big city and, besides, it keeps a lot of people off the relief rolls. Besides that, it makes a customer feel like he's getting something he's not paying for and that's important to business. We have to do things up in fancy packages.

For instance you want to get your watch cleaned. Now up in Douglas (my old home town), Wyo., you take your watch to the jeweler and, old-fashioned like, hand it to him and he hangs it up without putting a tag or anything on it, and two days later you go back and it's ready. The same guy hands it back and collects $4 from you.

But here in the big city you take a day off from work to have plenty of time to find parking space and all, then you drive downtown because you know you can't get a seat on any of the big comfortable buses we have here as another service you never hear of in the little towns. Then you go to the jewelry store and in about 15 minutes a clerk comes up and demands to know what you're doing in the place. You tell him you want a watch cleaned and hand it to him instead of the jeweler.

This clerk, he takes your watch and puts it in a little envelope with a number on it. Then he tears off one end of the tag and gives it to you to use when you come after your watch which will be ready in two weeks.

At that time you take another day off, go back and pick up your watch (if you can find the little tag), pay the clerk $7 and you don't have to waste time listening to a lot of questions about how's your wife and kids and your health and all that kind of junk. You just pay the man.

Only a few days ago I had a ring stretched to fit my finger and the job took two days. Up home a jeweler once did the same thing for me while I waited at the counter. It's these little extras that make city living attractive.

It's exciting to live in a big city. You never know, for example, what you'll get three weeks from now when your laundry comes back. Out in the hay tracks you get back the same old shirts with the same old buttons. Some laundries in the big city will take off the old buttons for free.

Even with its inconveniences, however, I like a small town. Take baseball. Orin Junction, a few miles from home, was so small when I was a kid, they had to borrow two men from Glendo

119

to have a team. Here in Denver where we have a half million people, we hire a whole team from back east and it's not near as much fun.

We used to play ball in a cow pasture when I was a boy, and I'll never forget the day one of the Sharps boys slid into what he thought was third base.

Lost: a Place to Sit

I don't know how you feel about this, neighbor, but danged if I'm not convinced that in our snatch-grab haste to adopt a lot of new-fangled things and ideas, we've surrendered a host of conveniences and solid, down-to-earth comfort.

This realization struck me like a tax delinquency notice the other evening and I must admit that I was considerably shocked. All this revolution, obviously inspired and carried out by kids, has taken place right under our very noses and has been so insidious that it's escaped notice.

The missus and I and all our relatives and neighbors had just completed a new concrete sidewalk in the front yard. It wasn't much of a job, perhaps, but to us it was on a par with construction of the Panama canal. After sending up a small dedicatory cheer the whole crowd wandered sort of naturally to a spot where our front porch should have been. There *wasn't* any! There was no place to sit! There were no chairs! And no shade.

Personally, I felt just a little conspicuous sipping my lemonade on the flower planter but I had to sit somewhere. And that was the only place. You see, our house is one of those modern doodads and they don't have porches.

For a minute I thought about going inside and getting a rocking chair to set on the lawn. Then I suddenly realized we haven't got a rocking chair. I put down my refreshments and went inside just to make sure. By George, there isn't a rocking chair on the place—just a bunch of bulgy overstuffed pillows with overstuffed sideboards to keep you from falling off when you slide down on your neck to make yourself comfortable. I went back outdoors.

Then it occurred to me to go over and sit down on the car parked in the driveway. They'd taken off the doggoned running-boards! The only place you can sit on our automobile—except inside—is on one of the bumpers and they're fixed so you get jabbed in the back if you dare to relax a little.

Well, *now!* It just seems to me we've gone far enough. What's wrong with having a front porch? And what's wrong with a rocking chair? And running-boards? Where do the kids romance their girls these days since they've spirited away the front porch? And how do mothers rock their little darlings to sleep? And where do you fishermen sit during those lively periods when—well, you know, when the fishing's not so good and you go back to the car?

Why, I remember when the whole family would go out on the porch evenings—grandad in his galluses and undershirt, bare feet propped on the porch railing—and greet the neighbors as they went by. It was a sociable spot, and that old porch swing . . . Wow!

She's a Jagalope

HRB

I came home wearing one of those English wrap-around roadsters the other night and people said I'd betrayed Detroit. Some others went so far as to say I'd been grazing on loco weed. Real friends offered excuses. Ferd Butler, wire editor of *The Denver Post,* said I'd been brain-washed by the S. C. C. A. (Sports Car Club of America) and Asst. City Ed. Don Davis explained that I was getting material for a book to be titled *I was a Spy for Standard Brands.*

Oh, what a furor! Sports car fans Barker and Baker of *Empire* magazine wanted me to eat a column of sneers I'd done some months ago on abbreviated automobiles and some of the neighbors acted like my whole family was somewhat more than slightly over-ripe.

And now that I think about it, possibly the missus and I do appear a bit eccentric to some folks. Admittedly, we once harbored a slavering but lovable Russian wolfhound big enough to eat a horse and did. (That's why we gave him up.) It is true that our present dog is a cute little psychopathic pooch with an undeniable phobia for devouring her cotton bedding. We likewise admit that our bird is a bit of a character. He's a parakeet named George. He says "Howd*ee* pard" to guests and he can whistle *Dixie*. Only he whistles it backwards and visitors who don't know this think he is whistling Beethoven's *Der Turken Hoppen.*

We favor western garb, like horseback riding, think *the complete* meal is steak and potatoes and wouldn't think of driving anywhere without carrying a muleshoe given to us years ago by Earl Pomeroy. Aside from all this and the fact we don't believe in telephones or airplanes, we're perfectly normal like anybody else.

But, boy! You'd think we'd really busted our cinch when we galloped up the other night in that gasolino mustang which we promptly named "The Thing." I'd spotted it on an American used car lot where they have a good sense of values i. e.: They knew what my Detroit monster was worth but grossly underrated the British product I wanted to buy.

I asked for a demonstration, pulled the car on like a boot and sunk my spurs in the throttle. When I had to go back two blocks to pick up my vest I knew this thing was what I wanted. They told me at the car lot that it was a Jaguar XK 140—MC—210 horsepower. The MC doesn't mean "much cash" as you'd think. It stands for "modified for competition," and is the hottest thing the Jaguar people have been able to come up with.

Right off, I knew, however, that The Thing was at heart a real Jagalope crossed between the Jaguar and Jackalope. Fellows out at my garage tell me it holds a scad of world speed records, so now I'm looking forward to a vacation trip but I've got a problem:

We don't know what we're going to do with George and the psycho dog. If we take a camera and some extra shirts there's no place to put them unless we do away with one of the cylinders. One concession I won't make, however, and that is to wear shorts and a beret. My old jeans and Wyoming crash helmet are good enough.

Dennis the Menace

We dropped rein just outside Santa Fe at the beautiful Del Monte guest ranch run by Barbara and Bill Hooton, and there— right out in public—was a jasper wearing a pair of those new high-water pants called onion country shorts. At first I couldn't believe that a full-grown man would go around with his bare knee-caps hanging out. But there he was big as life and I might have made the mistake of asking him where her husband was had it not been that the occupant of said Fauntleroy britches was sporting a Biblical beard that made him look like Moses in a track suit with no place to run.

Owner and wearer of the Seymour slacks, I learned on quick investigation, was none other than Patrick Dennis, author of the popular fun book *Auntie Mame.* I knew then that he was an educated man.

Really, though, Dennis looked right fetching in his Long Island Levis. He has rather attractive knees and there's just a hint of a dimple in the soft hollow behind the knee hinge. I think Dennis would put up a better appearance, however—and I hate to be catty about such things—but, honestly, you'd think he could shave his calves.

Up to the moment I laid eyes on Writer Dennis, I thought these new Ivy League leggings were strictly a joke and that they really were intended to be summer underwear for Eskimos. They *are* a bit shorter than longies, you know, although somewhat heavier than summer BVD's worn in balmier climes. But Dennis revealed not the slightest bit of self-consciousness.

These *Readers Digest*-size drawers do have advantages that are quite obvious. Take a man who is sensitive to unkind remarks about his balding head, bags under his eyes or burgeoning dignity.

He can wear these Manhattan chaps with absolute assurance of freedom from unkind remarks about his dome or physique. They sort of divert the interest. And they must be the greatest boon to the mosquito colony since the big nudist convention last summer.

It occurs to me as a precaution, however, that one should insist on only the highest quality in this new style. If these Bermuda bloomers shrink, a man certainly could get caught short in a rain storm.

I'm fascinated, too, by the stockings they wear with these half-mast zoot suits. How the devil do they hold them up? They fit snugly just above the big muscle of the calf and I must admit they do lend a rather enticing curve to a man's otherwise straight pins.

Dennis—that's only a pseudonym for some other real name— turned out to be a heck of a swell fella, however, despite his junior jumpers, and he downs a mean martini—or is it Scotch?

As I started to tell you, Dennis had volunteered to serve as bartender for the little guest group I had joined, and I guess he considered me a strange bird when I walked up and asked for a straight soda water—no Scotch, no Bourbon. He stared at the boots, jeans and ten-gallon hat and asked incredulously, "Really, boy, nothing in it?"

Patrick Dennis Rebutts

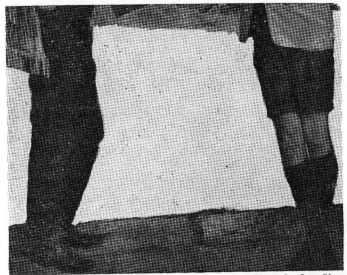

Photo by Lee Olson

Dear Red:

I am writing you from the Turkish bath that is New York. The temperature is 91, the humidity is 92. The steam is rising off Park Avenue just like those boring hot springs you people out in the Rockies are always showing to eastern visitors and the haze is so thick that you can't even see Grand Central Station six blocks down the street. You can, however, see a lot of knees.

New York has actually become a tropical city, although we wouldn't dream of admitting it. Ergo—we wear shorts: for that breeze around the knees. All it takes is courage and what my grandfather used to call "a well-turned calf."

And while we're on the subject of men's fashions, let's play Twenty Questions—more or less—about the outfit *you* were wearing.

1. Do you really have to grease your thighs to get into those tight Levis?

2. Is the true reason that western men never sit down is because they can't—without disrobing?

3. Do you honestly hide bottles of gin in those picture hats?

4. If you gents absolutely *have* to teeter around the streets in

French heels, why must they have that run-over look of a slow-moving item at the Methodist rummage sale?

5. Don't you ever long to kick off those high-heeled boots and just slop around the house in sensible wedgies? My wife does.

6. Doesn't all that turquoise costume jewelry weigh you fellows down?

7. About those fringed buckskin jackets—doesn't the fringe get in the way of things? I saw *yours* dangling into the guacamole at that cocktail party.

8. How are things in guacamole?

9. If those buckskin jackets are so all-fired, rootin' tootin', ridin', authentically western, how come they're all made in Milwaukee?

10. How do you tie those little string ties?

11. Why?

12. Now, to get to the shirts you men wear out there—are they really made from the tablecloths of bankrupt French restaurants?

13. Don't you find it exhausting to do up all those buttons—four on each cuff, three on each pocket, plus the essential ones? I'd be plumb tuckered out.

14. Don't they ever come in plain colors, white, say?

15. How come your waistlines slipped so far down? In the east we have ours between the pelvis and the rib cage—almost everybody else does, too.

16. Is it true that your pajamas are made of denim, buckskin, silver nailheads, turquoise and fringe?

17. Don't they itch?

18. Since you all seem to be got up for a masquerade ball 24 hours a day, what do you wear when you *really* dress up?

19. Have you ever considered shorts?

20. Or are you hiding something?

Well, I just thought I'd ask.

Best to the west,
Patrick (Gams) Dennis

Windy McGabe, Drummer

Now I hate to write so much about my relatives, but my Uncle Jeb (Windy) McGabe, the traveling man, does send me some interesting mail occasionally from out in the territory. And since

BB

he quit drinking he frequently turns out a fairly lucid bit of reporting on things and people in the Rocky Mountain Empire.

Some of our kinfolks regard Uncle Jeb as the black sheep in the family but I don't go along with that. He might be just a little bit off-color, that much I'll admit, but he's not a plumb black sheep, no siree.

Uncle Jeb's made a splendid effort to reform himself and the very cause of his sudden abstinence from hard drink indicates some of the sterling qualities that admittedly did become slightly tarnished through the years. He says plain-spoken, however, that he didn't take the pledge because he has anything against whisky —only the people who drink it.

He was sitting in a bar in Pueblo late one night four years ago, according to one of his letters at the time, when a sailor staggered into the place with two female "octopusses." (Uncle Jeb spelled it that way because he didn't know that the plural for octopus is octopi.)

Uncle Jeb said the sailor carried on something scandalously with the two girl octopi and he was so shocked by what he saw

127

that he swore off liquor. He said later that what sickened him about the whole scene was that both the girl octopusses were under the legal age limit and shouldn't have been drinking at all.

Then, too, times haven't been any too good with Uncle Jeb. Business has fallen off. He says there is practically no demand any more for magnetoes for Model T's and he hasn't made a really good sale in quite a spell. He's become far more optimistic, however since he lined up a new company that sells uranium stock and pneumatic horse collars. Uncle Jeb's enthusiastic over the rubber horse collar. Says it will revolutionize American agriculture.

As a matter of fact Uncle Jeb has become quite ambitious since he went dry. He's taken on some additional sidelines such as the "Blow-Out Sponge Rubber Cork for Limp Wristed People" and "Whiffomatic Formula X" to keep big dogs away from low-seated sports cars that have no windshield wipers. The sponge rubber cork's a honey. All you have to do to get it out of a bottle is breathe on it.

To keep him busy in spare time Uncle Jeb took up miniature photography as a hobby. (A fellow always does this when he quits drinking.) But he wrote from Orin Junction, Wyo., a few days ago that the hobby is so expensive he's begun to wonder just how much money he could save if he got good and drunk.

Uncle Windy's a great joker, too. Although he's at heart a fairly religious one, he wrote—kidding of course—that this year he'd given up Lent for mashed potatoes and gravy.

Saved by the Lens

Every so often somebody hauls off and just plain calls me a liar, usually in a letter. Then there's the type that interrupts with a sly grin just as I get in the middle of a tall tale, and asks "How old did you say you were, Fenwick?"

I don't bother to answer because I can understand how some young squirts who aren't even old enough to have a past could doubt some things. In my own case a lot of folks think I'd have to be at least 110 to have done and seen all the things I like to talk about.

Take this one for example. I tell it once in a while because it is a bit novel. Did you ever experience the thrill of having an airplane crash not more than 50 feet from you where you were standing? Well, I did. And I've got the proof.

It was one day back in the 1920's. I was standing out by the cow barn at the Wyoming state fair at Douglas (my old home town), Wyo., watching Edgar Todd scare the wits out of motorists driving across the Platte river bridge.

Todd was an excellent pilot—one of the best in his era. He built his own airplanes most of the time, but this day he was flying one that belonged to Mike Williams, Converse county rancher.

Todd would circle the fairgrounds, fly low up the river toward the bridge, then crow-hop the thing while folks in the cars ducked or jumped out and ran. You could jump out easily back in the days of the Model-T.

Well, I watched Todd have his fun, wondering all the time how long it would be before he hit the one-wire whoop-and-holler telephone line that crossed the river just below the bridge. Then it happened. The wire wrapped around the undercarriage, ripped off on one side of the river and pulled loose from a dozen or so poles on the other side.

Todd and his flying machine were ground-tied like a pigeon on a string. He was whirled in a magnificent circle around the entire fairgrounds, coming lower all the time.

I stood by the cow barn fascinated. It was easy to see that Todd would crash only a few feet away. I did what you would have done. I took off for parts distant. I'd only made a few steps when KKrrraasshh! Todd and the plane hit the barn.

That airplane stuck out of the side of the barn like an arrow. To my surprise, Todd stepped out of the ship, came over and said to me, "Don't let anybody near the ship." He was less excited than I was.

Prove it, you say? Only a few days ago, Cleo Randall of 10500 East Colfax Ave., Aurora, walked into *The Post* with some old photographs taken after the crash. Cleo and I were kids in school together. Now just to prove that Douglas has a lot of strange characters, listen to this: Cleo, a Denver house builder, lives in a trailer. The pictures were taken by a portrait studio at Douglas that went by the last names of the two owners—Merry & Love.

129

He Didn't Stay Long

Alkali S. Duntz, the political forecaster and windmill mechanic from Ruptured Falls, Mont., came down to Denver a few days ago trying to buy some dust inhibitor for water wells in his territory. Old Alky said it has been so dry up in Montana this year that the postoffice department is complaining about folks putting their postage stamps on with thumb tacks.

Alky had a real time in Denver. He took in the sights and observed that he had never seen so many women wearing shorts. Said they reminded him of a "bobwire fence." That is, "they protect the property without hinderin' the view."

We had him out to the house (we live over in west Denver), and after riding to work with me during the morning rush of traffic Alky said he could really appreciate Mayor Newton's desire to be elected to the U. S. senate. "With a problem on his hands like he's got, I'd want to get out of town, too," Alky said.

The last time Alky was here I took him for a ride down Alameda avenue, and I explained to him that the city was going to repave it.

"Well, guess that puts an end to any fear of a Russian invasion," he said. "When Denver starts tearing up the tank traps on the outskirts of the city I guess they reckon there won't be no war."

Alky said he would like to be exposed to a little culture while he was in town, so we went over to the art gallery they built over by the city hall when they tore down the garage there.

Neither one of us figured out what was going on until after it was all over. Then we found out that we should have got one of those little catalogs that tell what the pictures are supposed to represent.

Alky was impressed. He couldn't figure which way to look at some of the pictures and finally concluded that the whole array of modern paintings must have been sponsored by the paint companies to show off their new colors.

One picture that looked like a winged silo rampant on a field of pulverized alfalfa reminded Alky of the way the front curtain at the Bijou theater looked after the night the woman came out from the city and made a speech advocating birth control.

Over in one corner of the gallery was a framed canvas that must have been done by accident. Alky said it could have come through an explosion in a paint factory but on the other hand there was some vague resemblance to lightning flashes that seemed to form the tail of an aggrieved milk cow brooding over a three-headed calf. The lightning flashes were green, however, and the purple calf was trying to get in to four doors of a barn at the same time. We guessed that maybe we were wrong about the picture and spent the rest of the tour staring at a wood carving of a ga'nt woman dragging around a baby that had been mashed by something awful big.

This reminded Alky that we hadn't had any supper so we went down to the Windsor hotel and ate. And, say, they've got some pictures hanging over the bar down there that are dandies—if you like that kind of art.

Pass the Biscuits

I got to thinking the other day about how long it has been since I tasted good, old-fashioned home-made bread. And doggone if it hasn't been so long I can't remember when.

The thought occurred to me one evening as I was resting up for supper. (Some folks call it "dinner," but that's what *we* eat at noon.) I hollered out to the kitchen and said "What kind of bread are we having for supper?"

"Why, I hadn't looked," came the answer, "but I suppose it's from the same bakery we always get our bread from."

That did it. That got the tail in the milk bucket for sure.

"Why don't you knock out a few loaves of bread, yourself?" I asked. "Your mother used to make good bread. Your folks never had to subsist on factory food, pre-cast cookies and assembly line proteins. And look how long it was before your dad got ulcers."

Then it was that I made a horrible discovery. I was invited to look over the kitchen that's equipped with all the latest gadgets, modern cabinets and push buttons and things. But, do you know what, men? Nowhere in that kitchen is there a place to keep flour!

What's more. There isn't even anything there that looks like a bread board. Even if we had a flour bin, there wouldn't be a bread board to work the dough on.

131

My wife doesn't own a flour sifter and, come to think of it, I haven't seen one in the stores in a coon's age.

Then another thing dawned on me in all its awful significance: When my little woman makes coffee she just heats some water, gets a couple spoonsful of brown stuff out of a jar and puts it in the cups, then pours on the water. No more fancy striving for quality like putting in an egg, adding a pinch of salt and such like. Just open a jar.

This thing has been shaping up for years. First we let women vote. Then they overran the barber shops and the corner bar. Next, some joker came up with an electric washing machine, then he added an automatic dryer. All this was fine and dandy. It made work simpler for the sweet little things that brighten our days.

Next thing we knew we had canned biscuits, pre-cooked stews, packaged poultry and frozen desserts. All a woman had to do was thaw and heat. All this extra leisure thus created opened the way for women to take jobs and compete with their own husbands.

Then a few days ago I was reading an item by an eastern woman columnist who suggested that because both husband and wife hold down jobs these days, they would find it vastly more restful if each had individual bedrooms.

Now looky here, by George . . .

Our Daily Bread?

This report is being filed from a bomb shelter just back of the firing lines in the battle of the kitchen. It is being written at the height of a bitter counter-attack by a citizen army of females who were outraged when I merely suggested recently that we male citizens are entitled to homemade bread now and then.

At this writing I must admit to the loss of a couple of skirmishes. But I am happy to report three victories—two invitations to visit homes and enjoy homemade bread, and the actual receipt of one loaf from Virginia Baker, sympathetic wife of non-partisan H. Ray Baker, *Empire's* art director. (I'd be non-partisan, too, if my little helpmeet would bake bread like Virginia does.)

One Greybull, Wyo., reader invited me up, but she gave only a box number, the invitation and a suggestion that I should "go have seven or eight kids." That, she stated, would cure me of yelping about packaged foods like die-cut cookies and pre-digested stews. She signed her name Mrs. Art Schutte and she even endorsed the idea of separate bedrooms which I strongly oppose.

Mrs. Betty Nidey of Boulder, Colo., was real nice about the whole thing. She understands men. "After reading your column my heart bled for you," she wrote. "No homemade bread? You poor starved soul, drop in sometime and sample some old-fashioned, fresh-baked, nutritious homemade bread." Mrs. Nidey gave her address and reported that she bakes every Wednesday. I'll be there, Mrs. Nidey, and thank you, ma'am.

Mrs. Dorothy E. Beetle leveled at me from Laramie, Wyo., like she had just caught me trying to take away her washing machine. "After reading *Pass the Biscuits*," she wrote, "I am bowed in shame for the lazy mate of Red Fenwick and all the poor housekeepers across our land who use package mixes and electric washing machines. (Wait till news of this gets to my house.)

"Not feeding a man proper victuals to sustain him in his daily work is failing him pure and simple. Take Red Fenwick, for instance. He rises at 5 a. m. and, by candle light, primes the pump and hauls in water for his little woman. Then after a skimpy breakfast of powdered coffee and packaged pancakes he hitches up the team and heads for *The Denver Post*. The rumor up Laramie way is that Red is hard-pressed to turn out his copy by quill pen, that's how things are slipping."

Oh, pshaw, ma'am. It isn't really that bad, now.

She said some men had to use typewriters and talk on intercom phones between offices instead of moving around. Some men, she added, didn't know how to add, they use slide rules and adding machines. And shoe stores don't measure feet any more, they fit customers by X-ray.

"Ladies," she concluded, "a hard day at the office is a matter of pushing buttons. It's high time we investigated this dangerous situation. We can't have the men out-gadgeting us."

Encounter With the East

There is, of course, a certain limited appeal to simple country living. But it goes so far and no further. Compared to the social and cultural advantages enjoyed by our city slicker cousins, life in the sticks is about as beautiful as a box full of corn cobs.

This was brought home to me with considerable persuasion the other day when our Wayward Bill Barker invited me to accompany him on a shopping trip. It seems that Chipp, Inc., of New York, Cambridge and other points swish, had sent their man to Denver to sell tastefully styled clothing and men's items to us backwoods boys. Nothing would do but that Barker should see their offering.

Chipp enjoys a brisk business dealing with the college lads at Harvard, Yale and other eastern institutions of higher foreheads. But several times a year the firm sends a drummer into the new area bought by the United States under terms of the Louisiana Purchase, solely to satisfy the cultured demands of its old clients who have ventured into the western wilderness. Perhaps when the region becomes settled and safe, Chipp, Inc., will open a branch establishment here.

Chipp's man, Lester Ross, met us in his display room at the Albany hotel. He bowed and we stared and the dickering began.

All the time Mr. Ross talked, I kept thinking of Anthony Eden and Dean Acheson. His speech, manner and dress were impeccable, sir. I was afraid he might ask for references other than cold cash, and I don't know a soul in Boston.

He discerned immediately that Barker and I were a couple of outdoor Joes, true sons of nature. So he tempted us with a little item he had brought along for the colonial trade—a pair of plaid deer-stalkers. If he hadn't said so I would have mistaken them for detective's caps. They had two bills, one fore and the other a'hint. I guess the idea of the cap is to confuse the deer so he can't tell which way you're going.

We didn't buy any, but he showed us some snappy new things in the men's underwear line. They are sort of like a G-string and can be had in leopard skin or Scotch tartan. They would be chilly in winter, though, because they are made like cowpuncher's chaps with nothing behind.

He had a beautiful assortment of men's stockings including

Red, in a rare moment of serious expression.

Red, who was usually in hot water, or looking for it to get into, thought it appropriate to tie up in this caldron for a photo shot just to prove his point.

"Look at that filly . . . G-Boy! Come back here!"

Red, in 1950 as he traveled on special assignment for *The Denver Post* visiting the Governor of each of the 13 states covered by the *Post*. Red invited each Governor with one half of a pair of gold and silver spurs to visit the grand opening of the new Denver Post building in Denver on May 16, 1950 for which each Governor would receive the other spur.

If one particular photo best depicts the life of Red Fenwick, it is this photo. With his famed Stetson resting atop his Underwood typewriter, to Red, the two went hand in hand and life was not lived one without the other.

When old friends meet . . . Red, the first recipient of the March of Dimes Citizen of the West Award, pauses to reflect on times gone by with Citizens of the West Frank Ricketson and "Mr. Stockshow" Willard Simms.

Two close friends, entertainers and cowboys at heart, Red Fenwick and Pete Smythe (on horse) rode the Roundup Riders of the Rockies singing, "Why Oh Why Did I Ever Leave Wyoming?" in this 1950's photo.

In addition, they rode the rodeo circuit, county and state fairs and entertainment circles together throughout the years.

some that come clear up to the knees. These are worn with poplin shorts. And there were some "braces" that we used to call "suspenders," with pictures of naked women on them. These were pretty classy. Barker didn't buy one.

He did buy a cap with a little strap in the back, and a wool muffler that is longer than a halter rope. It hangs down to his knees and makes him look like his owner is trying to break him from crawling through fences.

It was an interesting shopping trip, though, and just one of the little things you can't do out in a hick town because Chipp's man positively would not think of going there. Not enough business, y'know.

Blessed Are the Meek

I think my folks brought me up with the wrong attitude. I grew up in the country and they thought I'd be a country boy all my life. They never knew, of course, that someday I'd find myself competing in a big city or they might have changed the rules a little.

As it was, I learned to respect ladies and my elders, to look up to my bosses, to wait my turn in line and always to take the smallest piece and, by George, that's about all I've ever been able to get.

I have learned, perhaps too late, that courtesy is its only reward. A fellow who doesn't push somebody will stay a long time at the hindmost nipple where the milk is lean and less. A gentleman will never find a seat on a crowded bus and a guy who's polite is usually the one stuck at the red traffic light. The same joker generally is still standing after the rush is over at the movies and always misses grabbing the only remaining socks off the bargain counter.

He's invariably the last guy to the table and the first everyone else thinks of when there's baby sitting to do. Strangers regard him as a sucker and the neighbors figure him for a weakling.

He's the kind of social misfit whose stomach always picks the very psychological moment when he's asking for a pay raise to commence an ominous and audible growling (My own stomach has a sort of nasal whimper.)

This type never beefs about taxes, he just smiles and hopes the

135

government can get along on what it gets. He never talks back to a plumber, so his faucets always leak.

He can work 40 years in the same office with 20 other people then drop dead at his desk and not be missed until somebody takes up a collection.

He'll never get in trouble by his own actions but usually because of somebody else's. He wouldn't think of getting into politics and apologizes for troubling the election judges when he goes in to vote.

He feels outraged most of the time but doesn't dare do anything about it. He's usually an hour late and a dollar short and can't find a collar that fits. The laundry recognizes this jerk's personality and sees to it that he never has buttons on his shirts.

In a restaurant he's lucky if he so much as gets the tools to eat with. He's usually served last and least, leaves the biggest tip but is regarded by waitresses as a sly, loathsome wolf and by the cashier as a gyp artist planning to lay a worthless check.

When he has a flat tire it happens either in the middle of the rush-hour traffic or on a country road right after he has loaned his car jack to a friend.

Dogs bite him, kids pester him, motorists call him things you can't print here; people shove him, women make him get out of their way; bankers and bosses frighten him and everybody borrows his money.

He is ridiculed, scorned, passed up, stepped on, knocked around and overlooked, but he's polite, he believes in his country and his fellow man. But what's more important, there are 75 million others in the country just like him.

Make Mine Winter

When *Empire's* staff was planning this travel edition, everybody sank back in idyllic dreams of the south seas, Mexico, Florida and southern California. Not me! I'm one of the local yokels who believes there is no place like home even in the wintertime.

To me, the sight of an evergreen tree, majestic in a cloak of purest ermine with frozen pendants glittering in winter's sunlight, is far and away more delightful than any palm. A snug log cabin piled high with winter's drifts and warm and cheery around the fireplace is more appealing to my makeup than all the beach cabanas of southern climes.

I like to buck a blizzard, fight a wind and watch the snow swirl wraithlike along lonely stretches of long highways. The big, deep drifts frighten me just a little, but at the same time they are fascinating, challenging, bidding you to come on and try. Hit one sometime, feel your car pull down, labor, kick, then break through and keep going and you've known a real thrill.

There are some precautions you should observe, however, if you're planning any extensive winter driving. Keep a shovel in the back end of your car. Take extra clothing—including dry socks—when you drive even on short trips. Nothing is more important when you're stranded than to keep your feet dry.

A good eiderdown sleeping bag takes up little space and may sometime save your life. A bucket of sand may spell the difference between spending the night on the road and getting through. Take along twice as much chocolate as you think you would need. Make a thermos bottle full of hot coffee a must on your list and, too, you will find if you become really snowbound, that an *empty* hot water bag is an almost indispensable convenience.

In an extreme emergency you will find that the upholstery in your automobile is first-rate fire material. And if you have no matches, dip a piece of upholstery, stuck on a stick, into your gas tank. Remove a wire from a spark-plug and hold it near the engine head with the engine running. The spark will light the cotton if it isn't too cold.

Carry a length of rubber tubing. Some gasoline siphoned into a can full of sand will burn for hours. Keep the windows open a crack to let the fumes escape. Otherwise you will be gassed.

But actually, few persons traveling the highways ever need to resort to such extreme measures. Snowplows get through in a hurry nowadays and winter travel is pleasant, scenic and relatively safe.

With the tourists gone for the season, western towns take on a homey glow. Winter confinement warms friendships, makes for greater companionship. Just walk into a restaurant or tavern sometime at the height of a heavy snowstorm and listen to the patter of conversation—how it picks up and sounds friendly. Me? I'll take mine right here in our winter wonderland—with friends.

THE WEST—
AS SHE WAS

HRB

The Lucky Stiff

In the old western tradition of good fellows, four men are gathered around a green-topped card table. A wearily flickering lamp suspended overhead lends a golden cast to the neat piles of silver dollars stacked professionally before each player.

These men are tense. This is no ordinary poker session. Their facial muscles are immobile, unrevealing. Each is wearing his stoniest poker face.

One player is particularly expressionless. He is dead.

But the game goes right on. The dead man is winning!

"Dag-nab the dad-blasted confounded luck," one exclaims with a liquored exhalation. "That doggoned Swede," he jerks a thumb in the direction of the deceased, "is taking his luck right to the grave with him."

● ● ●

That fabled poker game must have taken place in the backroom of one of Hartville's saloons. This Wyoming boom town certainly had never suffered a dearth of them, so the story goes. And besides, what more appropriate place could one find in which to hold a wake for a gambler with a slight case of rigor mortis?

The late departed was a well-known gambler. He is remembered as the "white Swede" they say, because of his almost invisible eyebrows, lashes and pale white hair. When he cashed in his chips, friends volunteered to hold a wake.

As the evening progressed and the bottle passed, a poker game just naturally evolved and someone dealt in the one being honored. It was a last respect, they agreed, but one they came to rue.

Ere the night was over and the time came to return the Swede to the dust from whence he came, he had cleaned up the game and had won more than enough to pay his own funeral expenses.

Some say the unfortunate losers snitched the balance and launched a binge that night that rivaled the one back in the 1880s when rival ranch cowpunchers shot it out in a saloon in Hartville, killing one man and badly scaring some others.

On that particular occasion the deceased was laid out on the barroom floor in great solemnity and covered with a blanket.

Towards morning another puncher who had surfeited at the mahogany, stretched out beside the corpse and when no one was looking, swiped the blanket for himself.

The next morning when the bartender roused him, the cowpuncher swore roundly and declared his bed companion was the "coldest and snorin'est derned human I ever slept with."

In those days, Hartville, the oldest remaining community in the mountainous country around Guernsey in east-central Wyoming, held many claims to distinction. For one thing it is historically famous as the birthplace of the "Hartville Rag."

Charley Ragan, fiddler extraordinary who played for dances, once held forth for a shindig that went on a full week in Hartville with only brief intermissions for community visits to the bar.

Ragan wore out all but one string. Its popularity caught on at once and he named it the "Hartville Rag," which still can be heard at some country dances in the more rugged areas yet to be penetrated by effete music.

Some weekend I'm going to meander up Hartville way. I want to get the story of Fletcher's Burlesque emporium, and I want to visit the grave of Charley Taylor, the only man in the whole west, as near as I can find, who was killed so the town could progress to the point of having a cemetery of its own.

Firemen's Trumpet
and sundry other mementos

There hadn't been such breathtaking excitement in Denver since the big rooming house burned down one night on Market street.

Eleven tense figures in ankle-length tights that looked like dropseat, long-handled underwear, were drawn up in team array on Chestnut place just east of Second avenue.

It was the Dodge City, Kan., exhibition fire hose team. And they were braced for a dash down Denver's streets that was to prove historic.

The brawny, fleet-footed fire laddies formed two lines along a length of fire hose. Each man was efficiently caparisoned with a broad leather breast strap. A rope from each strap connected each man to a tie on the hose.

They were the very picture of dash and verve. Their rakish mustaches, now tilted at determined angles, quivered with impatience and excitement. The lead man flexed his muscles, chafed under the delay.

A shrill blast split the silence. The signal!

Down the street scurried the nimble crew, snaking the hose along in the direction of a waiting fire plug. Their feet pounded the pavement in unison. They capered to a slithering halt and each man sprang to some new task.

One clamped the hose to the plug. Another snapped on the nozzle.

A lusty cheer went up from the throng that watched this spectacle of speed and efficiency. A stream of water powered its way through the rigid hose and squirted a remarkable eighteen feet.

That was March 21, 1887. The team had raced 450 feet, dragging 100 feet of hose in the record-breaking time of thirty-one and four-fifths seconds—a new world record.

The victors over Denver and other contestants in the fire games, took $800 in cash and a Gabriel-sized silver trumpet back to Dodge City as their trophy and reward for the astonishing demonstration of razzle-dazzle fire control operation.

What happened to the cash is not a matter of historic record. But the trumpet rests in resplendent glory in a glass case in Merrit L. Beeson's museum at Dodge City.

It is just one of a jillion or more relics of "the good old days" which Beeson and his wife maintain in apple pie order as testimonials to that never-to-be-forgotten era when there was "No law west of Newton and no God west of Dodge."

"Pop" and "Ma" Beeson's museum is by all odds one of the wonders of Kansas. Their collection is different.

The priceless aggregation, which returns a modest living to the couple, includes such fascinating little items as the double-barreled shotgun used by a bad man to blow off the head of a peace officer. That was back in the days when the immortal Sheriff Bat Masterson was chilling gun-slingers up and down the boardwalks of Dodge City's hell-for-leather Front street.

There are "side-wheelers" and "peacemakers" that once roared defiance of law and order; Sharps rifles, and a macabre collection of wooden coffins once destined for the only real "Boot Hill" in these western states.

AWOL for 80 Years?

I meant to write this piece several years ago right after I first met old Ed Ryan. Somehow I forgot about him until just the other day when I rounded a turn in the highway that twists through South Dakota's Black Hills. There, beside the road, was old Ed, whiskers bristling and his crinkly eyes shining under that battered sombrero just like they always did.

It's Ed's favorite summer hangout and his appearance beside the road gives motorists a start that usually causes them to stop. Ed looks like something that was left over from the gold rush days

—and that's exactly what he is or was or something. Ed's 98, gets around like a high school kid, is loaded with Black Hills lore (he's been there 81 years) and looks like a cartoonist's conception of the original Old Prospector.

He ekes out a living giving away rock specimens and selling his book *Me and The Black Hills.* He loads his old car with rocks and books each morning and hits for the Needles country to prospect for tourists. Sometimes the diggin's are good.

Ed claims he is the only real survivor of the Custer massacre and, oddly, a "casualty," too. He explains that he was with General Custer's Seventh cavalry and "we was explorin' the country." He j'ined up with the outfit in St. Louis, Mo., when he was 17 years old.

Well, it seems that Custer and his men had poked around the Black Hills for quite a spell and Custer was itching for a fight. So the Seventh ups with boots and saddles one morning and rode into destiny.

Except for Ed. The story is that Ed's tent mate was ailing and Ed was concerned with his health. As a matter of fact, the sick man's condition turned right serious and so Custer told Ed to stay with him until he recovered, then to rejoin the outfit. By that time the troops were well on the march.

Ed remained behind, he says, and the sick man got steadily worse. Finally he died. Then Ed saddled up and lit out in pursuit of Custer who by that time was going into battle at the Little Big Horn.

History records the rest. All of Custer's men were massacred and most of them were buried in a common grave atop a hill that overlooks the battlefield.

On the tombstone that was raised to mark the spot is the name "George Ryan." Ed claims that was the name under which he enlisted with the cavalry and that although he is a "survivor" he also was a "casualty."

I asked him one time if he had ever rejoined his outfit and pointed out that he had been AWOL from the army for 80 years, thus setting some sort of record that would excite the envy of any number of draftees.

"AWOL, hell," old Ed exploded. "I was told to rejoin my regiment and, son, that's pretty hard to do considering we wuz all wiped out by the Sioux."

145

Funereal Fun

Ever since folks have been kicking the bucket, disposal of the dead ones has posed a considerable problem. Now admittedly it is a somewhat macabre thought for a Sunday, but it seems unlikely that any of us is going to get out of here alive anyhow. So we should speculate on what's to be done with our remains. One prime consideration is the place and time of demise.

Over in Idaho years ago, a miner died in camp during the winter. The ground was frozen hard and the trails out of the mountains were packed with snow. There was only one thing to do with old Zeke's carcass. Friends put it on a woodpile safe from coyotes and let it freeze.

When spring came they brought him indoors, according to the story, thawed him out, put a keg between his knees and re-froze him. When he was good and stiff they sat him on a burro, tied his feet under the animal's belly, and led old Zeke to his final resting place.

Up in Fairbanks, Alaska, a few years ago, a stranger bought the funeral parlor there and inherited a problem. Some joker had died, I think it was fourteen years before, and left instructions that he not be buried in the north country. Inasmuch as he was broke and couldn't pay his own freight, the undertaker kept him on ice so long he forgot all about him until he sold out to the newcomer.

And, neighbor, this will kick up a storm. I know of an oldtimer in Denver who claims that Buffalo Bill Cody is laid away on top of Lookout Mountain, fixed to greet doomsday with a reviving snifter. Said oldtimer says in confidence that just before Bill's funeral, he slipped into the room where the deceased Indian scout lay in state, heisted up his coat and slipped a pint of good Kentucky bourbon into his hip pocket. My, what a tender thought.

Heard of a weird case up in Montana once. It seems some rancher's wife had passed away and they were taking her out to the graveyard for planting when the pallbearers accidentally bumped a fence post with the coffin just as they went through the gate. The lid flew up, the old lady let out an unearthly scream, jumped out of the box and ran home. She had suffered only a deceptive heart attack.

Several months later she died for real and as the pallbearers were taking her to the graveyard for the second time, the old man rushed out in front of the pallbearers, held up one hand in caution and cried "Watch out for that post, men!"

That story's quite in contrast with the one about the husband who was arrested for neglecting to bury his wife. His defense was that he didn't know she was dead. Said she'd been lounging around the house that way for fifteen years.

Just one more: They were giving a War I veteran a military funeral not long ago—I understand it was in Colorado. The vet's young grandson was impressed. A firing squad wheeled into position and let go a volley whereupon the vet's wife fainted. The kid ran out of the cemetery in wild excitement shouting "My gosh, they've shot grandma."

Mabel's Had Enough

Things are not going to be quite the same this winter up in the Togwotee pass country of western Wyoming. Mabel McFarland, who is just about as much of a landmark as the Tetons, is going to leave. Mabel allows as how 40 years of leaning into blizzards are enough for one woman so, on her doctor's orders, she's going to pull stakes.

It's not that Mabel's a quitter. She never quit anything she ever started. But she will be 64, come Halloween, and at that age Mabel reckons a gal is entitled to take it easy.

Taking it easy is not going to be the big plush cinch it's cracked up to be, so far as Mabel's concerned. She has fought the elements and out-lasted just about everybody up in the high timbered Togwotee pass country, and she's used to work and rough talk and bearded, sweaty mountain men. Now and then she enjoys joining with them in cussing the weather or whatever needs a good cussing at the moment. Mabel's no namby pamby.

When I dropped in on her one evening a few weeks ago, she was busy cussing the California tourists. We went into Mabel's roadside cafe and, over some high-octane coffee that would shock the senses of a dinosaur, she took a few well-aimed potshots at the Californians.

"Worst drivers in the world," Mabel exclaimed. "And the most demanding doggoned people you ever saw. Why they come through here by the thousands and derned if I'm not getting to where I can't stand the sight of a Californian. They think they own just about the only country in the world worth living in—and dad burn their hides, that ain't so!"

Mabel went on to relate some of her history. She came into the Togwotee country 40 years ago in a seven-passenger Stutz. The highway of today was then just two parallel ruts. Mabel homesteaded, built a shack, hunted, took care of herself in the best pioneer tradition and pretty soon bought the Long Creek ranch—all ten acres of it—for $1,000.

Mabel took advantage of sunny summers to build a small cafe on the main road. When winter came she would be snowed in for months. The only way she could travel was by ski. But Mabel stuck and, in time, expanded her holdings to include a service station, saloon and hotel.

It wasn't easy to do. There was gossip. There always is gossip about women who hew logs and shoot wild game and live alone like a man but without a man. Mabel didn't mind. There were plenty of men around—lumberjacks, cowboys, sheepherders and quite an assortment of traveling salesmen with whom Mabel became a great favorite. Mabel knew more lively stories than they did. Nobody who knew Mabel very well ever passed her place without stopping for a drink or a meal.

But now Mabel is leaving. She hopes to sell out and her asking price reveals the measure of the success she built on tenacity and $1,000. Mabel wants $85,000 for her holdings—cash or terms.

I asked Mabel where she planned to live in retirement. It was the first time I ever saw her blush. She lowered her head and mumbled almost inaudibly.

"California. If it's good as them Californians claim, it must be terrific."

How Sheep Tick Tom Got the Bird . . .

Women would have nothing to do with Old Sheep Tick Tom Tollison, the bashful herder from Flathead. There were several good reasons, too. For one thing Old Tick stunk. He seldom bathed. He seemed to hate water for any purpose.

Moreover, Old Tick's chin bristled with a goatlike beard that looked like it might have cockleburrs in it. The thing bore mute but indisputable evidence of long addiction to eatin' tobacco. So did the top of his long underwear that bore splatter marks and stuck out where his shirt collar opened at the Adam's apple.

But probably the main reason why women would have nothing to do with Old Tick was that Old Tick would have nothing to do with women. He hated them. He would spit and cuss every time a woman passed him on the twice-a-year occasions when he would come to town.

Some said it was because Old Tick had been jilted by a female critter when he left Ohio and came west to Montana to win his fortune. No one actually knew, however, or so the old-timer told me one night in the Log Cabin emporium and amusement palace up in Jackson, Wyo.

It seemed Old Tick's favorite town was Great Falls, Mont. He would come in and hang around the bars there for a couple of weeks, spend his money on bottled barbwire then hit 'er back to the wagon flat broke.

During his more loquacious moments, however, the old recluse would confess to a vast and intolerable loneliness—not for women, not necessarily for male companionship, but for something or someone to talk with.

It was understandable, therefore, that Old Tick was intensely interested to learn one time in town that an old retired sailor had died and that his possessions were to be auctioned—among them a well-educated, talking parrot.

Old Tick hurried right over to the auction. When the parrot went on the block, the lonely sheepherder opened for five bucks. Someone raised it to ten, and the race was on. Old Tick was finally overcome by the spirit of the competition and closed out all bidders with an offer of $75—all he had left.

He carried the bird home to the sheepwagon in a state of quivering anticipation. That night he sat it on the tarpaulin that covered his bed, and tried to engage the thing in conversation.

All he elicited was an ill-tempered "awrk" and a baleful glare from the bird's red-rimmed eyes.

Next day Old Tick went out with his sheep. That night he tried again. Again the bird just cocked his head, stared hard and stalked away amid a great ruffling of feathers.

A couple of days later the camp tender came and moved the wagon. Old Tick wondered whether to take the parrot along or leave him to the coyotes.

He reconsidered, however, and, still hopeful the creature would bring him the companionship he desired, took him along.

But one night as the hours waned, the old-timer sadly reported, Old Tick wrung the bird's neck. Killed him. Old Tick sobbed about it the next time he came to town and got gluey at the bar. Friends asked why he'd done it.

Old Tick explained simply that he had lost his temper.

"So ye cain't talk or ye won't talk, ye hammer-headed, yeller-feathered turkey. I ought to wring yore dern neck!" Old Tick had shouted at the parrot.

"Can't talk?," the parrot screamed. "Who th' hell d'ya think run up your bid to six bits?"

Too Proud to Walk

Phil Housieaux hated ranch chores. He was a cowpuncher and one of the best the west has ever seen. He told each successive employer the same thing: He would work. But he wouldn't do anything that couldn't be done on a horse.

One evening in an unguarded moment, however, he found himself standing on the ranch porch carrying two empty water buckets. When he realized what he was doing, he blushed clean to the toes of his bench-made boots. A foreman with a sense of humor that matched Phil's own had tricked the old waddie into going after water for supper.

Phil soberly contemplated the pump a full 100 feet from the house. Then he did the only thing a cowboy could do under the circumstances. He dropped the buckets, went to the barn, saddled up and brought in the water on horseback.

Ranchman "Zim" Zimmerman once put Phil in charge of a riding crew and left him and his men on a country lane beside a pasture where about 1,200 head of whitefaces were waiting to be moved to summer range. Zim drove to the ranch to have horses sent up for the riders but asked that, in the meantime, Phil and his boys open the gate and let the stock onto the lane.

150

Two hours later Zim returned to find Phil and the cowboys asleep in the shade of a barbwire fence. The cattle were right where they were when Zim left. Phil apologized: "We're afoot, Mister Zimmerman."

Phil was a legend up in Douglas (my old home town), Wyo. He was something of a mystery man, too. Nobody knew everything about Phil, and Phil went to extreme lengths to fabricate many a high sounding myth about himself—"just for the heck of it."

It was known that he was the best roper on the Laramie range. The lariat he used—a small one about the size of a man's little finger—came alive in his hand. He knew outlaws and peace officers alike and once was an Indian agency law enforcement man, himself.

Several months ago, Dr. W. A. Hinrichs interviewed Phil and tape-recorded a four-hour conversation. Phil unfolded much of his life's story to the delight of Doc, a young navy veteran who moved to Douglas after the war because he was attracted by the wealth of history there.

Then, one evening last winter Phil died as he dozed in his rocking chair at home. A relative gave Phil's most priceless possession, a frontier rifle sawed off to saddle size, to Doc.

Doc Hinrichs hung it in a place of honor in his den, but before he did he cleaned the gun. In so doing he removed the front stock and discovered nine carefully filed notches in the gun barrel.

Now Doc wonders: Did someone else put those notches there before Phil got the gun? Are those notches grim mementoes to the end of so many rustlers? Or is old fun-loving Phil carrying on his prankish myth-building from the big range up in The Sky?

Sagebrush Robin Hood

Underneath this stone in eternal rest
Sleeps the wildest one of the wayward west.
He was gambler, sport and cowboy, too.
And he led the pace in an outlaw crew.
He was sure on the trigger and staid to the end
And was never known to quit on a friend.

In the relations of death all mankind is alike
But in life there was only one George W. Pike.

Those lines are graven on a stone that marks the shaded resting place of one of Wyoming's most colorful outlaws. I memorized them when I was a kid because George W. Pike's tombstone was a favorite mecca for all small boys up in Douglas (my old home town), Wyo.

Pike was a legend and an idol in our crowd. We were told by oldtimers like Phil Housieaux and John Henry that he handled a six-gun and a lariat with equal dexterity. That meant he must have been pretty good with a rope for he could shoot the buttons off a man's vest the length of the College Inn bar. And that's a long way, brother.

He was a Robin Hood bandit according to the old stories. He rustled the big cattleman's stock and distributed the money among hungry homesteaders. He was a prankster, too. One winter he stole a stove out of a restaurant while the cook was up front taking a breakfast order. Pike threw away the legs and two of the lids, put the stove up on bricks and covered the holes with pie tins and defied the owner to identify his stove. He didn't, and Pike kept it.

Once he knew he was being cheated in a poker game, got up and disguised himself, then returned to stick up the game for $2,500. Later he returned full of sympathy for the fellows in the game. But Pike never was convicted of a crime.

Until a few months ago I thought Pike had severed all connections with this earth when they put him away on the tree-grown hill. Then, a few months ago, Roy Erickson, the Denver monument maker, brought a visitor to see me.

He was Claude Pike, George's brother. No two humans could be more dissimilar. Claude, now 78, is an extremely mild-mannered man whose eyes fill with tears as he remembers that George was "mother's most beloved son." Claude, long an office worker in Seattle, Wash., filled in some missing details.

George was red-headed, with 185 pounds of muscle distributed over a 5-foot 9-inch frame. He was born in Iowa, and left home when he was 13 on his father's orders to "make your own way son, you're now a man."

Pike roamed Texas, settled in Douglas and married. He had one daughter, Rose, who later married a Walter Myrick and lived for a while in Evergreen, Colo. She died in 1950 and her ashes were interred in Fairmount mausoleum, Denver.

Wyoming's most popular gun fighter never killed anyone. And no posse slug or gambler's gun laid him low. Pike died when he was 43 of a liver condition caused by drinking with friends who wished him a long life!

Intelligence from Tolliver

Had another good letter the other day from old Tick Tolliver, the Orin Junction, Wyo., traffic expert, weather prophet, political prognosticator and feed-room philosopher.

Tick, who also corresponds for the *Moneta* (Wyo.) *Mercenary*, says he's been reading some of the big eastern newspapers lately and he's made a few observations. Chief among these, he points out, is that there's only one thing we can be sure about today in modern society. That is simply that we can't be sure about a dern thing tomorrow.

Just about the time we catch on to how to use some new gadget, he says, up pops an inventor with a substitute that will do the same thing at about one-half the cost. Then, of course, we have to get used to the substitute and about that time some enterprising malcontent finds out how to do away with both gadgets and there we are.

"We are a great nation of folks for substitutes, imitations, knick-knacks and doo-dads," writes old Tick. "Ours is an economy of what-nots." Tick confides that right now he is working on a new-fangled contrivance made out of synthetics that will take the place of the electric shaver. It's called a razor.

"We've come a long way," Tick notes. "We have plastics, nylons, norlons, pyrex, prolons, neutrons and non-alcoholics; fibers, filters, compoboard, cellotex, celanese, sneeze cloths and ball-point pens; orlon, pellon, toupees, false fronts, snapons, zippers, vinylfilm, twin beds and, until a few weeks ago, we had Marilyn Monroe.

"Ours is a world of such wonders as X-ray, radar, chewing gum, television, drive-ins, the dial phone, vitamins, hormones, penicillin, tap water and the traffic light at the corner of West Eighth Avenue and Platte River drive in Denver.

"There are guided missiles, misguided youths, Bikini bathing suits, strapless evening gowns, 3-D, flying saucers, Hollywood and a Republican in the White House. This is an amazing age in which we live.

"We've come farther and accomplished more than any other generation since the nickel beer. But in spite of all this," old Tick went on, "nobody has come up with a sure cure for the common cold or a tonic that will grow hair.

"We've harnessed rivers, mastered space, split the atom, perfected the automatic transmission and broke the sound barrier, but nobody seems to be able to figure a way to cut taxes.

"We have 200-horsepower automobiles, Jeeps, Farmalls, home demonstration agents, REA and radio but nothing will make hay grow like good old cow manure.

"Sometimes I wonder where all this horsepower is taking us. It just seems to me that you never heard about anybody having stomach ulcers until somebody invented a wrist watch and the installment plan. Yours for better living, Friend Tick."

Never Say Buy

Old Pump McFarland's liver blew a gasket a few weeks ago and put old Pump away for keeps. They said a few nice things about Pump before taking him out to the cemetery. But no one paid him the tribute he would have preferred.

The deceased was conceded in his own circles to be the biggest tank in town. He had the capacity of a thirsty camel and the thirst of a Mallet locomotive climbing Sherman hill.

Pump was to the tavern crowd what One-Eyed Connelly was to baseball and the prize fight racket. Without a doubt, he was one of the world's most highly skilled barflies because he did, indeed, enjoy great success in this field of enterprise. To his dying day he never bought a drink.

At the height of his career, old Pump could strike up a conversation with a wooden Indian and, in less time than it takes to say "Make mine a double," he would have the Indian buying drinks.

Pump had a bag of tricks and a line of gab that would have

made a stage magician look like a first-day student at the deaf and dumb school.

One of his favorite "bet-the-drinks" tricks was performed with a baby's bottle nipple and a bobby pin. Old Pump would bet that he could pour a whole bottle of Seven-up into the nipple without spilling a drop.

No engineering degree was needed to see that the nipple wouldn't hold all the Seven-up. So, with the chips down and the bartender waiting, Pump would slip the nipple over the end of the bottle, plug the hole with the bobby pin and turn the bottle upside down. The nipple would swell with gas and swallow the whole contents.

Since this was back in the days when a shot glass was big enough to hold a quarter, Pump would drop a two-bit piece in one, heads up. Then he'd bet he could make it turn tails without touching either it or the glass. The trick was to blow on the coin.

He'd line up three empty glasses with two full ones in between. Then he'd bet he could move one glass and have three empty ones in a row—an impossibility. The trick was to empty one via the gastronomic tract.

He would put a dime under a bottle cap on the bar, then bet that when he lifted the cap a "heads" would be up. While the other fellow made up his mind, Pump would drop something on the floor. When he stooped to pick it up the bartender would turn the coin tails up and put the cap back. But when Pump lifted the cap, there was a dime with the heads up.

The secret was a friendly bartender and a cap with a hole in the cork just big enough to hold a dime until the cap was tapped with the finger.

Well, as I said, they put old Pump away. It is repeated now that the undertaker who injected Pump's veins with a solution far weaker than he had taken out, commented as he did so:

"This last one's on me, Pump."

Whose Rats?

Old P. Lee Skinner's place was so overrun with rats that even the rats were annoyed. They lived in marvelous congestion under

155

the barn and sheds, in the cellar and attic and all over the place. They scurried along the corral poles, haunted the hay mow, romped in the yard and bullied the ranch cats to the point where said felines took to the few small cottonwoods and stayed there.

At first P. Lee's rats were big and rangy and well fed. But as their numbers increased the per capita forage decreased. The result was the rat population grew gaunt.

The overcrowding finally became so aggravated that whole families of rats would up and leave the place, traveling overland to greener pastures.

It was about this time that one of P. Lee's horses came down with an ailment that called for the services of a veterinarian. P. Lee sent to town for old Doc Pritchard.

Now I know this to be a true story because it was told to me by none other than old Honest Ed Wright, the ex-rodeo hand who now owns all the winning horses at Centennial park. He is honest even if he says he has a good thing in the third race.

Well, Doc Pritchard showed up at the ranch, diagnosed the horse and treated it. Then he observed by way of conversation that the place had some of the most impudent rats he had ever seen. They had come right up to Doc's medical bag and had eaten generously of some horse salve Doc used.

It so happened, Doc said, that a customer a year or so ago had left on his hands an old sheep dog that had only one physical handicap. He was hard of hearing, but aside from that he was a good dog, mindful, extremely loyal and an extraordinary rat killer. Doc would part with the dog to no one, such was his affection for the animal. But he would, in this case, let him go to P. Lee for a lousy $10 because P. Lee needed the dog so badly.

P. Lee agreed and Doc delivered the dog a few days afterward. Everything went well until a week later when P. Lee summoned Doc to the ranch on another errand of mercy. P. Lee seized on the occasion to roundly criticize Doc's estimate of the dog's ability as a rat catcher and, in fact, hinted strongly that the sale of the dog was a put-up job. Then he took Doc to a cellar where the dog was holding forth—sound asleep and blissfully unmindful of the rats that ran over and all around him.

"Now just a minute, P. Lee. These here are *your* rats ain't they?"

P. Lee said they were.

"Well," Doc replied, "you just let a *strange* rat come onto the place and see what that dog does!"

Man of Courage

Al Peyton was one of the fairest sheriffs ever to fan a sixgun. Once he gave a known killer three chances against his own life before finally cutting him down in a blaze of gunfire. It is one of the most outstanding demonstrations of sheer nerve that I've heard about.

I saw Al a few years ago in Billings, Mont., and I think the memory of that shooting haunted him until he died early in 1956. Al was not the kind who could kill a man and forget it.

He was sheriff of Converse county, Wyo., a successor in the best western tradition to the famous Malcolm Campbell who captured Alfred Packer, the one they called "the maneater."

Al was identifiable as sheriff only by a badge. He packed his artillery only when there was trouble, and then his hips bulged with two silver six-shooters with pearl handles. His holsters were tied down to his thighs—the mark of a businesslike gunman in the old days.

Al didn't always rely on the guns, especially if the odds were too great in his favor. He once trailed an escaped prisoner to an abandoned coal mine near Glenrock, Wyo. He knew the man was unarmed, so he left his own guns in the automobile and went in after him barehanded.

They fought in the dark inside that tunnel and Al emerged as always, his prisoner meekly in tow.

But the night thirty years ago, when he traded shots with a crazed killer from Casper, was the most memorable of his career.

The man, whose name skips me, had slain his wife and another member of the family. He had hauled their bodies to the city dump and had thrown them there before leaving for Douglas.

At Douglas, the killer put his car in a garage, registered at the LaBonte hotel and was discovered almost instantly.

After stationing men at all avenues of escape, Peyton took up a lonely vigil in a room at one end of the hall where he could see his quarry emerge. The sheriff's patience was soon rewarded. The wanted man came out into the hallway. At the same time Peyton stepped out and called the man by name.

The killer whirled snarling, gun in hand. Peyton's revolvers, still holstered, leaped to his hands and the sheriff fired—once. The bullet smashed the man's gun-wrist. The man staggered, the gun clattered to the floor. Then he grabbed the weapon with his good hand and turned to fire. Peyton's gun barked a second time and again the killer's pistol fell.

It was only when the man grasped the gun with both hands and, in a fury that quenched pain, tried a third time to kill him, that Peyton did the one thing that remained to be done.

He blasted him but good. Then he left the hotel with his eyes streaming tears.

No Place Like Home

So you think your old Uncle Knitknick is a teetotaller, eh? Well, you better go look again. Colorado has a lot of mighty sneaky drinkers, and I can prove it.

Last year, as a matter of fact, the home-based imbibers outdrank the barroom boys almost two-to-one! What's more, the taste of the clothes-closet type alcoholic who keeps his liquor in liniment bottles and hides them in the hay mow when the preacher comes to visit, runs chiefly to the straight hard spirits. No beer or wine for this lad. He's strictly a high-octane consumer. (Just wait'll you see the figures.)

For this sensational scoop on Colorado's drinking habits, I am indebted to Myron Donald and Buck Wilson. They head up Colorado's liquor licensing authority, and I got the information straight (how do you like yours?) from them.

Among other interesting things, I learned that Colorado consumed twenty-four and one-half million gallons of wine, beer and liquor last year and that the drain on the national supply is even greater now despite the fact that last year was an election year.

Colorado is a beer-drinking state. We guzzled more than 16 gallons per capita in 1952. Man, woman and child, according to the statistics—we drank 1.38 gallons of hard liquor. Wine consumption was not worth mentioning.

The interesting thing is that 72 percent of all the hard liquor sold was take-home stuff. The public bouting spots accounted for only 28 per cent of total sales, and that's what I'm complaining about.

I can see only one or two reasons why people should hide out and drink at home. Either they're putting up a false front for the neighbors, or they're afraid they'll have to buy somebody a drink if they frequent the bars. (Donald and Wilson say they're looking at television. Pffutt.)

Down in Nevada, now, the west's reputation for robust flagon belters and come-howdy roisterers is being upheld right handily. I read in the *Territorial Enterprise* from Virginia City that one block and tackle joint there has installed an oxygen machine that breathes out life-saving ozone when a coin is dropped in. Two-bits-a-sniff is the going price, I understand.

This is supposed to increase a man's capacity for intake by leaps and pints. You'd think all the bars would have one.

Nevada, according to recent intelligences, is "the drinkingest state in the union." But I cry foul. If Nevada's using an artificial respiration system to stay on its feet, then I contend that Wyoming or Montana, either one, could outdrink 'em, and I'm an innocent bystander. I quit two years ago!

G. T. C. A. T. H. W. T.

Shortly after the Civil war, it was not uncommon throughout the south to see a scrap of paper bearing the initials, "G. T. T." tacked to the door of an unoccupied house. When, for any one of a number of reasons including honorable ones, some southern gentleman found it expedient to depart hurriedly without saying goodby, he merely left behind him the eloquent "G. T. T."

It meant simply "Gone to Texas."

At first, perhaps, the message was meant to imply nothing more sinister than notice that the former occupant had tired of carpet-baggers, taxes and whatnot, and had sought his fortunes in more favorable climes .

But eventually, G. T. T. began to appear repetitiously in court records almost always opposite the names of individuals for whom sheriff's officers had searched extensively and unsuccessfully. Soon, any man yearned for by the law was said to have left his G. T. T.

At this time there were a great number of G. T. T'ers around and about the Lone Star state, which undoubtedly accounted in part for the unpopularity of asking questions. To ask a man where he hailed from usually brought on right unpleasant repercussions. That applied to almost *any* man because anyone caring to settle in Comancheria must have had strong reasons for leaving his former place of abode.

Now I am indebted to Dallas newspaperman William Allen Ward for word that G. T. T. has come into widespread modern recognition. Texans, it seems, having run out of things to be proud of, are fawning on the dust of their ancestors who were G. T. T'ers and are forming G. T. T. clubs. The only membership requirement is that one's ancestor or ancestors was or were G. T. T'ers.

If old Grandpa Ellis escaped the noose at N'Orleans and came to Texas to make good and raise a derrick, all well and good. His descendants feel that it isn't what your forebears were. It is what you are, suh, that really matters.

So now a great number of Texas' most prominent families are members of G. T. T. clubs, Ward says. Considerable interest has arisen in blood lines and family trees. And unless your family tree has a rope on it, you're just a nobody these days down on the Rio Grande.

Books have been written about G. T. T'ers. Among writers on the subject are Thomas Hughes and *Empire* contributor, J. Frank Dobie. Newspapers, Ward says, are constantly being pestered by someone seeking to find a skeleton or at least a few old bones in the family closet.

But up here in Colorado we have a little club of our own called the G. T. C. A. T. H. W. T. which seems to gain popularity with each succeeding heat wave. It's called the Gone to Colorado and to Heck with Texas club. Membership is for free. Just bring your own oil rig.

Soft-Boiled Cop

People weren't complaining about the income tax at this particular time. No income! They weren't so much concerned about the value of the dollar as they were about the size of Salvation Army doughnuts. Hamburger was selling, if at all, for around 6 cents a pound, and the hock value of a good wrist watch wouldn't make a weak mulligan stew.

Let's see, now. That would be around 1929 or early in the 1930's

Well, anyhow, at the very nadir of that grim period when the backbone of the national economy suffered a slipped dollar, Patrolman Frank Ingraham was dispatched to the Denver railroad freight yards to investigate the strange disappearance of coal.

It was just a few days before Christmas and it was colder than the north side of 40 below. The wind screamed the call of the Alaskan Kee bird and Frank was mad clear through.

He and his partner had lain in wait for the culprit or culprits several frosty nights. Thus far the pickings had been cleaner than a baby's first tooth.

Then, suddenly, a shadow atop a coal gondola took the shape of a man. The shadow was tossing hunks of coal onto the ground. He had piled up a sizable load.

Frank crawled atop the gondola and shouted into the teeth of the gale: "Lay down that hunk of coal, you blankety blank robber. And come offa there!" He was ready to beat the guy's ears down to his shoulders like a pair of wings.

Meekly and in complete dejection, the coal thief dropped to the ground. Frank frisked him in approved police fashion then he asked him what in the name of Old Coalie's meatwagon he was stealing coal for.

"For my wife and five kids," the captured one sighed.

Frank's attitude was a big "Oh, yeah, let's see?" So they went to a little shack down under the viaducts. Inside, a pale woman and five skinny kids shivered around a kerosene lamp.

"You know," Frank observed of that evening not long ago, "it took us nearly to daybreak to get that coal picked up and hauled to that shack. And that Christmas sure bit a hole in the paycheck."

Yep, that's Frank—hardboiled as a picnic egg. You'll remember him. He's the cop on the corner of Fifteenth and California streets, here in Denver, who scorns a police whistle and screeches through

161

his teeth. He's capable of a whistled reprimand or an all-clear in the same breath.

He's due to retire in May. That's why it's permissible now to tell about the coal story. Good fishing, old-timer, and may you be plagued with no more jaywalkers.

The Heart Lake Monster

At the very foot of towering, bald-pated Mount Sheridan in the southeast corner of Yellowstone National park, nature blasted a yawning, heart-shaped hole in the earth millions of years ago. Subsurface pressures built up to an intolerability. The upper crust burst like a blownout tire. The volcano that formed must have been violent though short-lived.

The mighty opening it left has long since filled with clear, blue, glacier-cold water which was named Heart lake. No one knows exactly how deep Heart lake really is. But if the size of the fish there is any measure of depth—then Heart lake must be the deepest thing in all troutdom.

Few are privileged to troll the waters of Heart lake for two reasons: First, the lake can be reached only on foot or horseback. Second, it is little known and there is good reason for that, too.

Back in 1929, a careless smoker touched off an inferno on the lake shore that blackened 18,000 acres of the most beautiful timber you ever saw. And in three days, too. Floyd Gibbons, whose place in radio no one has ever been able to take, was in the park. He went to the fire and broadcast a dramatic, machine-gun-like description of its awful fury.

Heart lake's shores are heavily timbered with Douglas fir and Engelmann spruce. In dry season it's explosive. The park service prefers to keep out all except the *real,* woodswise outdoorsman.

Early in the 1930's a group of wealthy New Yorkers heard of Heart lake, formed a party and packed in for a siege. For weeks they whipped the placid waters for specimen trout and threw back fish so big that most Ike Waltons would have had them stuffed.

Telephone calls from the Heart lake snowshoe cabin are usually urgent. They frequently report fires. But there came a call

162

one day that concerned something that had happened on the lake. The New Yorkers had hooked a monster!

From all over Yellowstone, park officials rushed to the scene. A long, drawn-out battle was in prospect. They wanted to be in on the kill. When they arrived they saw two excited fishermen jumping about in a boat as though they had fleas, and grinning like a bear biting a bee. They were taking turns playing something on the business end of their copper line—300 feet of which was "out."

They had hooked "the thing" shortly before noon. It had zinged that copper line across the lake like it had tied into a submarine. Their friends ashore shouted instructions, offered advice, swore and prayed. The grim struggle went on for three hours and some minutes.

Exhausted, the pair in the boat edged toward shore, beached the boat and waded in. It wasn't exactly sporting, they agreed. But they hauled the monster in and gigged him—a thirty-two-pound Mackinaw trout. I don't think the record ever has been broken in Yellowstone.

One Word of Caution

Gunslick Tex O'Riley, professional soldier of fortune, was never in his life known to run out on a fight. In the first place, he hailed from Texas. In the second place, he was Irish. And whoever heard of a combination like that running from anything?

In both respects, Tex was like the son of Erin who was asked what race the Irish spring from. "We spring from no race," came the reply. "We spring at 'em!"

Therefore it was with considerable consternation that newspaper reporters noted Tex's unbecoming behavior that tense summer afternoon at Agua Prieta, Mexico. At the time, Tex was in the employ of some now-forgotten Mexican general fighting for some now-forgotten cause.

Tex's revolutionary force was drawn up in battle array in the general sector of the town's freight depot—prize in the day's shooting.

On a hotel roof a safe distance from the unpleasantries, a party of American newspapermen watched the show through field glasses and a mist of tequilla highballs. In the group was my old friend and correspondent, L. M. (Make Mine Water) Shadbolt.

Copper-clad .30-caliber bullets kicked dust spurts in front of the battling positions. Tex wore a broad-brimmed hat and Levis. He cut a singularly unheroic figure.

Suddenly he waved his arm in a sweeping arc. His little band of guerrillas yelled and raced to the depot under cover of fire. There they crouched behind protective boxes and crates and peppered their enemies.

The Mexicans in O'Riley's army seemed to shoot just for the noise and fun that was in it. But Tex aimed with slow deliberation. He was gunning for meat. Professionals of that prewar era were paid so-much-per-head.

Now a Krag rifle like Tex was using holds six shots and has a bolt action. Tex fired the six shots then ducked back behind his breastworks of boxes to reload.

Suddenly he did a strange thing. He threw down his gun and ran! He didn't waste any time. He got the hell out of there—pronto. He was still galloping like mad when he disappeared from sight.

Tex's unseemly retreat was the center of conversation that night as the newspapermen gathered in the town cantina to slake their thirst. Several theories had been advanced when, who should burst into the oasis but Tex, himself, O'Riley.

Shadbolt, who enjoyed a tippling acquaintance with the sharpshooter, questioned him bluntly about vamoosing when the fun was at its height.

"Just one word," replied O'Riley calmly, "just one word. It was stenciled on each of the boxes."

"And that word was?" Shadbolt asked.

"Dynamite!"

"Sure-Thing" Gamble

Back in the latter half of the 1930's when I was city-editing the old brass-voiced *Casper* (Wyo.) *Times,* we had an amazing writer on the staff named Ogden (Shutter Eyes) Rochelle. Now Rochelle was gifted at birth with a faculty most newspapermen dream of possessing—a pair of photographic optics.

In that one respect Rochelle was a human apart from the other fixtures in run-of-the-press newsrooms. In most other respects, however, he appeared to have been cast in the same mold which produced his inky brethren. That is, he shared all the minor vices and aberrations commonly discredited to reporters.

Chief of these little deviations from righteousness in the case of our boy, Ogden, was an almost fanatical yen to bring financial ruin to each and every member of a gambling gentry known to the trade as professional "21" dealers.

This uncontrollable impulse caused him to spend hours and a considerable amount of his cash in the city's then-plentiful gambling joints. And it also inspired and spurred him to perfect "Rochelle's unbeatable system for bankrupting the '21' dealer."

We in the newsroom knew Rochelle could do it. His remarkable memory was recognized by us—and how. Rochelle's uncanny ability to turn out reams of copy without once referring to notes was the eternal discouragement of all young reporters privileged to watch him operate.

He could scan a lawyer's brief for ten seconds, walk back to the newsroom via a route cobblestoned with barrooms, and copy the brief verbatim. He likewise could watch a blackjack dealer and remember each and every face and number in the discard, a valuable asset.

One night he hammered out twenty-some-odd stories packed with "quotes" and figures, relying entirely on memory. Another time he confounded an eye doctor by reading an eye examination chart through once, then turning in the chair and repeating the jumbled alphabet from his mental record. For an extra flourish, he recited the thing backwards.

He labored long and arduously on the "system" for making suckers of "21" operators, compiled charts and estimated odds down to tiny fractions.

"Nobody can beat 'Shutter Eyes' if he's in good form and has that system perfected," the boss observed. Everyone agreed. So did Rochelle who displayed an almost vulgar confidence in his Super Double X high-sensitivity glimmers.

Came the night the foolproof system got its initial test. Rochelle sailed into the game with $10 which, at the time, was considerable cash. He was back in the office in less than two hours to report:

"Only one thing I overlooked. It is a truth—the hand *is* quicker than the eye."

Blackie's Last Stand

Usually when a Wyomingite writes tenderly about an animal, said animal is a horse. But my favorite sagebrush philosopher, Doc. Walter E. Reckling of Lusk, writes about "Blackie," a tomcat.

One of Doc's patients introduced Blackie into the Reckling household to replace a child's pet that had been killed by an automobile.

"Blackie had little to recommend him," Doc writes. "I'd say that his mother was all-barnyard strain while his pop could have

166

been any one of the best twenty cats in Sioux county. A lady cat, in her amours, courts gentry from far and near.

"The year was 1936. Old Doc Reckling—that's me—had been stuck by a wife who had building pains. The year before, we had built a house.

"The spring of 1936 found me trying to landscape the yard. That year was dry. The city was short on water. The grass and shrubs grew poorly.

"Then other things began to happen. Insects!

"With each shift of the prevailing wind came another phylum of insects. They alighted on my shrubs and grass. The first batch were Colorado potato beetles. These chaps had the honeysuckle to a strip-tease in no time. But I managed to save a few shrubs by liberal helpings of Black Leaf 40.

"Then a batch of gray beetles moved in. They drank the Black Leaf 40 and grew fat. A bartender in entomology, I fed these chaps a Reckling cocktail of Black Leaf and Paris Green.

"Then came ants. My kids helped stomp out the ant hills. But the next pestilence was grasshoppers.

"They moved in by hordes. When I first noticed them, they were marching on me in divisional strength and in squads of eight abreast.

"I looked in vain for some feathered friend to help me. But bird life had been reduced by insect poisoning programs. When things looked darkest, I noticed an ally.

"Blackie was anti-grasshopper.

"From early morning to late at night, he stood on hind legs, waving both forepaws and devouring hoppers by the dozens. He observed no union hours. When the invasion was checked on the home front, he moved to the neighbor's yard.

"But poor fellow, he grew thin on the very diet which helped Elijah.

"We fed him milk, the same as the kids. But he grew thinner and thinner.

"Now my old dad taught me to have an answer to all questions and a price on everything I owned. But not on Blackie. A passer-by offered me ten bucks for the animal even in his emaciated state. I turned him down even though ten bucks in those days was quite a wad.

"A couple of days later old Blackie, weighted down with hoppers and weak from malnutrition, failed to cross the street with his usual alacrity. A car hit him.

"That night, the family gathered in the backyard for quiet funeral services. I think we all cried just a little that night."

The $3 Epitaph

Col. James Bulger had been going around and about the country for years shooting various and sundry individuals at random until he made a big mistake in Denver. Up to 1914, the people he shot had all been enemies of the United States or some revolutionist for whom Bulger happened to be working at the time.

Records show that he served creditably in the Spanish-American war with Teddy Roosevelt's Rough Riders and that he did all right in Central America. In Denver, however, he made the mistake of killing a hotel man and ended up with a life sentence to Canon City. Not long ago, after nearly forty years behind bars, the colonel asked for a parole. His story in *The Denver Post* attracted the eagle eye of my old friend L. M. Shadbolt.

Now few sharper newspapermen ever quit drink and went into a paying business than tall, fragile and inquisitive "Shad."

Instantly upon reading the story about Bulger's intentions, Shad's mind hearkened back to "about the time the Madero revolution had really gotten under way in Mexico." It seems he wrote in a letter to this corner, that Colonel Bulger, along with as choice a bevy of gun-runners, filibusterers, safe-blowers and gentlemen-on-the-lam as ever collected in one spot, converged on El Paso, Texas.

"One of the by-no-means lesser lights of this locust invasion was one Jack Neville. Sundry peace officers positively yearned for Jack if something less than a bushel of warrants is any criterion.

"Jack and the colonel," Shad continued, "were deep-dyed, to-the-death bosom pals. Damon and his buddy, (Greek Legend), whose name at the moment escapes me, were blood feudists by comparison.

"Well, at that time, I graced—if that is exactly the right word—the reportorial staff of either (A) the El Paso *Herald* or (B) the El Paso *Times*. I'm a bit vague as to precisely which since, in those

168

rather casual journalistic days it was the rule, when fired by one to be hired promptly by the other and, thank God, vice versa.

"Anyhow, word came to the city desk that the colonel, then an adherent of Madero, had called on the Maderista consul; demanded cash; got turned down, thereupon threatened suicide and, as evidence of good faith, pointed a gun near (but not too near) his head, fired and nicked out perhaps an ounce of scalp.

"I bounded out for the story. Returning, I ran into the aforesaid bosom pal of Bulger, Jack Neville.

"'Hey Jack—did you hear? Bulger just tried to kill himself,' I panted.

"'He did?' exclaimed Jack, startled. Then—'and that blankety blank so-and-so—he owes me three dollars, too'." (Your war and prison records are good, Colonel. Hope you win parole.)

Old Tip on Traffic

Tip M'Tavish, the Tie Siding, Colo., traffic expert and weather prophet, is upset no end about congestion on Denver streets. He writes that his conception of the average Denver motorist is a grim citizen sitting impatiently at the wheel of a 100-mile-an-hour automobile waiting for the lights to change so he can race the car beside him to the stoplight on the next corner.

Tip adds that since Henry Barnes took over as traffic engineer, Denver has broken out in such a rash of red lights that the town is getting a bad name.

"People are wondering what's going on down there," says Tip.

He declares Denver traffic is like politics. Only one-half the people are satisfied at any one time.

"The satisfied ones have the green light, and the dissatisfied ones are the other half who are waiting their turn to go," says Tip.

Now since Denver seems able to permit only one-half its automobiles to move at any one time, Tip suggests that half the people work nights or on alternating days, or just leave town.

Tip wonders, too, why it is that people who work on one side of town almost invariably live on the other side. He declares what Denver needs most, next to a repaving of West Alameda avenue, is a mass migration movement.

He went on to suggest a novel plan to speed up rush-hour traffic in downtown Denver. The plan is simple:

"Permit motorists to drive on the sidewalks at the peak congestion periods. The pedestrians could walk in the middle of the street and be just as safe because nothing is moving out there anyhow."

Then, too, Denver could just eliminate all its streets running north and south and make its east and west streets into alternating one-way arteries. That would do away with all cross-traffic and allow traffic to "flow" steadily.

Anything that wanted to move north and south could do so on an enormous, fifty-lane circle drive around the outskirts of the city. Such traffic could merely drive around out there until it came to the proper east-west street, then turn in and get to the destination in less than half the time it now takes.

Besides, that would make business better in Colorado Springs, Greeley and Fort Collins.

As it is, according to Tip, millions of dollars are needlessly going to the brake and clutch manufacturers in the east.

The plan could be financed, he said, by selling all Denver street signs and stoplights as scrap metal to the defense materials administration which could install them along potential invasion routes in such a manner as to protect this country from any aggression.

Hooray for old Tip!

Such Interesting People

Friendly letter from a reader down North Platte, Neb. way brought to mind not long ago a delightful little anecdote—true, of course. It was during the big flood of a few years ago. Traffic east and south of North Platte was cut off by turgid waters of creeks that had risen from their beds and had gone wandering about the country causing no end of inconvenience.

At the height of the isolation in North Platte, a newspaperman and an Omaha slot machine operator who was on the lam from inernal revenue agents, met in friendly fashion.

Their chance meeting came about in a place of mutual interest where each was seeking to stave off a possible attack of the muddy water jaunders. (Jaundice is perhaps correct, but my grandfather always insisted it was "jaunders.")

Since both were employing the same prescription in their medicinal precautions, they soon became well acquainted and, after a while, waxed chummy enough to embark upon an academic study of North Platte's seamier side.

They began a round of let's say dancehalls along the railroad that plows right through the middle of town.

In one of these off-street establishments they came upon a comely conversationalist who invited them to sit and chat awhile. Business had not been too good on account of the flood cutting off payroll checks for the railroad and a construction crew working out of the town.

Anyway, the three chatted amiably enough and the conversation warmed to a point where the slot machine operator thought introductions were in order.

"D'you know," he began, "that the man you're talking to is editor of the . . ." and he mentioned the name of a newspaper known nationally for its high journalistic morals.

"Izzat so?" she exclaimed, lifting a heavily painted eyebrow in the direction of the stunned newspaperman.

"Well, that just goes to show you. We do meet such interesting people in our business. Why, only a few years ago we had four fellows up here who stayed five days and gave us the surprise of our lives. We never dreamed who they were.

"They were wearing overalls," she explained, "but they spent money like mad. They even sent out for their meals.

"Well, two days after they left, we saw their pictures in the paper. They had been picked up by the FBI, and were escaped prisoners of war.

"Now one of the girls noticed they had some initials like P. O. W. on the backs of their jackets, but we just thought they were relief workers."

Pioneers from the Orient

Herman (the Hermit) Haskell, who is still hunting the mother lode just back of Colorado's front range, wrote the other day that we'd better stop this thing in Korea forthwith. Herman fears we are killing off the next generation's crop of laundrymen and ranch cooks.

He respectfully suggests that if science could take the noise out of war, the Chinese would soon lose interest and go home. Lacking somebody to fight, we'd come home, too.

Herman also advances the thought that one thing that has made the Chinese mad at us is Hollywood's consistent failure to give the Chinese any recognition whatsoever in western movies for the part they played in the taming of the west.

He's dead right too. Chapters of western history are colorfully tinted with the deeds and doings of the "Chineemen" who followed railroad construction, fought long wars, mined, built temples and mystified and confounded the early settlers.

Denver had its famous "Hop Alley." Rock Springs, Wyo., had a thriving Chinatown, scene of one of the bloodiest race riots in the country. Evanston, not far distant, boasted the only joss house within a thousand miles—reportedly one of only three in the nation—and Montana fairly teemed with Chinese population.

A good many of these pioneer orientals had sneaked across the Canadian border, bringing with them the strange ways of their country. They didn't set well with some frontiersmen of that era, and frequently incurred their wrath. In the fall of 1885 an angry mob in Rock Springs descended on the Chinatown there and burned every building. They dug the Chinese out of their underground warrens and killed thirty of them.

At Great Falls, Mont., a hot-eyed gang of bigots dressed like cowboys rounded up the city's entire Chinese population and headed them for the banks of the Missouri river. There the terrified prisoners were put aboard a raft and sent downstream to their deaths at the bottom of the falls for which the city is named.

Focal point for the Chinese in Montana seems to have been the rich gold mining area around Virginia City. The region abounds with "Lost Chinee" mines and yarns of hidden treasures concealed by the frugal "furriners."

Various tongs existed among the Chinese and disagreements between them were violent and noisy. One of these shattered the calm of the Montana hills in a particularly boisterous outbreak.

Pajamaed figures darted about in the streets, carrying rifles. Two large forces eventually met in combat in the thoroughfare Shots filled the air and the early hours were made hideous with high-pitched shrieks of singsong invective.

Enough rounds of ammunition were fired to lay low the entire Comanche tribe. But when the tumult was over and a peace treaty signed, only two Chinese lay dead.

Both had died of knife wounds.

They tell the tale up in Virginia City of the "Chinaman's luck" of an oriental accused of robbery.

Just to save time the jury took along a rope and hauled their hapless prisoner out to Pulpit rock, scene of most hangings of the period.

A bottle was passed while the judged apprised the culprit of his wickedness. Then he passed judgment.

"And now, you wuthless varmint, we're agoin' to give you a decent hangin'."

Just then a torrent from a heavy mountain rain washed out the earth that held Pulpit rock in its precarious perch for years. It tottered, plunged into the gulch. But not before judge and jury leaped to safety.

The bottle was passed again, and judgment revised:

"Prov'dence has saved yore wuthless hide. Now git out of Alder Gulch and don't never come back ag'in!"

The Last Stronghold

Of course, like others of my own generation, I am exceedingly grateful for the privilege of living in our particular era—history's greatest moment. We,—our generation—are exceptionally blessed.

We witnessed the advent of such marvelous scientific perfections as the atomic bomb, wonder drugs, bubble gum, the talking machine, television, yo-yo's, the automat, artificial insemination, the three-way stretch and the self-winding wrist watch.

We came a long way in one brief lifetime from the gramaphone to the singing commercial, galluses to braces, horse collars to Hydra-matic drives and from sassafras tea to aureomycin.

We observed the rise and fall of the jazz age, two world wars, honest women, old-fashioned bachelors, oratorical politicians, speakeasies and the swinging door. Let them lie where they fell. Mourn them not.

But I, for one at least, note with nostalgia and deep regret the passing of the last male institution which has for generations successfully withstood the powder puff influence as stoutly as have drop-seat long underwear.

I have reference to the fading art of chewing tobacco! There, gentlemen, we have the last sacred precinct of utter masculinity. The Sacristy.

Chewing tobacco does something for a man besides staining his chin. It gives him a reflective appearance, provides him with an absorbing pastime and distinguishes him from the weaker sex as only two or three other things can.

People for years mistook my old grandad for a genius or at least a very wise man, just because he was an inveterate and practiced user of "eatin' tobaccy."

Asked for an opinion on any controversial or difficult subject, he always employed the same technique with devastating effectiveness. He would stare silently and contemplatively at the ground. Then, with a great show of reflection, he would shift his cud from one cheek to the other. All this took a great deal of time. His listeners thought he was deep in cogitation. Actually he was just looking for a place to spit.

Finally, he would jerk his head up, emit a thin stream of tobacco juice and sagely observe: "Wal, now, that's a tol'able question. That's something that deserves a lot of thought. Yessir, a lot of thought."

He was quoted at the barbershop and around the bars. He would have made a great politician. He never committed himself on any question except one and then he would always say: "Don't care if I do. But just one."

On lazy summer afternoons out in the shade of the barn where we talked about fishing, grandpaw was great fun as he "target spat." He could pick off a fly at seven paces on a windy day, and farther if the air was calm.

Winters, however, always frustrated grandpaw. He never quite succeeded in expectorating his initials on a snowbank.

Few of his listeners know it, but Gene Amole, the genial newscaster, mastered the art of chewing when he was in the army. He says he could at one time, expectorate over the windshield of a Jeep while driving forty miles an hour against the wind, and never splatter the machine or himself.

Dan Partner, one of *The Denver Post's* more wholesome looking lads, chewed tobacco until he married himself off and was talked out of the habit, and I've often suspected that former Gov. John Vivian now and then secreted a cud in his jaw.

But then, that's a tol'able question, and one that deserves a lot of thought.

Seth Gets an Earful

It was hotter than a grass widow's kiss out there on the Lazy-J spread. Heat waves shimmered over the bunkhouse roof, and the ranch dogs snored in the cool under the floor.

The only thing that moved in the afternoon stillness as I tied up at the ranch was old Seth Cowperthwaite. He sat on the front porch in his rocking chair, mopping his brow with a red bandana and whittling on his false teeth with a pocket knife.

Seth had been "deef as a post" for years, as the neighbors would say. So I ups with a big intake of breath and yells, "HOWDY, SETH!"

"Save yer lungs, Bobby," Seth breathes softly. "I kin hear ye. I ain't deef no more."

The simple pronouncement was like a sudden clap of thunder. Up to now the only way you could get old Seth's attention short of setting off a dynamite blast, was to holler as loud as you could as close to his ear as you could get.

"Yep. It's been some experience, sonny. Got back my hearin' just like the doc said I would."

He sliced a thin strip from the inside of his uppers, curled a probing finger inside his mouth and extracted a cud of tobacco. Then he inserted the molars, clicked his jaws together, and sat back smiling.

"Dern things never did fit just right," he observed "Have to cut 'em down now and then."

Hearing Seth talk in tones lower than the roar of an enraged donkey was a surprise. His ability to hear was as amazing as seeing the devil in a trick riding get-up.

Folks had always allowed as how old Seth probably would have to be jerked awake on the judgment day because he never would be able to hear Gabriel's trumpet even if the mighty angel blew the thing right in his ear.

I curled a cigaret and leaned against the porch post while Seth elucidated.

"Yessir, Bobby, I'd tried everything—ear horns, electric gadgets, skunk oil and soapweed juice—but nothin' worked. Then when the doc got the trouble cleared up I wuz never so susprized in my hull life.

"Why, I heered that there Benny feller on the radio t'other night. Went to church, too. Listened to the first sermon I'd heered since I wuz a shaver.

"That there preacher shore wuz givin' 'em fits. He hollered about hellfire and brimstone till he scared me plumb outa muh skin. Said we wuz all a'headin' for perdition.

"Hand me that there demmyjohn, Reddy boy. I'm hankerin' for a snort of Taos lightnin'."

He drained off a heavy sluice from the jug, wiped his mouth with the back of his hand, and continued.

"Yep, that there doc shore had things figgered out." He was talking louder now. He tipped up the jug again.

"Th' old lady got through to me, too. Said I wuz going to have to change muh ways—git some store clothes and quit swearin', especially when the preacher is here.

"And say, Reddy, I turned on that dad burned radio t'other day and heard some pollytician named Whaft or Baft or sunthin. He said the hull country's goin' to th' dogs—war, taxes and starvation." Old Seth was shouting at this point.

I got curious as all get out what the doc had done for old Seth's hearing, so I up again and makes inquiry.

"MADE ME STOP DRINKIN'," he bellowed. "HEARIN' COME BACK IN JIG TIME. BUT I BEEN THINKIN', RED-DY. HAND ME THAT DEMMYJOHN AG'IN. STUFF I

176

BEEN HEARIN'S WORSE'N THE STUFF I BEEN DRINK-
IN' . . . CARE TO HAVE ONE, REDDY BOY?"

Winner by a Natural

If it hadn't been for the Cheyenne, Wyo., baseball team, Colorado might never have become a state. Well, maybe that's putting
it a little strong. But it is on record that the team and a raft of
boisterous Cheyenne boosters, did help Colorado into the union.

They came down to Denver to play the local nine the day Colorado voted on the question.

When the game was over—the outcome was never recorded—
the team and the Cheyenne rooting section marched uptown in
a body and, with considerable hoorah, joined Coloradans in cast-
ing the ballot that brought the Columbine territory into the federal tax system.

Colorado has been sore at Cheyenne ever since.

Authority for the sly, unneighborly trick is J. W. (Doc) Howard's memoirs, an altogether too-small booklet written in captivat-
ing style for limited circulation among members of the family.

Doc Howard was the father of my old friend, Sam Howard,
who retired from the Denver police force a few weeks ago.

Doc came west to Colorado and Wyoming as an Indian fighter
with the old Fifth cavalry. He stayed on to become the second
marshal to hold office at Cheyenne. He also was a member of the
Cheyenne baseball team and, as such was one of the pranksters
who helped make Colorado a co-conspirator in the big, continuing
plot on the Potomac.

Another party to the deed was none other than Cheyenne's
mayor, D. Fisk. He came down with the baseball team. The way
Fisk got into office is interesting.

He and another Cheyenne citizen, Abe Simmons, finished the
election for mayor in a dead heat. The vote was tied. The two
candidates ran off the tie in a crap game—winner take office, and
Fisk rolled a natural.

A vivid assortment of colorful characters trod the board sidewalks of Cheyenne back in the 1870's when Doc was the constable
there. Among them—and all sufficiently close friends of Doc to

177

borrow money from him—were Buffalo Bill Cody, Wild Bill Hickok, Calamity Jane and a French female gambler known favorably to the menfolk of the community as Madame Moustache.

The name sort of grew on her, so to speak. She got it because of a sassy little hirsute growth on her upper lip which she groomed to two dagger points with the use of imported wax.

It was Doc who drove the first stage from Cheyenne to the Black Hills country. And it was the same Doc who, in the finest tradition of a hard-fighting ex-cavalryman, successfully defied big cattle interests that threatened to tar and feather him when he homesteaded near Cheyenne.

Threats were not to be taken idly in those days. They weren't idly made. But the town had a remedy for bad men. It gave them a fair trial and then hanged them.

There were some miscarriages of justice, but no one can recall that any victim of quick rangeland justice ever walked back from a necktie party with a rope around his neck to voice any complaints.

One such, Doc says, was strung up to a telegraph pole down by the Crow creek railroad bridge. After the hanging, they caught the guilty party and hanged him, too.

Doc met his downfall at Douglas (my old home town), Wyo. He heard about a shortage of vegetables up there—up to this time they et nothing but beef—and began freighting the finest garden varieties to that heart of the cow country.

Among the shoppers for the vegetables was a young Michigan woman who had been visiting in Buffalo, Wyo. They got married and she forced Doc to settle down. That's when they moved to Colorado.

Old Fashioned Xmas

Maybe you've noticed it, too. But it seems to me as I grow older, that Christmas comes on like a freight train—only quieter, almost unheard until it's upon us. Before one knows it, it's Christmas again and for one brief moment in the hurrying rush comes the flood of mellowness, the pleasant memories and the sparkle and good cheer that only the Yuletide can create.

178

Why, it seems only yesterday that we were in the midst of a national election campaign and I was calling the fellow up the street an incontrovertible, nickel-plated nincompoop over some disagreement that skips my mind right now. And already it's time for us to exchange Christmas greetings. It affords a study in contrasts, in a way. One minute we're shouting slogans and the next, singing carols. We were poles apart on politics, but united again come Christmas. And speaking of being reunited. One of the great things about the old-fashioned Christmas was the family reunion. Although we can cross the nation in a few hours and can drive from Denver to adjoining states in less time than it used to take to get into town, the family reunion seems to have become a thing of the past for some reason.

And it seems Christmases used to be colder and the snow deeper. Can it be that the climate has changed or that you and I are taller?

Decorations on the tree were prettier then, too, when Mother made them by hand out of cranberries and popcorn. Necklaces of enchantment they were, for a magic evergreen that bloomed overnight with simple delights made of old-fashioned wood and iron and plaster.

A mistletoe sprig had authority, too! Any girl who ventured under the gay sprout in those days got herself kissed by whoever was handy and sometimes by a whole crowd if she happened to be exceptionally pretty.

Everyone, way-back when, was conscious of the coming of Christmas for weeks and weeks. First indication of its nearness was arrival of the mail-order catalog all done up in bright holiday colors and filled with pictures of a jovial Santa. Remember how you'd study those pictures and wish, and then spend hours—endless weeks that never passed—waiting for that big bundle to come through the mail. Then you'd know that somewhere in the house —you didn't dare peek—were the makings of Christmas.

Of course that package contained only the things for Mama and Daddy. Santa Claus brought yours. And he was real, too, and many nights you saw him just before you dozed off to sleep on the feather tick, bundled under a beautiful and dreamily warm crazy-quilt grandma had made.

I know there was a Santa when I was a kid. I heard his sleigh bells and the pawing of reindeer hoofs on the roof many a time. I don't think I saw a dressed up Santa Claus in a store until I was nigh onto 21, and the first time I laid eyes on him and his false whiskers, I knew right then that there was something funny, something deceptive about the whole thing. I've been wondering about it ever since. You can't fool me. The real Santa never shows himself. Merry Christmas, friends.

Grampf Loft Hif Teece

HRB

You remember how it always used to be over at Grandpa Elmo Twittinger's place on Poison Spider during all the holidays. Remember the big Halloween party, for instance, when Grandpa Twittinger dropped the live salamander down Mrs. Lufe Ferguson's back just as she was bobbing for apples? Everybody laughed for hours because Mrs. Ferguson dived right into the tub of water. And remember how, later that night, she put horse liniment in Grandpa Twittinger's hard cider?

Well, there was a Thanksgiving day that will be remembered for some time to come. It was to be the biggest Grandpa Twittinger ever observed and plans were made weeks in advance.

All the lavishness was due to the unfortunate fact that the year previous, Grandpa Twittinger had to eat mush while everybody else loaded up on turkey and things. The dentist had jerked all Grandpa Twittinger's choppers only eight days before Thanksgiving. All during the meal he muttered about the starving Armenians and what hogs people could make of themselves in the face of his misery.

Well, this year things were going to be different. He kept telling everybody about it as they would drive up and unhitch that Thanksgiving day morning. As he told them he'd take out his new store teeth and show them off.

Luke Thatcher and his wife and kids pulled up about midmorning. Uncle Luke unloaded, sent the kids and the missus running to the house while he and Grandpa Twittinger and the Milner boys disappeared inside the barn as usual. Uncle Luke said something about fixing a loose shoe but he didn't seem upset about it. In fact he and the others seemed quite pleased as they went inside and closed the door, probably so the horse wouldn't get out.

When Grandma Twittinger heard that Luke and Grandpa Twittinger were fixing a loose shoe out in the barn, she just snorted and said something about getting dinner on the table before it was too late.

Later on some of the hired hands drifted over to the barn from the bunkhouse. You could hear them and Grandpa Twittinger holler and laugh once in a while.

Once grandpa yelled "Hide the horse collars men! Old Twit's a starvin'." About then somebody called from the house "Come and get it." Everybody ran out of the barn—everybody except Grandpa Twittinger.

When the barn door swung open I could see Grandpa inside trying to get the cork out of a cider jug. Finally he gave up, ran to the house and sat down to the table. He shoveled off enough turkey and things to founder a hound dog, then a look of dismay came over him.

"Muh teece," he mumbled. "Lost mu teece fomewhere."

Grandpa Twittinger was fit to be tied. He hunted and hunted and got maddder and madder. He was madder than ever when everybody started home and he went back to the cider jug in the barn. He grabbed the cork and it bit Grandpa Twittinger with Grandpa's own teeth.

New Year at Poison Spider

About the most successful New Year celebration I ever heard of was the one back in aught-eight at which somebody shot off Grandpa Twittinger's big toe with a .45, and one of the hired hands burned down the bunkhouse.

Grandma Twittinger was responsible for the biggest joke of all, however. It was so funny that nobody laughed about it until next year when everybody talked about it for the first time since it happened. Up to then, nobody dared bring it up without danger of being struck dead by Grandpa Twittinger who was mighty upset about it.

The celebrating got under way earlier than usual that year. Uncle Jake Torgerson drove over in the bed wagon before noon, and brought along the cousins and a couple of small kegs of hard cider for the party.

It seemed the corn crop had been especially good, and Uncle Jake had cooked up a batch of it up to his place beyond the loading corrals at Poison Spider, Wyo. He and Grandpa Twittinger spent a long time in the barn unhitching the team. Occasionally you could hear them cough and laugh real loud.

They went back out to the barn right after the noon meal to look at the horses again and see if they were all right. They stayed a long time again, and this time instead of just coughing and laughing, they got to yelling and singing.

The women folk stayed in the house and got everything ready for that night. They cooked up some taffy candy late in the afternoon and set it out to cool before it had to be buttered and pulled.

Grandma Twittinger popped some corn in the fireplace and set out a big plate of nuts and hog cracklings in the center table but none of the menfolks paid any attention to these things. They kept walking between the kitchen and the barn.

Even after supper they went out to see how things were getting along. Once Grandma Twittinger had to go out to the bunkhouse to break up a wrestling match that had gotten a good start. She had to go out again and take care of Elmer Wilson who had fallen off the bunkhouse roof.

Uncle Jake must have had some mean horses because everytime one of the kids would go out to the barn, he would tell them to run back to the house so he wouldn't get kicked.

Just before midnight, Grandma Twittinger went out to the barn and called all the menfolks to the house to join in the fun. It was awful chilly that night, and Grandpa Twittinger's face was bright red from being out in the cold.

He made a little speech and told what a grand year aught-eight had been, then somebody hollered "Happy New Year" and Uncle Jake grabbed a .45 pistol and all of a sudden it went off and so did Grandpa Twittinger's big toe.

About that time everybody noticed that the bunkhouse was on fire.

Next morning Grandpa Twittinger said the whole thing boded ill for aught-nine because of all the trouble.

It was then that Grandma Twittinger told him not to blame it on aught-nine because she had set up the clock an hour and a half so's everybody could get home early.

Christmas on the Range

It was one of those driving blizzards that stockmen dread. An angry north wind whooped down the narrow defile between the Big Horns and the foothills to the east, and burst upon the defenseless plains around Kaycee like a blast from some supernatural shotgun.

The biting gale blared in the arroyos, whinnied like the mares of hell in the rimrock and sent the furiously cascading snow to whirling in ghostlike dances around chalk pinnacles. It seemed bent upon ripping up every bunch of sagebrush between Buffalo and Crazy Woman creek.

Swallowed up in the storm and almost oblivious to the falling of night, two bundled riders fought to herd a hundred strays into the comparative shelter of a tiny valley.

They had been riding since daybreak. Their overshoed boots had frozen to the stirrups. Numbed feet were like heavy hunks of ice.

Honest Ed Wright shifted his reins, removed a mitten and blew on his fingers.

"Green blazes of hades, Pete," he yelled. "We'll never make it."

His words were blown back into his mouth and lost. Pete, unhearing rode on, slumped against the frigid rukus that blew all about him.

It was dark now, a miserable darkness that cut off vision and hemmed a man into his own small world of pony, saddle and increasing cold.

Suddenly Ed jerked erect in the saddle. He spurred his horse beside Pete, yelled something into the wind and pointed to a splotch of yellow light that twinkled in the swirling snow.

"Homesteader," Pete shouted to Ed. Without another word the two spurred their mounts to a gallop and, minutes later, scraped to a noisy stop in front of a battered shack that creaked and groaned under the impact of the storm.

They tied up and stomped inside. A wall of heat from a cooking stove slapped color into their cheeks. They swept the frost from their eyes and surveyed the interior.

A tall, emaciated individual regarded the two narrowly but with just a suspicion of welcome and obvious relief.

"We ain't ordinarily blessed with visits from cattlemen," he murmured. "But in view of th' weather, I reckon yuh're welcome." He nodded toward another corner of the room where a pale figure lay in a sheeted bed.

"I'll hafta ask yuh fellers to be a mite quiet, though. My wife's —uh, sick. And in a way I'm glad yuh fellers happened by. Yuh see, I'm a dry farmer. But I don't know much about caring for stock and such like. I reckon, mebbe, yuh can be of some help— iff'n yuh understand what I mean."

Ed and Pete did understand. They didn't have much time, and there wasn't much to work with. But it was not entirely unlike some of the cowpunching chores they had done before.

Ed admits even now, that he was a little awkward—and embarrassed. But the job was done with skill born of rangeland practice, while the anxious homesteader hovered near with kerosene lamp in hand.

Afterward, they were smacking their lips over a boiling pot of coffee and congratulating themselves, when the shack door jerked open for the second time that night. In stomped the irate figure of Jeff Stone, range foreman.

"So!" he exploded. "This is where yuh ding dang catawampuses have been roasting yore shins while them there strays are a'driftin'. Why, I oughta . . ."

His fist-shaking was interrupted by a tiny cry. Startled, Stone stared toward the bed which he had seen for the first time. Then he walked closer, grinned.

"Why, dang me. It's a—what is it? A boy!"

Outside the storm had subsided, the wind had died and stars shone through ragged clouds. Three cold cowpunchers tailed up 100 strays. Jeff Stone mumbled something.

"Yuh know what?" he said. "Merry Christmas, yuh hyenas!"

Zeb Rankin's Thanksgiving

HRB

"Yuh know what, Jake?" Zeb Rankin said. "This here's Thanksgiving day. Yuh betcha. Frost's on the punkins and the fodder's in the shock as the poet fellers say. It's time you and me was cal-clatin' our blessin's."

His brief sermon over, Zeb shrugged his shoulders deeper into the warmth of the old sheepskin coat, adjusted one leg of his chaps to shut out a breeze and lapsed into a meditative silence.

Jake just gazed off into the distance where a little bunch of steers stood bawling complaints at the edge of an ice-sheathed water hole.

185

It was indeed Thanksgiving day. But it had begun like any other except those summer days when the sun got up earlier and it was hot by this time of morning.

This particular morning it still had been dark—and plenty cold, too—when Zeb woke up, threw back the warm soogans and reached for his boots beside the bed.

He pulled them on over the wool socks he hadn't bothered to take off the night before, then he lit the oil lamp and put a kitchen match to some kindling wood in the cookstove.

By the time he got into his Californy's and wool shirt, there was warm water on the stove. He poured some into a pan, washed his big calloused hands and sloshed a little on his face. His toilet was complete.

Pretty soon the coffee pot was giving off happy sounds and was filling the kitchen with aroma. The flapjacks were browning and a half dozen thick slices of bacon curled and crackled in the skillet.

Breakfast was man-size and soul-satisfying. The coffee was hot and strong like a man wants it in the morning.

Zeb had noticed the date on the calendar while he buttered and syruped his 'cakes. He had intended to say something about it then, but he waited until they were out in the open where a man can think better with the help of a hand-rolled smoke and the frosty smell of sagebrush.

His speech had been somewhat less than he had planned, though, but he thought a lot about the significance of the day as he rode along that morning.

About the middle of the day he and Jake stopped at a place along Elk creek where there were some scrubby cottonwoods, and Zeb brought up the subject again.

"Them Pilgrims must have had it purty hard the first few Thanksgiving days—nothing to eat but turkeys that they had to go out and hunt. Maybe there was plenty of 'em, though. Times shore have changed, huh?"

About the time the sun was turning the skies all gold and red and sort of purple, Zeb and Jake returned to the homestead shack there at the crook in Bitter creek.

On the way to the shack Zeb stopped at the smokehouse and cut off some thick chunks of meat from the deer carcass hanging there. Then he got the flour sack, poured some water into it, added the rest of the makings and put together the biscuits.

As an afterthought he wrapped some bacon around the steaks just to lend a festive touch to the occasion.

Then he sat down to the table, lifted his knife and fork and stabbed at one of the steaks. He stopped, put down the knife and fork, lowered his head and said a few words to his Lord.

Then he did a strange thing. He got up from the table, put the steaks back on the stove to keep warm, got into the sheepskin and went out to the little leanto barn he had built.

There he shook down some more hay to an appreciative saddle horse, and even tapped the sack of oats for an extra can full. As he pushed out the stall past the animal, he slapped him on the rump and said:

"Eat a gutful, Jake. This is Thanksgiving day."

Sheepherders' Eulogy

Well, the "gummers" are most all off the open range country now. The sagebrush wears a lacy white morning frock of frost. The first snows have come, and the nights are getting colder and colder. The fire in the old sheepwagon stove feels pretty good.

Out on the rimrock in the still of night, a coyote points his nose at the frozen moon and yap-yaps a lonely plaint.

For one instant, perhaps, the cry strikes a responsive, sympathetic chord in the heart of the sheepherder.

Then all of a sudden he's up and going for his sheepskin coat and the .30-30 carbine by the door. Coyotes are bad business for the sheepmen.

Times have changed considerably since the historic period when the only thing sheepmen and cowmen had in common was a hearty dislike for each other. In those days they maintained gunshot distance between each other and the only greetings exchanged consisted of high-velocity lead.

Nowadays the sheepmen and cowmen drink over the same bars —I'm talking of the sheep and cow owners. Sometimes they even lend each other money, belong to the same clubs instead of carrying same.

Not so the sheepherder. He is a soul apart on this earth. He frequents no club, his visits to the tosspot tepees are few and far between (but of long duration when he does come in) and he fraternizes with few, if any, when in touch with civilization.

His is a lonely life and an arduous one. There are no telephone booths out on the winter range, no corner drug-stores or coffee shops and chances are that a hundred miles or more may lie between him and the nearest town of any consequence. That's big country, neighbor, where they raise sheep in herds of more than a thousand.

There have been some few modernizations, of course. The canvas top sheepwagon that resembled the old Conestoga of pioneer days has been replaced by a wagon with metal top and automobile tires. But the sheepherder is still his own cook, doctor, counselor and even conversation partner.

His wagon has a better radio. With today's better roads he may get his magazines and newspapers more frequently—say about every two or three weeks—but the winters are just as cold, the snow as deep and the task as difficult.

Hardly a winter goes by without a report from somewhere in the west of a ranch owner finding the frozen body of a sheepherder near the flock he had tried to protect from bunching in a storm.

Sheep follow the leader, you know. They'll crowd in one on top of the other until hundreds may suffocate. They'll drift in a storm, get themselves pocketed in a canyon or fence corner and die like flies.

It takes a good man to shepherd a thousand animals through the slashing onslaught of a plains country blizzard. And it takes good husbandry to nurse a herd's wobbly legged, helpless offspring through a temperamental spring. But the sheepherder does it.

At times eccentric, the butt of crude jokes always, occasionally given to long conversations with himself, frequently bewhiskered and unbathed, the shepherder is, nevertheless, a picturesque and highly important character of the west, albeit a vanishing one.

Weatherbeaten as a split cedar fence post, challenger of the elements and months of solitude on end, conscientious, loyal and faithful even to death, the sheepherder finds his work little changed since the time of Christ. Small wonder sheepmen find it difficult to fill the thinning ranks of this band of stalwarts in full-crowned hats .

You'll see their handiwork on the hilltops—mounds of rocks

patiently gathered and piled in symmetrical heaps. It's the only monument to their memory. Long may they stand.

Where'd the Color Go?

Old Honest Ed Wright, cowboy, yarn spinner, former king of the rodeo clowns and race horse owner blew into Denver a few weeks ago with his string of bangtails and cheered my heart like nothing had since 1952 when Lou M came in winner in the six-furlong.

What made me happy was Ed's hat. It was an oldtimer that he had rescued from the attic of his home in California, and had restored in all its Seven X glory. This bonnet is a real ten-gallon-er. Its crown is big enough for a jack rabbit to nest in with ears up, and the brim would shade a span of mules. It reminded me of the days when Ed and I worked the rodeos together, he as all-around rodeo hand and I as camp tender to a brace of jackasses and a pet monkey Ed used in the show.

Big hats were the style in those good old days. And there was no lack of color. I can't help but notice with a touch of regret the change in rodeo cowboy styles.

Boots were high-heeled and sharp-toed. They weren't usually as fancily stitched and colored as today's lower-heeled variety, but there was an appearance of sturdiness about them that testified with dignity to the rigors of range life.

Then, the fashionable bronc stomper bought his Levis as long as he could get them in his waist size, and would make a bottom cuff about six or eight inches high up the leg. The color contrast created by the fold plus a slight warp which the cuff put in the bottom of the denims, romantically enhanced whatever saddle bow the cowpuncher had in his legs.

Chances are that if he were a riding contestant he wore a leather belt about his midriff which was at least eight inches wide in back. It usually glittered with silver and ruby spots and was fastened in front by three or four silver buckles. Another bejeweled leather item was the wristlet which sometimes encased a cowboy's arm almost to the elbow.

Shirts? In those days cowboys wore turtleneck sweaters with

loud stripes running around, or shirts that screamed for attention. On top of all that was a bandanna kerchief that might be any color of the rainbow or some garish sunburst hue that no self respecting rainbow would claim.

Today's rodeo contestant is by comparison a colorless, almost drab individual at least so far as dress is concerned. Only the boots are universally bright, giving the impression that all the flash of yesteryear is draining down and out of the rodeo cowboy. He usually wears his denims without a fold, appears in a white shirt occasionally spotted accidentally with corral green and has even forsaken the flaming western hat that was in vogue a few years ago.

Gone are the bandannas and the radiant sweaters, and the pink angora chaps of T-Joe Cahill's day are not even a memory. In fact, as rodeoing becomes gradually more of an athletic sport than a combination brawl and wild west roundup, even black eyes and red noses are fewer among rodeo contestants

These Changing Times

HRB

Boy, how times do change. About the only things that remain the same are Denver's streets. And that reminds me, I wish to thank Mrs. Joe Moe for suggesting that the state game and fish department stock West Denver's bigger chuck holes with trout this summer so tourists won't consider their visit here a total loss.

What prompted this discourse on changing times was a letter from Bill Graff up Worland, Wyo., way. Bill wrote that he was stretching leather with a couple of new-generation stockmen the other day. Seems they had just returned from a "caboose trip" to Omaha with their cattle and they and Bill were comparing notes on how such trips have changed in the last 20 years.

Years ago, Bill says, the railroads used to give one free pass for each two cars of stock, to the same destination as the stock. The passes were for the drovers and were good for a ride in the caboose or waycar, sometimes referred to as the shack or crummy in rail parlance. The trip usually started from some unheard-of side-track where the cattle were loaded.

These shipments were preceded by a roundup and cattle drive to the loading chutes and there always was about these occasions the atmosphere of a college football victory, two Saturday nights in town and a family reunion at a barn dance. Some of the boys had to be poured onto the caboose when the engine picked up the loaded cars.

The drovers accompanying the stock were expected to keep the cows on their feet throughout the long trip to cut down on the kill for which the railroads assumed responsibility. But after nearly being left behind at a couple of water tanks and forced to jump on the nearest car when the train started unexpectedly, everybody decided they were needed in the waycar to keep the game going. The life of a man running in high-heeled boots the length of a swaying cattle train just isn't worth an election-year promise.

Usually the boys wound up in Denver, Omaha or Chicago in their range get-ups, packing their summer's pay in their pockets. In boots, big bonnets and jeans they'd invade the big town. "You could see the panhandlers crossing over to your side of the street two blocks ahead," Bill wrote. "They didn't have to ask where you were from or even how much you were carrying. They knew.

"But, gosh, it made a man feel first-class to be met in the yards by a genuine limousine ordered by the railroad, and hauled up-town to the best restaurant for a feed at railroad expense. Nobody seemed to mind that the real concern of the railroad was to see that the rannies got back to the yards and eventually home to make another shipment next year. On their own, the boys never would have found caboose No. 38 among 200 others scattered over ten square miles of yard tracks.

"But nowadays if you ride the train *you're* responsible for kills and the loss of one steer will pay for an airplane ticket. But who th' heck cares to make 'little Joe' in the aisle of an airplane and, by George, a man feels plumb conspicuous unless he's carrying a briefcase. So, I reckon, there goes the last of the good old days."

THE WEST—
AS SHE IS

Schoolboy Spellbinder

I've always been of the opinion that country kids, far from being underprivileged in the matter of education, are the luckiest of all. This belief was considerably strengthened the other day when I went out with Shutters Sealy, the photog, to take some pictures of the inside of a modern city school building.

All I can say is that it is a dirty trick on the kids. Oh, the interiors are pretty and nice with green blackboards (that doesn't sound quite right does it?), pastel colors on the walls and new type desks and chairs. But do you know what? Nowadays the teacher sits in the *back* of the room.

If there ever was anything made me nervous, it was a teacher staring at the back of my neck. A fellow can't study her mood and thereby learn when it is safe to make a wisecrack or wink at the girl in the next aisle. He can't determine whether the teacher is peeved, pretty or perverse. And think what a discouragement this will be to the coming generation of psychologists.

Teachers are the finest subjects I know of for knee pants psycological studies. (I made a study of one once up in South Dakota but that's a different story.) The bad thing about it, however, is that a boy, like myself, can become so well versed in his teacher's mental workings that he neglects his own.

I became so adept at sensing the right moment to cajole teacher out of a little better grade that I actually managed to get from one class to the other by this ruse. I climaxed my career in grade school by making a speech before the class on salesmanship. The teacher assigned me the subject and I've always wondered why.

I'd never sold anything except a few garden seeds and washing machines in my life.

But our teachers were really interested in me. One used to insist that I stay with her a short while almost every night after school. I don't think there's enough of this nowadays in city schools.

Eau de Schoolroom

Now this may prove to be somewhat startling to the county school board. It may provoke considerable eyebrow raising at the next meeting of the Parent-Teachers association, too.

But, come what may, I'm here to declare myself on the side of the kid who contends pungently, and perhaps with an unfortunate choice of verb, that "School stinks!"

What he means, of course, is that "Schools stink." I know. And I sympathize. I've smelled them, myself.

Schools possess a distinctive and memorable redolence all their own. It seems to comprise a thick consistency marvelously blended from the separate smells of lead pencil shavings, sweeping compound, apples, chalk, stale lunches, art gum erasers, writing pads and oceans of smelly ink.

It could be that I suffer an unpleasant thought association with that smell. Anyhow, it never fails to spark some psychological mechanic in my innards each time it assails my olfactory nerves. It causes a quick sinking feeling in the pit of the stomach. I have to fight again that old battle against an impulse to run outdoors and seek the sanctuary of some hidden place like a fishing hole or a tree house like we kids used to build.

When I confided this to a friend he said, "Yeah, I didn't do so well in school, myself."

My aversion to this malodorous atmosphere could not have sprung from a dislike for school. On the contrary I enjoyed school tremendously.

Three rows back and two to the right of where I sat in the eighth grade, there was the cutest little blond you ever saw. By turning sidewise and pretending to be absorbed in the contents of a textbook, I could catch her eye and wink.

School fascinated me.

Our mathematics teacher was out of this world. She had a physique, let us say, that was a dream. Had it not been for her I never would have cultivated an interest in figures. In fact I would never have mastered the multiplication table. She held the complete attention of the entire class for one reason or another, depending upon one's personal interest . . . in mathematics, of course.

In some respects I excelled the entire class. I stood head and shoulders above my classmates when it came to target shooting with a bean blower.

I was always first in line—when the line formed to go out to recess.

Moreover, although my individual recitation on the class floor may not have measured up to par, my examination papers always were identically as high as the girl who got the best grades in school.

She sat just in front of me.

In addition, I was never satisfied to put in just a full day's shift I worked considerable overtime, staying as many as four and five times a week to help the teacher after school was out. She spared me embarrassment in this respect, usually by insisting that I remain on.

But that funny classroom odor—it should go. If only someone could perfect an airconditioner that would blow "Old Swimmin' Hole No. 2" into our schools, he would make a million.

In Love with a School Marm

Of course, Red Jr., and his speckled-face brother, Brian Timothy, are definitely not looking forward to the opening of school with any marked degree of happiness. Like most young jaspers who still are in the decimal-point and fractions stage of book learning, they anticipate that first Monday morning bell with all the glee with which their father contemplates March 15.

Fellow youngsters, I know! That sound is death.

It used to be. But not any more. With me, now, it's different—now, I mean.

197

Nowadays, I instinctively look forward to the opening of school with a quiver of excitement for just one reason: Someday, somebody is going to bring back the age-old practice of box suppers at the country school house!

Never so long as I live will I forget the first box supper I attended. My good old dad took me. It was at Cedar Grove country school in Meade county, Ky.

I had 50 cents in my pocket, and with it I succeeded in buying the box supper—with dad's help, of course—of the prettiest girl in the whole world at that time. She was our "Miss Cora," the brunet school teacher.

Now, many years later, I must confess that I switched the ribbons on her box supper with that of the oldest spinster in the county, knowing somewhat precociously, I admit, that Miss Cora's boy friend would bid for that ribbon.

My, that was wonderful. I was in love. Naturally she was a little older than I. But what does twenty-five or thirty years matter when you're in love?

We sat on the school steps. That other guy sat nearby, alternately glaring at me and looking gooney-eyed at Miss Cora.

The lightning change of expressions on his countenance has always amazed me. He was two-faced, I knew. He certainly was not the man for our Miss Cora.

Moreover, I was sure Miss Cora could detect this shiftiness. I was convinced that spring when she sent me a valentine. It was not one of those things you can buy in the stores these days. She drew this one, herself, with pen and ink in two colors. There were some flowers on it, and—boy oh, boy—a heart with an arrow through it.

My conviction of everlasting affection grew apace with each understanding smile during those months in grade school. Then one day, wonder of wonders, she let me ride home behind her on her big bay mare.

Then, I knew, we were never to be separated.

That was just before she flunked me in English!

My hurt was insufferable. I could see our great love shattered on the cold, hard rocks of text book reality. I crept home. My heart was cold.

I sulked for days, dipped little girls' pig tails in my ink well, chewed gum in school and in general behaved obstreperously. I vowed that someday when I got to be a general, I'd march my army past that schoolhouse out in the country, and I'd never even acknowledge Miss Cora's waves.

I'd show her.

I'd never again study English. I'd quit school.

Sometimes I think all that is why dad took me out to Wyoming to grow up and forget my great heartbreak.

Well, I grew up out there although I never became a general and never had the satisfaction of marching an army past that country schoolhouse.

But, by George, I went to work on a newspaper, and I learned how to bang up the English language.

And, with luck, someday some country school will have another old-fashioned box supper and I can begin all over again—brunet school ma'rm and all!

Lingo Learnin'

I allow as how this might not set too well with your English teachers, but here goes, anyhow. I'm talking about you young city waddies with the Cassidy clothes and the nickel-plated Roscoes. I figure it this way: You might just as well sit in on this class on cowboy lingo along with the tourist folks who plan to visit the Rocky Mountain Empire this summer.

First off like, it is only fair to say that this Sunday piece is being written from the first *Cowboy Encyclopedia* that I've ever encountered. It is the work of Bruce Grant, a one-time cowpuncher turned newspaperman down Texas way.

Grant, I admire to say, has done a nice piece of work on his dictionary of oldtime western terms and manners. He has cleverly worked in some lore and a considerable amount of accurate history. Jackie and Fiore Mastri have credited themselves with the illustrations, too.

Do you know what a cowboy meant when he referred to an *Airtight?* Why that's his talk for canned goods, particularly peaches, his greatest delicacy. Here's a good one: *Alforja* (alfor'hah) : Spanish for saddlebag or knapsack. A bag in which the oldtime cowpuncher carried his "plunder." *Auguring:* Cowboy

199

term meaning "talking big" or bragging. *Brushpoppers:* Name given to early-type cowpunchers who "popped" longhorn cattle out of the dense brush and chapparal where they would hide.

Buck tie: A method of tying up a prisoner in the old west with hands tied together, arms passed over the knees and a rifle stuck between the joints of the knees and over the arms. *Cabestro* (cahbes'tro) : A rope of horsehair.

Calaboose: Keep out of this, you young waddies. *Circle riders:* Cowboys who ride in a wide circle and round up cattle. *Collected:* A "collected" horse is one that does not "wing" but travels smooth. *Coulee:* A deep gulch, usually dry, with inclined dirt sides. Different from an arroyo because the latter is usually a stream bed.

Coupling: That part of the horse which connects the hindquarters with the barrel. If the space between the last rib and the hip is narrow, say three fingers in width or less, the horse is said to be close-coupled. Otherwise he is long-coupled. *Dally:* To take a counterwise hitch with the throwing rope on the saddlehorn. *Doggone:* Cowboy's cussword used in the presence of womenfolks —when he could remember it. *Dry shooting:* Gun practice including the quick draw. *Earing down:* Method of holding a horse's head while a rider mounts. Used on bucking horses and one ear is usually held firmly in the teeth. (Note to older persons: Don't try this with China clippers.)

Fuzztails: Wild range horses. *Horseback opinion:* Rangeland gossip. *Hurrah town:* Town where cowpunchers had fun. (Look me up when yuh git to Denver.) *Line rider* and *line camp:* When a cowboy "rode fence" to keep it in repair, he stayed at night in a "line camp." *Outrider:* Cowboy of the old days who made a general tour of inspection on range or ranch to look over stock. Sometimes a gunfighter who accompanied wagon trains as a scout.

Who's Underprivileged?

HRB

Possibly it is because I am one at heart, but I like a country kid. Give me a kid with sunburned face, freckles, tousled hair, bare feet and an old pair of overalls, and I'll show you an American champion.

Maybe he is rustic. He might even be a little awkward and embarrassed in the presence of strangers. Those are qualities, not shortcomings to be overcome by progressive education.

One of the things that irks me is to hear folks express sympathy for the kids who are growing up in our small towns and on our farms and ranches. It makes me feel just a little sorry for the person who voices such sympathy.

No playgrounds? No amusement parks? Shucks, there's a "sody fountain and moom pitchur show right downtown." Besides that, the little feller you see on the streets of the average country town has access to some of the finest recreation any youngster could ask for.

He knows the meadow lark's song, he knows where there's the biggest ant hill in the world and he has watched them work.

Somewhere out there in the country not too far to be reached on foot, is a fishing hole where the trout jump.

He knows how to watch out for wood ticks and rattlesnakes, and if you are smart enough to make friends with him, he'll maybe catch one for you with a stick and a rag.

Nature holds no mystery for him. He knows how calves are born, where little colts come from and how they get up on their wobbly legs and start first off to look for something to eat.

Right out at the edge of town there's a haunted house. Of course only he can see the "ha'nts." But he knows they're there and the thrill he gets from tip-toeing through that house is far greater than that derived by any city kid from a visit to the fun house at the amusement park.

Naturally he respects a horse's heels. But he knows how to handle one. Once in a while, even, he gets to saddle up and ride out alone where nobody can see him and he can take down his saddle rope and toss the loop over sagebrush clusters that really are genuine calves.

When he gets to thinking he's good, he'll maybe reach down and thumb the old roan's neck to make her buck.

His is a world of infinite wisdom. The chances are that he can even make a slingshot and can throw almost a quarter-mile with it. He can walk barefooted across the prairie and never step on a cactus.

Sports? Did you ever try to catch a greased calf, win a pie-eating contest or climb a greased pole?

And just wait till winter comes. Soon as the first snow is on the ground, you can betcha he'll be out in the hills with his .22 rifle. He knows just where the cottontails are. What's more, he can hit 'em on the run, too.

Ducks? Same place where those trout were jumping in the summer. Sneak out there some winterish morning, and maybe you'll find him there when he's old enough, bringing 'em down with his dad's shotgun.

Sure it's a long way to school, and there are no buses. But there's old roany and a warm fur cap and overshoes that are made to fit right over a man's cowboy boots.

When a man gets to school he can help carry in the wood or coal, too. A fellow doesn't have to depend on a custodian of buildings for his warmth.

And when he grows up he probably won't have to depend on anybody for anything. He'll make it on his own. He's got initiative.

What's more, he's lived closer to God.

Asafetida Time

Along about this time of year many moons ago, my mother used to run me down, put shoes on me, tie a sack of asafetida around my neck and get me ready for school. The asafetida was to keep away such things as measles, whooping cough, bad colds, diphtheria and the droops. If you've never smelled asafetida you'll never understand how effectively it worked.

We were talking about home remedies the other day and our editor, Bill Hosokawa, told about the time he called on a Colorado ranch family to get material for a yarn.

An impressively big dog met him at the gate, uttered some unpleasantries, then nailed him in the fleshy part of the leg. The ranch woman rendered first aid—turpentine and lard poured into the wound.

When they caught Bill just before sundown that night, they explained that this was a long-established home treatment that never failed. Bill agreed. He had already run off any poison he might have gotten from the dog's bite.

In some quarters the ranch people would have run into the cow corral, grabbed a handful of the most available stuff and plastered it over the cut. That's designed to "draw out" the infection. It does work miracles on jaws swollen from toothache. You just wrap the medicament in a rag, place it on the jaw and tie it to your head.

Oh, there's no end to what you can do right at home to cure almost any type of calamity. Turpentine and coal oil for the croup; boiled cherry bark for coughs. Speaking of coughs, I heard through my old adviser, Dr. Walter Reckling of Lusk, Wyo., about a man who once made a most unorthodox prescription for a persistent cough. While not indicated as a lung sedative, the recommended laxative did make the patient afraid to cough.

Sassafras and mullen leaf tea for a tonic; a copper wire around the joint to cure rheumatism. You can make a good ice pack out of an inner tube in an emergency, and I know of one instance where a wheat straw, used as a catheter, brought heaven-sent relief to a stricken man who was snowbound.

I heard of another man who boiled up a concoction of horse hair, hog fat and goose grease flavored with liniment to cure pneumonia. He, too, won heavenly relief. He looked so peaceful when they laid him out.

My old grandad used to believe strongly in many home remedies. He believed a man should "get his iron" every day. Accordingly, he used to stop at the blacksmith shop each evening and take a long swig from the tub of water used for cooling heated horse shoes.

He also used to take shotgun pellets, put them in a glass of water, allow the mixture to set over night, then drink off the water the next morning for its medicinal benefits which he said were numerous.

This was all right until he thought to add a little Kentucky bourbon to the mixture. He got overly eager one morning, swallowed shot and all and danged near ruint our plumbing.

Mother's Little Helper

Because I always was a helpful cuss, and because this is Mother's Day, it was decided that this Sunday's effort should be a column of useful information for the housewife. Let's get right with it.

Did you know, for instance, that a good stiffener for cuffs and collars can be made by boiling one ounce of isinglass and borax, one teaspoon of white glue and two teaspoons of egg white in two quarts of starch? Try it.

Now here's a dandy recipe for gall soap, and what house can afford to be without gall soap in these times? Get a pint of bee's gall from the butcher, cut fine two pounds of common soap; pour into one quart of boiling water; boil slowly, stirring until well mixed. When the gall bottle is empty, get fresh. (My information source doesn't explain that last sentence.)

A good general household soap is simple to make. Strip the fat from chickens and hog entrails and save all your bacon rinds. Separate the wood ashes from the coal ashes, build a leach and secure a good supply of lye. Now put one pound of lye into an iron or stone vessel, pour on slowly one and one-third quarts of cold water, stir with a stick until dissolved, then allow to cool. When cool, pour the lye into eight pounds of melted grease and stir until well mixed. Pour the whole into a box lined with paper. When the soap has set, cut into convenient bars.

Now every woman should have a good black dress for weddings, funerals, Sunday and special occasions. Alpaca is good, but cashmere is better although the alpaca does take dye nicely and doesn't shrink. To restore the color to cashmere, make a solution by boiling logwood chips in a little water, strain and boil the cloth in it. To clean alpaca, sponge with strained coffee (if you can afford coffee). Iron the wrong side. To clean black kids, add a few drops of ink to a teaspoon of salad oil and apply with a feather.

A teaspoon of castor oil rubbed well into your shoes by the fire will prolong their life. And a good shoe blacking can be made with four ounces of ivory black, three ounces of coarse sugar, a teaspoon of black oil and one pint of beer.

Always wash your hair in cold sage tea. A good hair oil can be made from two teaspoons of castor oil and glycerine. Add alcohol, keep in a bottle of rain water. For freckles. Grate horseradish fine. Stand four hours in buttermilk, strain and wash the face twice a day. (Just what benefits are derived from standing in buttermilk is not explained.)

Chapped hands can be cured by grinding a pumice stone and rubbing the powder on the hands while wet. Next rub on honey and dry. (?)

The aforegoing information is authentic as a Sharps rifle. It came from a cookbook which Caroline Lockhart of Cody, Wyo., says was found in a cabin on the Salmon river in Idaho, which was abandoned during Chief Joseph's reign over the Nez Perce tribe.

Ladies' Home Companion

Ever since first publication in this column several months ago of Fenwick's Friendly Philosophies for Frustrated Fraus, I've had a great number of requests (well, two, to be exact) for additional advice on how to be happy though married.

This advice, you may remember, consists of little household hints for the wife. (You can't get anything across to the average husband by merely hinting.) First off like, let's take a few medical items.

Stiff joints: Oil made by frying angleworms and applied to sinews drawn up by sprains or disease is recommended by those who have tried it. (It should be added here that you can't hardly find them kind no more.) This same old home remedy can be used for sore throat with good results.

Tapeworms: Refrain from supper and breakfast and at 8 o'clock take one-third of 200 minced pumpkin seeds—remove the hulls—and at 9 o'clock take another third. At 10 take the remainder. Follow at 11 with a strong dose of castor oil and watch results. (Stay home that night.)

Drunkenness: Sulphate of iron, five grains; peppermint water, eleven drachms; spirit of nutmeg, one drachm. Swallow twice a day and a cessation of desire for drink will follow. (At first you may find it difficult to swallow only twice a day. But stick to it! Perseverence pays. Pretty soon you won't be drinking anything.)

To stop bleeding: Apply wet tea leaves or scrapings of sole leather to a cut. Fresh barnyard droppings can be applied in poultice form to swellings.

Sea sickness (and, nowadays, air nausea). Make a pad of wool or horse hair and bind over the stomach if you can locate same.

Morning sickness: Just be more careful next time.

The first thing the young housewife should learn, although there is some dispute on this question, is how to prepare a good breakfast for her husband. An excellent menu is as follows:

Hot rolls, broiled sirloin steak, Saratoga potatoes. Corn pone, stewed tripe, potatoes a la lyonnaise, buckwheat cakes, sausage, breakfast hominy, crust coffee. For this last, toast some stale bread very brown, pour on boiling water, strain, add cream and sugar with a dash of nutmeg if desired. It is sometimes advisable to put on the table a few left-overs from supper, particularly if your husband plans to break wild horses that day.

Easy way to clean silver: Set fire to some wheat straw, collect ashes and, after sifting through muslin, apply with soft leather.

A wife should keep busy. In spare time she should make candlesticks, rid the house of flies, bedbugs, roaches, fleas and ants; boil new lamp chimneys before using to keep them from breaking; sew rag rugs, mend clothes, keep flour and coffee sacks in neat pile and checking the lightning rod.

Of course the source of this information is an 1870 almanac, but if up-to-date dope is needed I'm available for private consultation.

Oh, My Aching Epitaph!

Do you remember the big wind of 1950? I distinctly remember it and always shall, because it blew me clean across thirteen states. And that's no figure of speech, either.

It gripped me by the differential in Denver the morning of March 26. It blew me that first day to Sterling, Colo. Next day it swept me on into Nebraska. On succeeding days it rolled, jerked, whipped, pushed, snapped and fanned me into Kansas, Oklahoma, Texas, New Mexico, Arizona, Utah, Idaho, Montana, North Dakota, South Dakota, Wyoming and back into Colorado.

In some sections of the country my inseparable companion was a thick, gritty cloud of dust. Elsewhere it was snow, sleet, rain and mud.

Misery, numbness, the little woman, numbness, a Lincoln automobile, numbness, a yellow trailer, misery, and a horse named G-Boy were with me everywhere.

It all started two weeks prior to that fateful morning of March 26 when the boss greeted me with an affability that should have aroused my suspicions immediately.

"Got a great assignment for you, Red," he beamed. "Probably the greatest you've ever had." He rubbed his hands in what I thought was a gesture of warmth. Later I learned he was trying to restore his circulation which had suddenly stopped at realization of what he was doing to me.

"We are going to send you all around the Rocky Mountain Empire. You'll visit each state capitol and invite each governor to come to the grand opening of our new building May 16. Now, isn't that wonderful!"

There were exclamation marks in each of his eyes.

207

"Now you are going to get to hand each governor a silver and gold spur. That's his invitation. When he comes to Denver we'll give him the other one.

"We're going to let you start on this (get a load of that 'let you') as soon as you can get the necessary equipment."

"Yeah? What'll I need?"

"A horse, a horse trailer, saddle and the other things you'll have to have."

I walked out of the office in a trance. I was to ride up to each state capitol in thirteen states and deliver the roweled invitations in Hopalong Cassidy style.

I did. Period.

And ever since I've been acclaimed as the character who outdid Paul Revere. People still shake my hand and exclaim over me. I've been asked so many times to write the story of that trip that I've decided to get it over with. The thing promises to outlive me. At one time I thought the trip itself would kill me. Times were when I wished it would bring on a quick and painless attack of rigor mortis. My boss would have had to bring home the body anyhow, and it would have served him right.

But now that death has been staved off a few fleeting hours, I resignedly expect that when my obituary finally is written, all the really worthwhile accomplishments of my life will be completely overlooked.

Yessir, Fenwick rode a horse! Rode him all over the west.

All the small works of kindness I have performed for my fellow man, the money I've spent buying liquid solace for down-and-outers, the dough I've loaned and never got back, the friends I've sprung from jail, the sick ones I've sat up with all night, the big stories and scoops I've scored—all will be forgotten.

Instead I'll be remembered as a man who lived seven weeks with misery, numbness, his little woman, numbness, a Lincoln automobile, numbness, a yellow trailer, misery, and a horse named G-Boy.

Introduction to G-Boy

The first thing you must have if you're going to ride horseback is a horse. Sounds simple, doesn't it? But it isn't. Try riding

208

horseback without a horse sometime and you'll instantly discern the difference. That's why I went to see my old friend and saddle buddy, H. John Eastman.

"This gelding of mine, G-Boy, is just the animal for your big roundup of governors for the grand opening of *The Post's* new building," he assured me in a silky voice. "He's flashy—a well marked pinto, you know—and he's as gentle as a housewife."

That should have aroused my suspicion but it didn't.

"Is he trailer broke?" I wanted to know. "Does he load and unload easily?"

"Why, shucks," John purred, "he's just like a dog. Show him a trailer and he jumps right in." That satisfied me. (Oh, what a dummy!)

The next two weeks I spent accumulating a silver-mounted saddle and trappings, a trailer with appropriate signs on it and chaps and buckets and currycombs! I had my car springs reinforced with overloads and had a big trailer hitch attached to the rear.

This wasn't going to be a bad trip after all. I'd have a horse for a pet, could make like a cowpoke again and, besides, the weather showed great promise. The sun shone all during that preparatory two weeks. In fact it was hot.

I was too busy to get acquainted with G-Boy. But then he was gentle, anyhow, and was well broke despite his tender age of 3 years. We didn't meet formally until the afternoon before we launched our horseback attack on the Rocky Mountain Empire.

"Jump in the trailer?" Not this kangaroo. He wanted to jump over the thing. And with me on him, too. He humped his back when Gary Garrison, John's wrangler, saddled him. He disliked the photographer. He didn't want his picture taken. He was aware of his role and had gone temperamental like a veteran movie star.

I looked upon him with great misgivings. I thought about switching suddenly to a motorcycle or making the trip by helicopter. It was too late, so bright and early the next morning we pulled the family car up in front of our hotel and loaded it.

By great dint of pushing, repacking and perspiring, we squeezed in the saddle, cameras, oats, chaps, silver spurs for the governors, then pulled from the curb while small kids on the sidewalk gave a tiny cheer. They were awed.

The trailer was out at Eastman's horse ranch waiting to contain G-Boy who hadn't yet been persuaded to get in it. Moreover, he wasn't about to.

We coaxed, promised extra oat rations, cursed, pushed, heaved and pleaded. G-Boy saw something sinister in the bright yellow contraption. He balked. I alternately swore at G-Boy and at H. John Eastman.

When he thought, to his surprise, that he could jump clean through the trailer and out the little hole in the front, he made a flying, four-footed leap.

Bango! We had him.

Then, relieved at least momentarily, we lit out for Nebraska. Just then the balmy weather ended and the worst blizzard and wind storm in years descended out of the heavens with a vengeance.

If you've never tried to pull a horse trailer over icy roads in a tornado, you've never appreciated life. We skidded, slithered, jerked and slid to Sterling, Colo., where the wind blew the water out of the bucket I brought for my shivering charge. When I did get water to him at the risk of life and limb and the expense of being half drowned—he wouldn't drink.

We stabled up that night in Sterling—and prayed for strength.

Love Comes to G-Boy

We recruited three husky ranch hands the morning we left Sterling, Colo., to help load our pinto, G-Boy. We plotted the task carefully, turned the trailer in the proper direction, opened the barn door and the wind blew him right into the thing.

That afternoon it all but blew him out of it. It whipped up dust on the eastern Colorado and western Nebraska plains in thick, soupy clouds that reduced vision to a few yards. We drove with the headlights on.

A fine silt sifted through the sides of our automobile and settled on us, our clothes, the lunch, my bridgework and the gal's cameras. (She said some things which indicated she must have known a cavairyman before me.)

Never in my life have I seen so much acreage in the air. With a little moisture and a couple of days of sunshine a man could have grown grass up to an altitude of a thousand feet.

At McCook, Neb., we exercised G-Boy at noon and G-Boy developed an Adonis complex despite certain precautions previously taken against that very thing. He fell in love with Mrs. J. M. Willis' young mares.

He declined to travel farther. He spurned his trailer—again. He exhibited a distinct preference for remaining precisely where he was. For him the trip had ended.

That's where I invented the new words. It was cold—colder than a well digger's watch. The wind blew the buttons right off my shirt and the words right back in my throat.

I offered to ride in the trailer and let G-Boy drive. He refused. I thought of saddling him and riding him clean to Lincoln. After thinking it over I decided it best to try once more to put him in the trailer.

Then it was that I spoke to him about his future and how I could be provoked to reduce that future to an extremely short span of moments. That and some persuasion with a rope used on his fundament turned the trick and we set out anew, to the great relief of the Willis family who by then showed some alarm.

About 9 o'clock that night we rolled into Lincoln and began searching for the Hudson stables. We arrived half frozen, put G-Boy to bed, luxuriated in the hospitality profferred by the Hudson family, then partially expired until sunup.

Next morning G-Boy and I reached a permanent understanding about that trailer. His owners now will tell you that he is "just like a dog. Show him a trailer and you simply can't keep him out of it."

Shortly before noon I decorated the pony with his silver saddle, mounted him . . . and wished I were Jim Shoulders. We put on a limited, one-event rodeo on the Nebraska capitol lawn while excited office workers cheered, snickered, and outright laughed.

The caretaker tried to shoo us off the lawn. We jumped right over him and he took off for obscure recesses in the boiler room. When Governor Val Peterson appeared with a cute secretary, G-Boy and I charged up the steps right at 'em. I was never so happy to get off a horse and shake hands with anyone, including a governor.

211

Consternation in Kansas

Well, we got out of Lincoln quicker than it would take to drag a hayrack up Pike's peak, and streaked south toward Kansas. G-Boy gave out a long-winded whinny just as we passed through the busy part of the city, striking consternation into the hearts of some farmers who were in town to buy gasoline and oil for their tractors.

That night we stopped shortly after dark at a little settlement just outside Topeka where, it appeared, we wouldn't have much trouble finding quarters for our family nag.

We were wrong.

We searched and probed, frightened Kansas citizens by the dozens with our odd request for a place for our horse to sleep, and finally found an abandoned barn at—of all places—an airport. A unit of the Kansas civil air patrol was in session when we whinnied to a stop.

The meeting promptly broke up and a horde of airplane pilots flocked out of the building near the barn to stare at G-Boy as though he were Pegasus, himself.

Fellows who could do spins, Immelmans and power dives at 8,000 feet, and never bat an eye, gave G-Boy's heels more room than they would a hot prop.

I swaggered into the dark interior of the ramshackle old barn with G-Boy trailing on his halter rope, feeling every inch a red-blooded hero. Then the missus and I shook out some hay, dished a few oats, and I puffed on a cigaret, leaned against a tired bronc stall and listened to a symphony.

Anyone who has never heard a hungry horse munch oats in the still of night, who has never thrilled to his nicker of thanks and contentment, and who has never felt the appreciative and affectionate nuzzle of a horse's nose against his chest, just hasn't lived—doesn't know music.

Although there were moments when I could have killed him with glee, I began that night to develop a feeling toward G-Boy akin to love—if you understand what I mean, and you will if you've ever liked a horse.

Obstinate, proud, handsome and resentful of the saddle, G-Boy was more like a pup than a beast of burden.

Next day we saddled up on the parking lot adjoining a ham

burger stand not far from the capital. The "monster," an appellation we adopted for G-Boy, was particularly averse to being ridden that day, and I'd like to apologize again to the woman we nearly scared to death.

She was hanging up her wash in her back yard when I mounted. G-Boy charged down the alley to a wild sort of chopping lope, broken now and then by his attempts to turn somersaults.

She dropped her clothes basket, ran for the back door but finally recovered to return to the fence and ask questions.

G-Boy had quieted down somewhat by that time. My little woman was headed toward the state capitol building to summon his excellency and I was trying somewhat breathlessly to make sure that my mount would be well behaved during the presentation of the second pair of spurs.

"What in the world are you doing?" the woman demanded curiously.

"Going to see the governor," I said simply.

She headed for the back door and this time shut it behind her.

How Much Car-Power in a Horse?

The next few days after leaving Kansas, G-Boy was in horse heaven. That's a place where all good little horses go when they leave this world. It's in Texas. We reached a decision that we'd like to live in horse heaven. At least we'd like to live there in the spring when the wind is blowing in Kansas and Nebraska.

The weather was nice. The grass was green. Texas was hospitable. The Texas rangers were more than nice to us. That's one reason we got so sore at a fellow named Will Harrison when we went to Santa Fe. Will wrote in his newspaper that we didn't know one end of a horse from another.

Will is a likeable cuss.

In Arizona the wind blew. Fine sand erupted from the desert arroyos and blasted the paint off the car. G-Boy got acquainted with palm trees and a little filly with a traveling horse show.

In Utah we hit a blizzard and were hit by a truck. We carried out a barn and fence rebuilding program for the state that should have been subsidized by the U. S. agriculture department. Mostly the project was carried on in snow and bitter cold.

Idaho was its usual beautiful self and Montana was more than hospitable. The governor, however, could not come to the grand opening of *The Denver Post's* new building because of a heavy schedule. We learned later that he, or someone by the same name, had showed up in Louisiana and was a guest of New Orleans.

Montana seemed to have three kinds of roads—muddy, dusty and bumpy. We hit all the muddy and bumpy ones. At one point we were stuck four hours in a mud hole that was listed on the official state map as a highway, and had to be pulled out by a bulldozer.

The frame of our old automobile suffered three fractures, an injured reputation that would have made the adjusters blush, and established as an engineering fact that 160 horses under the hood is not equal to one in a trailer behind.

North Dakota was flooded (you've no idea how wet it can get up there), and South Dakota was the scene of a continuous blizzard. In Custer State park, at the famous Blue Bell lodge, we holed up finally and just about let the boss dedicate his new building without an invitation to the governor of Wyoming. It's that pleasant in the land of Pahasapa.

Then we crossed into Wyoming, home of Jim Griffith's Lusk *Herald* and Barney's Bar. At Cheyenne G-Boy undertook to emulate the infamous Midnight, so we walked to the capitol and gave Governor Crane his silver spur and invitation to our grand opening. It was a good thing we still had two feet left by this time because riding horseback was painful and our old Lincoln had all but expired.

In Denver the boss welcomed us home. He was highly pleased with our Paul Revere foray into the hinterlands.

He said, and I quote, "Hi, Red!"

A few days later, with busted knuckles, saddle sores, bowlegs and a threat of divorce hanging over my head, I rode with that great gang of guys, the Roundup Riders of the Rockies, to deliver the last invitation. Gov. Walter Johnson was the target for the day.

The governor was impressed.

He said, and I quote, "Hi, Red."

No Limit on Jackalopes!

Always at this time of the year I begin to feel a twinge of pity for that common, ordinary, unimaginative species of sportsman called fishermen.

While these tireless stream-whippers concern themselves with the prosaic practice of luring pan-size trout to their spinners, we more-discerning, high-level outdoorsmen turn our thoughts to the Jackalope season.

The privilege of hunting these elusive little critters is reserved by statute to an appreciative few. Fortunately I am one of them.

My license for the Jackalope hunt arrived just the other day. It was sent to me by my old friend and Jackalope authority, Jack S. Ward of Douglas (my old home town), Wyoming.

Jack's letter, which came with the hunting permit, was encouraging. It said there is more than an abundance of the cagey little animals this particular season. This is on account of the great amount of lightning in the hills last fall.

You see, unlike ordinary animals that prefer a full moon, these fur-bearing prong-horns mate only by the glare of lightning flashes. It seems to electrify their sense of romance and shocks them into realization that there are boy Jackalopes and girl Jackalopes.

The back of the hunting permit gives some arresting facts about this unusual game:

"The Jackalope," it says in big print, "is perhaps the rarest animal in North America. The strange little fellow defies classification. Were it not for the horns it might be mistaken for a large rabbit. Were it not for its shape and coloring it might be a species of deer.

"It is not vicious usually, although coyotes have a fine respect for the sharp menace of its horns.

"An odd trait of the Jackalope is its ability to imitate the human voice. Cowboys singing to their herds at night have been startled to hear their lonesome melodies repeated faithfully from some near-by hillside.

"The phantom echo comes from the throat of some Jackalope.

"They sing only on dark nights just before a thunderstorm. Stories that they sometimes get together and sing in chorus are discounted by those who know them best."

My permit authorizes me to take one one-tailed Jackalope within the boundaries of Converse county, June 31, between the hours of midnight and 2 a. m. only.

Holding the Jackalope permit is a distinct honor among men. It certifies that "The holder of this license is attested to be a man of strict temperance and absolute truthfulness." The one exception is that "in cases where the number of Jackalopes he has seen or slain is under investigation, he may occasionally, at his discretion, take such lingual evasion or loud rebuttal as the occasion may require."

Adam Lyre and Jack Ward both sign the hunting permits.

Hunting the crafty critters is an art. A novel glass gun is invariably used. It is of the double-shot variety and must be aimed at the mouth to be of maximum effectiveness. Shots may be had as frequently as the weapon can be loaded.

It is necessary that you start early in your quest, else the chances are that you won't even see any Jackalope.

And when you do, brother, have somebody drive you home quick like.

More About Jackalope

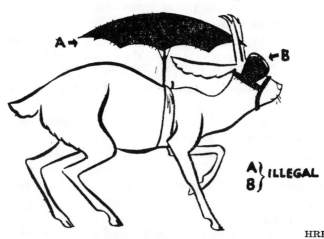

HRB

Until recently, I had labored under the delusion that Wyoming had a monopoly on the Jackalope. You will remember the Jackalope. He is the prong-horned animal that breeds in the glare of

216

lightning flashes, imitates cowboy songs and bears a slight resemblance, except for size, to the jackrabbit.

This apparently fool notion that Jackalopes grew only in Wyoming was entertained without giving a thought to California. You'd just know they'd have them, too.

Sure enough, Jack Foley of Universal City wrote me that he was "surprised" we still killed Jackalope in Wyoming. Out in California, he said, they domesticate the critters and teach them to pitch hay.

This California jasper even went so far as to make the ethnological origin and blood background of the Jackalope sound like a cross between a Thesaurus and the Encyclopedia Britannica.

Now it wouldn't be too difficult to imagine the California species of Jackalope is larger than Wyoming's variety. But I seriously doubt their speed.

Accordingly, I am arranging, with the help of a strong committee, an event which may become a great American institution. Next summer, I am sponsoring the first annual International Jackalope Derby, pitting California Jackalope and Wyoming Jackalope against each other.

Winner of the event will be matched against "Rusty" at the Denver dog track, and the International champion will automatically be required to challenge Bing Crosby's entire stable of thoroughbreds in a unique and highly exciting competition. This will be run off at Madison Square Garden between rounds of a heavyweight championship prize fight.

This Derby, neighbors, is going to be no one-town, one-night stand. It will be a countrywide spectacle of regional magnitude.

I have tentatively selected a course through neutral territory. Under present plans (suggestions are welcome, of course) the race will begin at Scottsbluff, Neb. They sell nothing but beer in the bars over there. I want everybody to see the start of this race.

From there the course will proceed over the highway which Mark U. Watrous promised to build, but didn't, to Fort Morgan. Thence it will continue to Denver allowing two days here for the Jackalope to make their way through traffic.

From Denver the course will continue to Steamboat Springs, with a brief stopover at the basement rumpus room of Maurice Leckenby, to Craig and then over the Million Dollar Highway to

217

Silverton where the generous miner folk are free with their hospitality in a manner which pleases certain of us gentry no end.

The course will continue through Durango and end somewhere in Nevada where the gambling folk can bet on the outcome and the state can collect some revenue.

Through Colorado the race will be supervised in part by the Colorado racing commission. An appropriate investigation is already promised.

Jack Ward of Douglas (my old home town), Wyo., and Mr. Foley of Universal City will enter their favorites in the race. Weight handicaps, it has been suggested, will consist of bottle corks, Hoover buttons and liquor labels.

Because he is such a good hand at assembling specialists, Quigg Newton, mayor of Denver, has been named to head the committee. Henry Barnes, traffic engineer, was considered for a time, but the committee has since dropped his name and barred him from the entire course because of his penchant for wanting to stop everything once it gets started.

Gene Cervi, Denver newspaperman, will be official starter. He can start anything. Other committee vacancies will be filled by popular demand. Spectators at the race will take care of their own individual filling along the course.

Proof, at Last!

Now there are a few unenlightened killjoys out of strait jackets around and about the country, who continue to shout there is no such animal as the American Jackalope. Such uninformed, flatland foreigners wouldn't know which end of a bottle to put the cork in.

These doubting Thomases probably sneered their disbelief, too, when they read in *The Denver Post* not long ago that a boy from Douglas (my old home town), Wyo., had actually killed a Jackalope in Germany!

This lad who thus covered himself with glory, is known to one and all as Sgt. Darwin B. (Badwater) Peebles. In the finest tradition of Jackalope hunters, Badwater Peebles made his kill wih a well-aimed canteen.

Most important, however, is the boy's scientific discovery and his invaluable contribution to the defense department's archives on espionage and strategy. This lad's going places!

Before detailing Peebles' account of his thrilling kill—on which I take some pride in having scooped all foreign press services—let's backtrack a ways on the Jackalope:

It is a small animal, you'll remember, that closely resembles a jackrabbit. The difference is that it has horns, is exceedingly fleet of foot, can be seen only at night, breeds by the glare of lightning flashes and is noted for a unique ability to imitate the human voice.

The Jackalope has surprised cowboys on many occasions by repeating back the songs sung to the cattle by night herders. They have excellent voices but are not believed to be given to group singing or barbershop harmonizing.

Now for the story: Peebles wrote that he was on maneuvers with his company. It was late at night. Moonlight filtered through the trees. All was quiet. Peebles' scouting platoon was halted momentarily.

Everyone was tense, he reported, expecting the opposing element to attack from somewhere out in the shadows of the forest. It was nigh onto H-hour.

"Suddenly, across the low land below, a small dark animal jumped from an opening on my right flank.

"Then all of a sudden, their .50-calibers opened up and the blanks began popping all over the place. I heard someone shout 'Give 'em h-l.' Then I saw the animal darting toward me. Still I never imagined what it was.

"For a second the moonlight seemed to come brighter. I could see the silhouette of the horns! It zig-zagged toward me.

"My eyes were glued to the object. I was paralyzed. The sounds of battle fell on deaf ears.

"I faintly remember snatching my canteen from my belt and throwing it—at the Jackalope. Then I fainted and when I regained consciousness, I was the center of attention.

"I crawled to the spot where I had thrown my canteen—which was full, no foolin'—and there lay the Jackalope, his neck broken.

"I am sending you the mounted head as proof."

Now this clears up two great mysteries, both of inestimable value to the defense department. For one thing it confirms my suspicion that Isadore Heinrich Von Schnitzelheimer was a German. He was, moreover, a German agent. What aroused my suspicion was his thirst for suds and a way of saying "Yah" when asked if he wanted some.

Schnitzelheimer spent many months in Wyoming prior to War II.

The other mystery: Many times American troops fired thousands of rounds of ammunition at the enemy lines during World War II, after hearing shouts of "Dizzy Dean is a big so-and-so." But never did they find any enemy dead after these withering blasts. Invariably, these infuriating taunts were flung from Nazi lines on moonlit nights.

Schnitzelheimer, it nows emerges, smuggled live Wyoming Jackalope into Germany and taught plattoons of them to shout insults at the American troops!

Try to laugh that one off you disbelievers!!!

Derby Day

It may not have come to the attention of the United Nations yet, and the president may not even make it a national holiday. But plans are just about complete now for the first annual running of the original, exclusive and unique International Championship Jackalope Derby, Field Day and Fun Festival.

Of course you are familiar with the Jackalope—world's fleetest animal. He is that extremely elusive, vocally gifted and speedy-to-the-point-of-invisibility creature that follows the cow camps of the west.

He loves to imitate the songs the cowpunchers sing to their herds at night. Aside from that little is known about him.

It is known, however, that they are few in numbers possibly because of the short duration of the mating season. Jackalope of opposite sexes are never attracted to each other except during the glare of a lightning flash late at night and usually toward the end of the summer months.

Speed and their vocal talents are perhaps their outstanding characteristics.

For this reason it was decided last fall that about the biggest thing this department could contribute to living generations would be a matching of Jackalopes in a giant race—a race so big that it promises to be outdone in size only by the human race.

There have been some hitches in plans, however, and a few changes. Site of the starting point still is up in the air. Right now it is a toss-up between Scottsbluff and Haig, Neb. More about that later.

There are no entry blanks. But despite this seeming handicap, entries have been coming in even in the absence of a formal announcement.

Eddie Bohn of Denver, boxing commissioner and long a Jackalope fancier, has offered to enter a speedy contender. "Split-Second Gonzales," possibly a long-shot number, has been entered by the Fish and Culture club of Scottsbluff, and an untried entry is in training at the stables of the Roundup Riders of the Rockies.

Another entry is expected to be sponsored by the Pipe-Layers club of Casper, Wyo., an association of oil men, and Jack Ward of Douglas (my old home town), Wyo., is certain to be on the starting line the day of the race with an outstanding runner from the Equality state.

Contrary to an unfortunate report being circulated in some quarters, there will be no barbershop quartet made up of Jackalope singers. Jackalopes have never been given to choral groupings. They are strictly soloists.

It is hoped that at least twenty of the fleet-footed animals will be entered on Derby day.

Entries will flash over a fast but difficult course from a point in the Scotts Bluff country of Nebraska to Reno, Nev., where betting is legal.

Roy Petsch of Stateline, Wyo., will be the official starter for the occasion, and Henry Barnes, Denver traffic engineer, will be the official stopper. Timing will be done exclusively and officially by his mechanical brain traffic controller from the city and county building in Denver. Mechanical mental telepathy will be employed for communication between the starting barrier and the finish tape.

It first was decided that Scottsbluff should be the starting point of the long distance, speed and endurance competition. But there may not be room enough there to accommodate the crowds, so

221

the Haig Chamber of Commerce's offer is being seriously considered.

The date? Oh, that has been set for midnight, sometime during the week of Sept. 14 to coincide with National Truth week.

"Here Comes Trusty"

The hinges sure flew off the gates of Hades the day this corner announced the date of the forthcoming International Jackalope Derby, Field Day and Fun Festival. New developments have been piling up like teething time troubles in a nursery full of quadruplets.

I'm as confused as a high school boy courting twins!

First off like, there was the big attempt to fix the race. (More about this scandalous thing later.)

Then the Civic Society and Improvement association at McKinley Beet Siding, Wyo., an important railhead on the C. B. & Q., offered to send in 250 state highway maps (with pictures of former Gov. Nels Pearson on them) if the race could be run through their town.

Traffic Engineer Henry Barnes promptly offered to have the Denver city council subsidize the race with an appropriation of 2,500,000 street signs. A Kentucky politician said he had a bunch of leftover coonskin caps the judges could wear for identification. And one Washington source said a fellow named McGranery probably would want to investigate the whole thing.

Rocky Ford just heard about the race and had planned to enter two crates of competitors until they found out it was a JACK-alope race and not a melon-judging contest. (Boy! How thick can you cut this stuff?)

On top of all that, there was the attempted "Fix." No one among the committee was at all suspicious at first. That was when one entry owner obtained permission to outfit his racer with a unique set of blinkers. These blinkers would limit his vision considerably and were completely glare-proof.

To understand the nature of this underhanded trick, it must be known to the fan that the Jackalope enjoys only the briefest of mating seasons. He breeds only by the glare of lightning flashes.

These onerous, double-dealing dastards were already negotiating with a Denver rainmaking company to conjure up a big rainstorm the night of the race—complete with lightning and all!

Their Jackalope would be the only one that wouldn't see the lightning. And a second or two gained in a Jackalope race is tremendously important.

Now the polecats responsible for this unseemly conduct have not only been thrown out of the race, but barred from the entire course from Haig, Neb., to Las Vegas, Nev.

They will not be permitted the courtesies of the track clubhouses along the way, at every town and hamlet the length of the run. So as to identify Jackalope Colonel's club members and prevent scapegoats from sneaking in, the committee has issued the membership card printed here.

It entitles the bearer to all the privileges of the exclusive Colonel's clubs along the course, and permits them to stand (if they can) without charge in the special spectators' area just off the paddock at the starting point at Haig.

Cut out official card, paste on cardboard

WORLD JACKALOPE WATCHERS SOCIETY

This Certifies That

COL. _____

is a Jackalope fancier, that he has seen Jackalope in their native habitat and has, on occasion, heard them sing songs of the old west. It further certifies that he is fully qualified as

A JACKALOPE COLONEL AIDE-DE-CAMP

on the committee of the International Jackalope Derby, Field Day and Fun Festival, and entitled to all club privileges.

By _____

Pres. World Jackalope Watchers Society.

Bush Time Coming Up

Things have been hopping right along with the big International Jackalope Derby, Field Day and Fun Festival scheduled for this week.

First off, it should be reported that a last minute change has been made in the starting point. It was planned originally to launch this spectacular, unprecedented demonstration of fleetness from Haig, Neb. But a geodetic survey shows that Haig is considerably lower than high-altitude Colorado, and this event is not one that can be permitted to get off to a lowly start.

Accordingly, the attractive invitation of the Honorable Pat Waterton, mayor of Tin Cup, Colo., was accepted, and the starting post already has been installed there.

The term "starting post" is somewhat of a misnomer. Starting posts are used only in horse and dog races. Because of a Jackalope's radically different nature, a "starting bush" will be used to start the first derby of its kind ever undertaken in history or anywhere else.

Bush time in the race has not yet been determined and probably will not be known in time for publication. This is necessary because of the need for absolute assurance of clear weather along the entire course.

Under the new arrangements, the course will run from Tin Cup, up over Tin Cup pass, thence to Lone Cone, Colo., and Split Lip, Utah, and on to the finish line in front of Harold's club in Reno, Nev.

Perhaps the biggest development to take place since arrangements first were made for the International Jackalope Derby, Field Day and Fun Festival, is completion of the radio broadcasting contract.

Sole rights to broadcast the race have been snapped up by the Tin Cup Development Corp., and the broadcast will be by stimulated remote control direct from Tin Cup over station KTLN of Denver.

A pre-race broadcast describing the colorful event will be made shortly before bush time by Pete Smythe, Tin Cup radio man. It will feature, among other things, an address of welcome to all Jackalope lovers by Elmie Elrod, bachelor about town who will speak for Mayor Waterton. The mayor hopes to be in Canada by the time the race starts.

The KTLN broadcast will be on one of Pete Smythe's regular Tin Cup periods between 9:30 and 10:30 a. m., and 1 and 2 p. m., Monday, Sept. 29.

When the twenty fleet-footed entries hit the gravel as soon as good weather is assured, a rapid-fire, jump-by-jump account of the race will be offered from Tin Cup, Lone Cone and Split Lip— all by stimulated remote control. Race officials and Jackalope owners, including yours truly, will make guest appearances on the program.

Two of the speediest racers have been named after the presidential candidates, Eisenhower and Stevenson. Permission to carry banners saying "I Like Ike," and "We Need Adlai Badly" was denied, however, but already political wiseacres are saying "As the Jackalope goes, so goes the election." Well, we'll see.

As followers of this column know, the Jackalope originated on the plains north of Douglas (my old home town), Wyo., but many have been transplanted to other regions, notably California. Out there they claim to have taught some of the wild creatures to pitch hay with their horns.

Up in Wyoming they are noted for their fine voices which enable them to mimic the songs cowboys sing at night to their herds.

Among peculiarities of the Jackalope are his penchant to sing just before storms which always signal the beginning of the mating season. Jackalopes mate only during the glare of lightning flashes, you know, and stormy weather during race time may cause the Jackalope to stop running and take to singing.

Here's hoping for fair weather and a fast track this week.

They're Off and Running!

They're off! Yessiree, Bob, it's true. The big International Jackalope Derby, Field Day and Fun Festival (after being delayed a week by bad weather) is actually under way.

For the first time in history, a field of the world's fleetest creatures of the animal kingdom are matched in an exciting speed competition that promises to go down in the annals of time as the greatest race in the world.

Twenty eager, well-conditioned, well-matched Jackalope, ears back and horns whistling a merry tune in the breeze, hit the ozone out of Tin Cup, Colo., early last Thursday morning like a gang of candidates heading for a free barbecue and beer bust.

It was speed—speed such as the good folk of Tin Cup hadn't seen since the time Ezra Hitchcock lit for the hills after getting the first glimpse of his newly arrived mailorder bride.

If those Jackalope had been wearing vests—which, of course, they werent—the pockets would have been scooping dust.

Low to the ground and spread for speed, the twenty Jackalope entered in the big sprint to Reno, Nev., sprang from the starting bush like divorcees after alimony.

Up and over Tin Cup pass they whizzed in a dizzy bid for lead position, then took out for Lone Cone, Colo., with the longshot, "Short Change," well in the lead. At last report they were well on their way toward reaching Split Lip, Utah, before midweek.

Fair weather prevailed. And to those who know their Jackalope, that's good. There was not a cloud in the sky.

Tin Cup was in a state of high excitement. The whole town turned out to see the race start. Bush time was exactly 5:15 a. m., Mountain time. (Tin Cup has two kinds of time, mountain time and a good time. Four a. m. is not a good time.)

The Tin Cup Consolidated and Rearranged band and color guard turned out for the occasion. You could hear Bill Juplin's French horn clear over to the Busted Knee mining camp.

A colorful parade passed in front of the Town Hall during the celebration, which took place at noon the day the race started. It consisted of Mrs. Mamie Jupin's grade school children, the Women's Independent League for Better County Government and the Volunteer Fire department with both pieces of equipment.

Pete Smythe, Tin Cup radioman, broadcast a description of the race over KTLN by stimulated remote control, and will maintain constant contact with the running all the way through to the finish line in Reno.

He can be heard now and then at 9:30 a. m. and at 1 p. m. with vivid descriptions of the running.

Great political importance has been attached to the outcome

226

of the race because many of the racers bear the names of political candidates.

"Long Talk" was a decided favorite over "John Metzger" as the race got under way. "Dan Thornton" may not place because handlers said he runs best in only one direction, and "Eisenhower" was getting a big nixing by the "Stevenson" backers who claimed their Jackalope had better wind.

"Split Second" was scratched because of rumors of unwholesome connections, and "Junior Pott," entered by some young Denver businessman, ran off to New Mexico before bush time.

Derby's Dastardly Disaster

The big Jackalope derby is over. And this final report is being relayed to the office by smoke signal from a lonely hogan on the farthest part of a Navajo Indian reservation somewhere in Arizona.

When things settle down, I hope to return to home territory. But until then, it will take directional radar, two packs of bloodhounds and an agent from the internal revenue department to find me.

You'd feel like getting lost, too, if you had the troubles I had. The shame of it! Oh, what an ending!

Everything went wonderfully for a while. Then, *whammo!* It happened. Lightning struck, you might say.

Twenty Jackalope, speediest animals in the world, raced with might and main to outdistance each other. Up through Lone Cone, Colo., on to Split Lip, Utah, the pack charged like something pursued by the devil himself.

They were beautiful to watch. Streamlined, perfectly conditioned, well-matched and responding furiously to the great test of endurance, they ran like no other creatures can run.

The weather was perfect on opening day a week ago. It was one of those typical Colorado fall days. Aspen were an artist's mixboard on the mountainside, and the air was crisp and invigorating.

Just twenty miles out from Split Lip, up in the high country of Utah, the first trouble developed. Menacing, black storm clouds gathered and rain began to fall.

The two Jackalope entries, "Eisenhower" and "Stevenson" were neck-and-neck. "Thornton" and "Metzger" were tailing up the pack. Others were changing position quicker than a pea in a shell game.

Just as the sun went down, the first dread flash of lightning streaked through the thickening dusk. What happened after that is anybody's guess.

All I know is that the storm continued most of the night. The Jackalope forgot about the race and commenced singing from the hilltops, romance uppermost in what the Jackalope use for brains during the heavy weather.

The next morning they had vanished. Pete Smythe, the Tin Cup, Colo., radioman, and I checked the course for a sight of them but to no avail.

We went on to Reno, Nev., where the race was to end, thinking the fleet animals might be ahead of us.

But the timers and judges were there as per schedule, waiting for the end of the race. There were twenty judges, one for each Jackalope in the race.

They reported no sight of the racers. Some Renoans were outright insulting. They accused us of framing the thing.

Actually, as we learned later, some California mobsters had contracted for that disrupting thunderstorm with a rainmaker whose name both Pete and I would like to learn. The Californians had a blindfolded Jackalope in the race, and expected him to get through the thunderstorm ahead of the pack.

We were just discussing the dastardly trick when into sight hove one of the strangest visions ever seen—even in Reno.

One hundred and sixty-three Jackalope, bouncing slowly along in formation, descended upon Reno like a plague of horned locusts. Gifted with the ability to imitate the human voice, the critters were singing in chorus, *Whoopie Ti-Yi-Yo, Git Along Little Jackalopes.*

The original twenty had subdivided or something. End of smoke signal message; over and out.

Bores-A-Hole With Bullet

Beyond the land of rolling prairies, near the forests of Pahasapa, on the banks of the Big White river in the heart of the Pine Ridge Indian reservation, is the home of Willie Bores-A-Hole and his wife, Isabelle Pretty Cloud Bores-A-Hole.

They are proud people. To some, their family name may sound strange. But among western tribes it is known that Willie Bores-A-Hole is a great grandson of Chief Bores-A-Hole-With-Arrow, a famous Sioux warrior.

Chief Bores-A-Hole-With-Arrow fought at the Battle of the Little Big Horn when Custer's Seventh cavalry was wiped out. It was Chief Bores-A-Hole-With-Arrow, too, who tried to kill Chief Crazy Horse. He shot Crazy Horse through the cheek.

But withal, Willie Bores-A-Hole and his Cheyenne Sioux wife are taken with a bitter sadness. Several moons ago the heartbreaking rumor reached the reservation . . . their son, Glen Bores-A-Hole, an infantryman with the Second division in Korea, had been captured by Chinese Communist forces.

Grief and despair came to sit in the house of Willie Bores-A-Hole, and the birds sang no more in the land of his warrior ancestors.

Pretty Cloud Bores-A-Hole goes about her household tasks with a heavy heart. But she speaks no word of sorrow to her mate. Theirs is a common burden that words can not lighten.

Theirs is a sadness that has sat many times in the teepees of their ancestors—and theirs is a story that has been told and retold down through the centuries, of great battles and the fortunes of war.

One morning soon, however, Willie Bores-A-Hole's wife will awake at the break of dawn and will go to a high hill there to sing the song of her people for her brave son.

It will not be a sad song, either. It will be a chant of triumph, ancient, primitive, symbolic, legendary and traditional.

She will sing it because Jake Herman received a newspaper clipping out of *Stars and Stripes,* sent home by a relative, Cpl. Rex L. Herman, part Sioux Indian from No Flesh creek, who has been in the thick of the fighting in Korea.

When Jake Herman read it, he wrote about it for this corner of *Empire:*

"Three battle-hardened infantrymen on ambush patrol Tuesday were credited with smashing a company-size Chinese attack.

"The three, Sgt. John Freeman and PFC Kenard Napier of New York, and PFC Glen Boresahole, a full-blooded Indian from Oglala, S. D., had to fight their way through thirty Chinese to get back to their own lines and in the fight broke up the Chinese attack.

"The Chinese got so close to the three infantrymen before the shooting started, that one asked Freeman a question in Chinese.

"That's when the shooting started. Freeman blasted the Chinese soldier with his automatic rifle.

"Then it happened," according to Napier. "They blew a whistle and Chinese came out from everywhere, from the draws, from behind trees, down a road.

"The three infantrymen used up all their own ammunition and grabbed burp guns from dead Chinese to finish their battle.

"Their company claimed fifteen Chinese dead, two wounded and a Chinese company attack stopped before it began."

Jake Herman pays this honor.

"To you and your buddies, PFC Glen Bores-A-Hole-With-Bullet, our war bonnets are off in tribute."

The Indian Wheel Mystery

HRB

If you'd like to step momentarily out of this world and live a thousand years ago; if you'd like to thrill to the faint echo of ancient tom-toms and the weird chant of ghost voices raised in savage supplication to departed gods, then drive your automobile next summer into the Big Horn mountains of northern Wyoming.

With the aid of a map, and by making local inquiry you'll find this enchanted ritual ground at a point just south of the Montana border on the highway between Ranchester and Kane.

It is known as the Indian Medicine Wheel, a place of worship for some vanished tribe and so old that its origin is lost even to Indian lore. No man knows when it was put there on the western edge of the mountains. No man knows who the prehistoric architect was.

But, whoever he was, he seemingly possessed a strange knowledge of mathematics and astronomy.

The wheel is about 245 feet in circumference and is made of limestone slabs. Across it extend twenty-nine stone spokes, obviously representing the days of the lunar month. Six altars, apparently dedicated to the planets, surround the wheel.

There are evidences of other altars and of shelters for the high priests of the ancients.

The whole looks out upon a huge, breath-taking panorama. In the foreground to the west, the high mountain country drops away to foothills. The scene from there on encompasses the vast space between the Big Horns and the purple heights of Yellowstone National park, nearly one hundred miles away.

To the east and the north and south, the country is a pine-covered fastness of high peaks, deep gorges and canyons, mountain streams and snowbanks that linger far into the summer.

Across all this and extending visibly for miles distant are the travois trails of a yesteryear, locked in the musty vaults of time. Over these trails the sun worshipers came from miles around to participate in fantastic rituals—to beseech the gods for good hunting and, when the hunting is over, a place on the other side in the happy hunting ground.

A breeze that now and then mounts to a buffeting fury, alternately whispers and rages around the rocks and in the rustling heights of the evergreens. It carries to the ears of a listener who can project himself out and beyond the intervening pale of centuries, the faint echo of man's unending, eternal striving to understand the imponderables he can only sense—but knows are there somewhere.

To such person the winds carry the murmur of strange prayers, the pseudo defiance of tom-toms, the smell of pine smoke arising from ceremonial fires. The voices rise and fall away and seem to blend somehow with other tongues that chant their praises down the centuries to the mysteries of space and time that primitive man cannot understand, so fears.

It is an eerie place, a place for meditation. It seems even today to be as removed from the earthly order of things as it must have appeared to those who first gathered there and, in awe, built their altars and made their first offerings.

Your reverie is soon interrupted, however, by the drone of a plane overhead or the roar of a motor on the highway nearby. Thoughts come back to atom bombs, machine guns and warplanes. You suddenly realize these are merely improvements of the primitive weapons used by your predecessors on the magnificent spot where you stand.

Their power is only a power to kill, their employment attributable to impulses as old as the Medicine Wheel itself.

Oh, Sun God, pity us—the primitives.

Dance of the Man God

It was a typical New Mexico night. There was pinon incense on the air. The skies sparkled with heavenly jewels. A peaceful silence ringed Farmington like a stage curtain.

Tom Kimball and I—he was then mayor of Durango—climbed into our automobile and headed for the bluffs that held the roadway to a remote section of the unbelievably big Navajo Indian reservation.

We were bound for a Yebichai dance somewhere out in that dark distance which remains to this day unbroken by either fences or telephone lines. The Navajos have their own means of communication. Telephones simply are not needed.

I had never been to a Yebichai dance. I didn't know what it was. Neither, I might add, does an accepted reference book which lists it as a dance of prayer for rain and good crops.

The Yebichai is a "dance of the man god—a dance for a dying man."

We drove miles across a great emptiness. Then suddenly we were atop a high mesa which dropped away to a broad expanse dotted by firelight. There was our Yebichai dance, out there on the sprawling space of land where even sagebrush has to fight for its very existence.

The wagons were drawn up in a huge semicircle around a number of glowing campfires which cast a soft red glow on the stony faces of the spectators and threw their shadows behind them in a flickering pattern.

We squatted cross-legged with the others. No one noticed our presence. It was then that "the oldest man" strode out of the hogan of the dying man and vanished into the desert night. It was a part of the primitive old ritual.

The "tallest man" then strode into the center of the campfire light after being announced by an eerie wolf call from one of the dancers, and asked in Navajo that "the bears please leave because the Yebichai dance is about to begin."

He assured the bears that they were friends of the Navajos, but that this was a solemn moment and they could not participate.

A few moments later one of the strangest sights I have ever seen materialized before my eyes. The dancers came out of their hut at the far end of the semicircle, and began their weird chant. This was no mere spectacle put on for the benefit of tourists. These people were asking their ancient gods to spare the life of a man who lay in that hogan at the verge of death.

In unison they chanted their song to the accompaniment of tom-toms. It was a chant that echoed far back somewhere in the soul, to some primitive ancestor, perhaps, who may have done some similar dance. It made the flesh crawl on the back of my neck.

Then we were invited, for some strange reason, to enter the dying man's hogan. It was done with due solemnity.

The relatives of the ailing man were lying on the dirt floor of the hogan.

The medicine man kept up an endless chant while pounding on a small tom-tom, reciting a savage hymnal, the words of which he had memorized and which never were repeated, although the supplication continued without error for thirty-six hours, or until the man went on to the great hunting ground. There could be no error in that recitation. To err was tragic. Few medicine men ever have erred in it.

We got up to depart. Then I witnessed one of the most amazing phases of the entire ritual—something that spoke eloquently of another era.

I don't yet know whether it was a universal practice of all Navajo Yebichai dances, or whether it was a part of only the one arranged by this spectacular medicine man.

But it had sense, and it made me feel guilty because I was a member of a race that had failed in one respect and possibly in many others.

Ancient Wisdom

A tiny tom-tom in the hands of an intent Medicine man throbbed its prayer on the chill New Mexico night. The air was heavy with the intense heat of ceremonial fires. The Medicine man sat cross-legged at the feet of a dying Navajo. His voice was raised in a weird, tremulous chant intoning primitive intercessions for the dying man's life.

This was a solemn occasion that could last thirty-six hours during which the praying and tom-tom beating would never cease until the ceremonial ended in the sick man's recovery—or death.

The Medicine man continued his sing-song supplications. The prayers he said were so ancient their origin was long ago lost in antiquity. They never were written—just handed down through the centuries from one Medicine man to another.

The Navajos have never had any written history, and there has never been any recorded religion. Still, that religion has persevered through the ages—persevered, perhaps, since the age when the Navajos' ancestors began a trek from somewhere along the coast of China, up to and across the wastelands of Alaska and on down to their present place of confinement.

Confinement it is, too, because no Navajo relishes the idea of leaving the place of the great bird and the fallen giant we whites know as Shiprock.

They know that their ancestors were brought there by the great bird. They know, too, that when the big giant took away many pretty girls, the great bird and the big giant fought to their death there today.

Outside the hogan there was a small wolf cry from one end of the ceremonial oval, sounding as if it had come from a great distance. It was weak but it carried far.

Next there came a series of hoarse shouts. Then the Yebichai dancers pranced to the door of the hogan and began their dance. Around the outside of the moving circle of twelve or more dancers there jumped and cavorted the devil dancer whose purpose it was, as the representative of evil, to deter the dancers from their chosen pattern of movement.

Presently the dancers ceased their wild circling and returned to their hut of sticks to remove the fantastic headdresses and to rest for the next challenge of the forces of evil.

Tom Kimball and I had remained in the hogan while the dancers cavorted. We sat cross-legged like the Medicine man.

Suddenly we arose to go and there happened that strange thing that set me wondering.

I had been told to do exactly as Tom did. So when he got up to leave I walked from the hogan with arms crossed, then bent down to dip both hands into an empty tea kettle which had been placed near the door and which I thought was just there by happenstance.

Tom explained it was part of an ancient ritual, this symbolic washing of the hands.

A symbolic ritual that began when? And why? Could it be that somewhere in the dim past the Navajos knew that it was necessary to wash the hands when leaving a sick man's house to avoid carrying the danger of infection?

I believe that the case. Somewhere in unrecorded history the Navajo knew these things. We have failed in that we have not taught them the basics of sanitation or anything else for that matter. We have simply been washing our hands in an empty vessel so far as the Navajo is concerned.

White Crow's Downfall

Art is a great thing for the soul but it does practically nothing whatsoever for the stomach and that's why Miles Horn took a job one summer on a ranch—a few miles north of Sheridan, Wyo. Miles, known as White Crow to his red brothers, the Sioux, the Arickara and the Cheyenne, is a big Indian.

It takes a lot of pork chops, indeed, to keep White Crow's ribs apart for any length of time. But being an artist, White Crow knew some lean days and since he has a somewhat keener appreciation of pork chops than he does even of art, he elected to accept employment doing chores around the ranch.

Well, White Crow took his canvases and easels and oils out to the ranch and pitched a big teepee not far from the main house. He ate with the ranch family but slept and painted in the teepee.

Now it is generally accepted that the Creator endowed Indians with a great many talents almost exclusively their own, among which is an uncanny ability to forecast the weather .

The ranch foreman, being a man who knew much about Indians, capitalized on this knoweldge the first morning at breakfast. "Chief," he began, "what's the weather going to be today?"

White Crow blinked, sensed opportunity and replied:

"Indian forecast weather only on full stomach. Still hungry."

A second and a third helping of flapjacks and bacon went to White Crow who looked up presently and declared all would be fine that day. It was. Next day he foresaw scattered rains in the afternoon and wind that night. Again he was right. White Crow proved almost infallible in the days that followed.

Accurate knowledge of what the weather has in store is important to ranch people, so White Crow was held in high esteem and favored lavishly at the table. All this pleased White Crow no end. He garnered many extra pork chops during the ensuing weeks.

Then one morning a small tragedy took place. The foreman wanted to drive into town and had to have a reliable projection of the weather. Miles turned his head, changed the conversation and ignored a second helping of bacon and eggs.

Each time the question of weather was put to him, White Crow's face went blank. He was obviously upset. So was the foreman.

"What's the matter, White Crow? You haven't said anything and you haven't given us your weather forecast for today. Are you sick?"

White Crow looked at the foreman helplessly. Then he answered: "Not sick. Radio heap broke."

Miss White Eyes Would Baffle Brooklyn

Phyllis White Eyes' eyes are as soft and warm as an Indian summer night and are contradictorily as brown as a luscious wild berry. Miss White Eyes, who hails from the Sioux Indian reservation at Rosebud, is really an eyeful even to the most unappreciative observer of feminine charm.

Miss White Eyes sells milk shakes and Indian novelties to the tourist trade up in Custer state park at a Black Hills store only an arrow's flight from the game lodge made famous as the summer White house when silent Cal Coolidge sojourned there in 1927.

Incidentally, the summer White house is being managed this year by Mr. and Mrs. Harry Herbst, widely known Cheyenne, Wyo., restaurant operators. They invited me to spend the night and sleep in Cal's bed. I accepted the invitation with much the same anticipation with which I would look forward to wearing a neon-lighted dinner jacket. It was the first time I had ever slept formally and felt genuinely apologetic for snoring.

But getting back to Miss White Eyes. She differs greatly from her Navajo sister, who is identified by a somewhat flashier but admittedly original adaptation of the "new look" in women's dresses. Miss White Eyes is a shining (and how!) example of what the American Indian could become universally if given a break. She is modern, educated, polished, knows how to use lipstick and nail polish, dresses neatly and speaks with such pure diction that she is certain to be misunderstood by Brooklyn tourists this summer.

Carl Burgess, who was then park superintendent, wanted me to look at the Buffalo herd which he claims is the largest in the country. I wanted to look at Miss White Eyes. She held a certain academic interest for me because of my previous studies of Navajo ways.

She constituted living proof that something can be done about the Navajo problem. She is one of a great many Sioux who annually leave the reservation after careful training and good education, to take their place in the world. You can find them everywhere up here in South Dakota and in Nebraska.

It's the handling of the raw material, the child Indian, that is predominantly important. Unguided, the American Indian will naturally follow age-old pursuits and ways of life. Take a look at the boy I dubbed Little Hungry Buck:

Little Hungry Buck is 8. He was shivering, cold, hungry and sleepy when I found him huddled in the hotel lobby at Hot Springs, S. D. He had missed a bus connection while returning from Rapid City to his home.

I talked to the little fellow a short while, determined his plight, and we went out for ham and eggs. Little Hungry Buck's sister was in a hospital in Rapid City. He had visited her somehow, although the whole thing was not quite clear. But I learned something from Little Hungry Buck.

He was without quarters or funds, and a gentleman in need must be helped. So I invited him to spend the night with me. First, however, I insisted he take advantage of my bathing facilities.

Little Hungry Buck scrubbed himself with soap. He scratched at his elbows and ankles, studiously avoiding his ears, which I later had to scour for him. He told me he had no floor in his home, and he had no bathtub.

"Where do you bathe," I asked.

"In the river," he replied.

"Which do you like best," I inquired, "the river or the tub?"

"The river," he said.

Why I Don't Fish

Colorado fishermen have at least one thing new to look forward to this year. They can always talk about the lower license fee that got away. But that's small consolation to me. The only part of fishing that I enjoy is the eating and frankly, brother, I don't even know which end of the pole you use to beat the fish to death.

It's not the fishing that I dislike, exactly. It's the work connected with trying to land a few minnow-sized trout. I hate the idea of getting out of the sack in the middle of the night to drive 200 miles just to go wading and get bit by mosquitoes. Even worse, I hate fighting Sunday drivers all the way back to Denver.

I wouldn't mind fishing if the fish would come into town where we could get at 'em easier. My idea of a perfect fishing trip is to lie down in the shade with my head resting on a friendly lap and the line tied to my big toe just in case a fish should want to come up and join me.

My Uncle Jeb (Windy) McGabe, the one who travels for the Dobbin's Rest Pneumatic Horse Collar company, was telling me the other day that fishing is so popular up in Wyoming that the bars had to close down on Sunday.

But Uncle Windy admitted even that tragedy has failed to make a fisherman out of him. He swore off of fishing a few years ago when he read the handwriting on the wall. Everybody knows, he said, that the Colorado river and all its tributaries belong to

California and that, therefore and to-wit, the fish in said streams must belong to California, too.

"Now," he continued, "I don't want to go out fishing and run into some darned yokel in a California cop suit standing on a Wyoming stream and demanding to see my California fishing license.

"I'm just naturally hot-headed. I'd probably poke or shoot the native son and this would lead to complications. They'd send more fish wardens to Wyoming and because there's no love lost between the people of our state and the people of California, a civil war probably would break out.

"It would be total war. Women would get in it and fight alongside the men. Now you know that your Aunt Ellie, the one I divorced, lives in California. They'd probably draft her first thing into the California army and she'd get in the front lines of our enemy.

"And I'll be darned if I ever want to lay eyes on that woman again—ever."

The TRUTH About Fishing

All I know about fishing is that you get up early on Sunday, take along a quart-size container, (full, of course), drive into the mountains, wade into the stream, scare the fish onto the bank then beat 'em to death.

That's the old Wyoming formula.

Reason I happened to remember is because I was sitting in Morris Sunshine's health and recreation emporium a few nights ago sipping my yogurt, when the conversation got around to the proper pursuit of piscatorial practices (how to fish, to you).

"Fishin'," I snorts in disgust. "Why there hasn't been any good fishing in this part of the country in years." From there on I enlightened these creel-toting sagebushers on fishing as it used to be.

Young as I am, I still can remember when real honest-to-gosh fishermen wouldn't be caught sober in a bootleg joint decorated with all the fancy folderol so-called fishermen use these days.

We used to just float a jackrabbit out on a wood raft then shoot the fish with a .30-'30 when they'd come up to get the rabbit.

It was real sport—hunting and fishing at the same time. And that way you didn't have to bother with the fingerlings.

Why, I remember when, after all the really big ones had been caught out, we had to resort to fishing with hook and line. Up at Heart Lake in Yellowstone national park, we had to stand behind a tree to bait our hooks.

I recall one occasion when Sam Ballard of Douglas (my old home town), Wyo., was fishing on the upper reaches of Antelope creek. Sam had fished all afternoon with moderate success. He had pulled in a half dozen ten-pounders or better, but decided at last to try for a big one.

Sam needed some big bait. With typical good fortune he espied a six-foot rattler a short distance away. The snake had a frog in his mouth.

It just so happened that Sam had a quart of Kemmerer Kicker in his hip pocket. He uncorked the bottle, poured a small snargle into the snake's open mouth, then captured the frog.

He used it for bait, hauled in a fish the size of a young antelope. Then he felt something tap him on the leg. It was the grateful snake packing another frog.

You can hear all sorts of fish stories. The one that makes me maddest, however, is the intendend exaggeration about the fellow who had to tie his pole to a tree so he could climb up it, slide down the line and stab to death the trout he couldn't land. Boy's stuff! Kid's play!

Cowpunchers in the LaPrele country used to suspend a half-grown steer from a limb overhanging the creek, then rope the trout as they leaped into the air to snatch the critter. It took a quick hand and a good eye, but some fairly nice fish were caught in that manner back when fishing was fishing.

History records that one necktie party, with a fairly prominent rustler as the guest of honor, was interrupted abruptly in pretty much the same way when some ignoramus picked a tree for the hanging which overhung Bear creek on Dead Horse gulch.

A fairly good sized cutthroat broke water and swallowed the guest, boots, spurs and Stetson, just as the guest hit the end of the rope.

About the best fish yarn I know, however, went the rounds back in 1938 when the bureau of reclamation drained Alcova lake.

The water ran lower and lower with each succeeding day. Then one night one of the larger fish set out across country for Seminoe dam where, he was sure, there must be enough water to keep him.

He tore out four spans of a barb wire fence, stampeded a herd of cattle and wallowed out 857 acres of wheat.

The farmer caught up with the culprit and was so mad he harnessed that trout and ploughed 1,409 acres with him by leading him across the field waving a wet gunny sack in front of his snout.

And you think there's fishing today?

For Good Old Dad

According to the almanac, this is Father's Day. And that's something, at least. If Mama can have a new refrigerator, Daddy is entitled to a "day." On this auspicious occasion it is the national custom for the missus and the young 'uns to show the old man the respect and consideration he is entitled to but doesn't get on the other 364 days. So let's all be kind, affectionate and quiet.

Tomorrow we can all get back to normal.

This Sunday, Dad gets first crack at *The Post's* sports section. The car is his, too. He can also exercise seniority in the choice of radio and television programs. And if he wants to sleep out on the front porch with his galluses hanging down, that's his own business. (You keep your nose out of this, Sis.)

Then along about 3 p. m., the breadwinner should be permitted to indulge in a small snort. (It's safe by now because he won't be driving the car anyhow. Junior will have it in spite of the orders of the day.)

And speaking of snorts (how about a quick one right now?) this end of the bunkhouse is indebted to Mrs. C. F. Youberg of Hayden, Colo., for a dilly of a Father's Day suggestion.

It came about as the result of publication here on Mother's Day of a list of valuable household hints. The household aids, it must be admitted, were taken from an old cookbook which, I learned later, has now become somewhat outmoded.

So Mrs. Youberg delved into an ancient cookbook in her own collection and came up with this little recipe which she claims should interest a great number of males: It is called Cherry Bounce.

"Mix together six pounds of ripe morellas and six pounds of large black heart cherries. Put them into a wooden tub or bowl and, with a pestle or mallet, mash them so as to crack all the stones.

"Mix with the cherries three pounds of loaf sugar or of sugar candy broken up, then put into a demijohn or a large stone jar. (Now brace yourself.)

"Pour on two gallons of the best double rectified whisky. Stop the vessel closely and let it stand three months, shaking it every day during the first month.

"At the end of the three months, strain and bottle it off. Stop shaking the bottle and just shake."

If you can't wait three months, it is suggested that similar results can be obtained by pouring some ordinary household ammonia, wood chip whiskey, and weed spray into a cement mixer, shooting the mix with two sticks of dynamite and hitting yourself on the head with a hammer.

It won't taste as good, but we said only that "similar results" can be obtained.

But just in case you happen to be like my own good dad up at Douglas (my old home town), Wyo., and you don't go in for violent celebrations, here's a happy Father's Day to you, anyhow. Me, I'm going out to the crick.

For A.A.-uld Lang Syne

What I like most about New Year eve is that it's not compulsory. You don't have to if you don't want to. You can say to heck with it and go to bed and not make any silly resolutions and keep on being the same old monotonous heel you always were and nobody will really give a hoot.

Pursue this course and a few will call you an old fuddy duddy but you'll begin the new year with more money in hand and fewer noises in the head. Your pockets next morning won't be stuffed with mysterious telephone numbers, confetti, corks and party doo-dads, and you won't be required to explain that the lipstick on your shirt is nothing more indicting than tomato catsup.

There are those of another school, however, who seem to be pretty sot in their ways when it comes to New Year celebrations. They believe strongly in wringing out the old year and sluicing in the new. Each year end they rise to the occasion and fall on their ear.

Custom dictates that they go out on the town, eat stuff they can't digest at prices they can't afford, then drink things they don't need in volumes they can't contain. This form of celebrating seems calculated to push the victim at last across the threshold of bankruptcy to which he was led by the Christmas spirit. Any observance short of ending the old year with delirium tremens and beginning the new amid the chaos of financial disaster is considered a libel on the new year's promise of great fortune to one and all.

Up at 1311 York street in Denver, however, a great crowd of merrymakers will throw a party that's just a shade different. Don't get it wrong. There will be perhaps more noise, more all around fun and more cutups than at any public blowout in Denver.

It will be a most democratic crowd. This set knows no social barriers. Doctors, boiler makers, dentists, bricklayers, lawyers, machanics, newspapermen, carpenters, merchants and whatnot. There usually is no shortage of cuties either. There are young ones and old ones, newcomers and oldtimers to the organization.

The festivities will get under way with a clamorous beginning and end with a crescendo sometime in the dawn. About midnight a little character in three-cornered pants will appear on the scene to symbolize the new year and the crowd will give with a welcome that will be heard halfway down to the Union depot.

One of the best jazz bands that can be hired for money is usually retained for this special occasion which annually rocks the old York street mansion. The place becomes a very jungle of streamers, and confetti showers down in blizzard proportions.

No crowd in Denver enjoys the skilled planning of so many oldtime, professional party throwers as the crowd at 1311 York street. That's the address of Alcoholics Annonymous.

Street Scene, Dec. 24

"Christmas," croaked the pudgy stool rider in the gabardine top-coat, "is strictly for the kids." He poked an empty shot glass across the bar with a manicured finger and said "Fill 'er up again, Mac.

"Y'know," he paused thoughtfully, "the whole thing has become too commercialized. It's nothing but a business gimmick—a racket, if ya ask me. The stores make a big killing, the old lady spends all your money and you're left holding the sack and a dime store necktie.

"The big idea is to grab all you can offa the Christmas tree, get by as cheap as you can and then beat it down to the stores the day after Christmas and exchange the stuff you got for things you really want. I'll be glad when it's all over. Fill 'er up again, Mac."

Somewhere in the joint the jukebox blared *He's a Real Gone Guy*. The drone of barroom conversation lifted stridently to meet this competition. A woman in one of the booths laughed just a bit hysterically. Her male companion guffawed. Suddenly the place seemed to become hot and sticky. It didn't smell good.

Outside, a gentle snow had been anointing the city with a new purity, concealing most of its ugliness and softening its sharp edges. Here and there the soft white pile glowed with the gaudy pastels of reflected neon signs and shimmered with the dancing brilliance of moving headlights.

Through the gathering darkness of the late December evening, a dwindling trickle of last-minute shoppers hurried homeward. Across the street a little crowd of exhausted store clerks could be heard putting up a small cheer as the manager cleared the place and locked the front door.

The streets became almost deserted. Traffic diminished and a strange quiet settled over the streets, broken only by the incongruous grinding of the now-distant jukebox.

Farther down the street a man and woman dismantled a tripod, took down their donation kettle and walked toward Larimer St. It was pretty much the same scene there. The gin mills were doing a desultory business, however, and there didn't seem to be as much hilarity.

The wind was damp but it blew color into the wan cheeks of arthritic pensioners who moved jerkily along the sidewalk. Down in an alley a short distance from the faded splendor of the Windsor hotel, someone had built a roaring fire in a garbage can. It glowed cheerily and soon drew a tiny crowd of news vendors, chilled winos and bedraggled figures in overalls and cast-off overcoats.

Some street urchins raced by, teased the crowd around the fire for a second, then disappeared up the street laughing and shouting in the gloom. A semi-trailer truck thundered up from Market St., turned and headed out-of-town. Idlers in front of the mission turned to watch it disappear in the distance.

As the roar of its Diesels died a new and glorious sound drifted faintly from uptown. A church carillon pealed forth the heraldic *Joy to the World*.

The song was only dimly heard on Larimer, but everyone stopped to listen.

Words Without Music

Brother, when you tore that December page off the calendar and threw it into the discard, you traded comparative peace and quiet for discord and clamor.

This is an election year! And seeing as how two of the most notorious political states in the Union figured importantly in my upbringing, if any, I love it.

You see, I issued forth from the feudin', fightin' family of Fenwicks down in the hilliest section of the Bluegrass state of Kentucky, and grew to manhood in the cactus and rattlesnake country of Wyoming.

One of my lifetime heroes is Davy Crokett, whose boast it was that his father could whip any man in Kentucky and that he could whip his father.

That was before the time of my granddad.

Crocket boasted that he could "run faster, dive deeper, stay under longer and come out drier than any chap this side of the big swamp." He was strictly a short-breathed frog-styler compared with modern political aquabats.

Today's free-style platform performers can coast farther faster, jump higher, talk louder longer, lie quicker to more people, promise more and deliver less, steal slicker, vote oftener and come out fatter than any two of yesteryear's champions.

In Crockett's time the range of a campaigner's field was the sweep of a fast mare in light harness. Today's air-borne ballot-bagger can wind up a campaign on election morning by coming out for ham and eggs in California, reversing himself in Denver and voting in twelve Kansas City precincts before noon, backing Bricker in Ohio and Stassen in Minnesota and then voting legally in New York and getting home in time to hear the results.

It must be admitted, however, that politics of yore lacked the subtlety that prevails nowadays. A certain heavy-handed crudeness existed then.

Crockett, for example, was charged during the white heat of a dark congressional campaign with a quite understandable indiscretion with a member of the opposite sex. The most serious intrigue of which a man can be accused in this year of polite political finagling is one in which a mink coat is the medium of exchange.

Crockett's reply to the grievance against him was that he "never ran off with anybody's wife that wasn't willing."

To date the replies to the mink coat charges abroad in the land have been limited largely to mere mumbo-mumblo.

Crockett and his opponents alike must be credited with the laudable quality of direct charge and forthright reply.

A quite similar but hitherto unreported exchange took place a few years back between two political figures up Wyoming way.

A political bigwig leveled a blast of verbal grapeshot at a trembling party smallfry who was seeking appointment to a government sinecure. In a letter (never intended to fall into the job-seeker's hands) the challenger indicted him on each and every one of the human delinquencies from belching at the table to blowing the foam off his beer.

He climaxed the bill of complaints with a slur on his morals. While a hospital patient, the writer charged, this aspirant to the party trough once carried on a clandestine romance with one of the nurses.

The battered applicant replied heatedly. He said his reputation had been badly damaged and his ability questioned. He felt a deep hurt.

"There were fourteen nurses in that hospital," he wrote angrily. "Which one did you have reference to?"

So I'm glad this is an election year. The spirit of good, clean fun in the offing tempts me sorely to enter the political arena myself.

I know all the words and that's no Crockett, brother.

Comes the Resolution!

Man and boy, for more years than I care to contemplate, I have made it an annual practice during this season to take my soul into a bright corner, look it in the eye and make what I considered the necessary resolutions to improve it and me.

The annual examination this year has had some queer results. I find by cross-examination that my own faults are innocuous, intriguing little things by comparison, which should, if anything, be cultivated.

I haven't given anybody a fur coat to take care of a loan or get my taxes squared. I haven't put the shake on any of my friends for business reasons, and I haven't sold my vote for favors of any kind.

I haven't stolen a tax dollar, bribed a congressman or run down a pedestrian, and I've made an honest effort to earn my pay.

I haven't dealt in war contracts, sponsored legislation to put gelt in my own pockets, and I haven't lied to the public.

It won't be necessary for me to swear off drinking. I can't afford the price of liquor, anyhow. And I won't have to forego any luxuries. I can't afford them either.

Thanks to the best efforts of the office of price spiralization, my vices, and those of a good many of my countrymen, have been reduced almost to the vanishing point.

We—the whole of us—are tax-cleaned and price-polished. Anything we can get, and get honestly, I believe we are entitled to. Swearing off, cutting down and doing without seem to be fine for everybody except the government.

So I'm not making any major New Year resolutions this year. I'm going to flaunt a complete disregard for the conventions and customs.

A pose of independence is about all a man can afford in these times, and don't noise that around too much or the government will slap a tax on it.

I promise only a few things during 1952.

For one thing I promise to do a better job of answering my mail.

I hope to do such a job *at* my job that I can hold my job and, perhaps, win a little something in addition from the boss.

I promise to report every waste in a tax dollar that I encounter —and with a vengeance. The government has got my dollar-three-ninety-eight, and I want to get value returned for it.

Aside from that and one other promise, I'm not going to give up anything—not even cussing!

I've been a Democrat all my life and now I've got a good reason to cuss.

Cook's Christmas Comments

Got a letter a few days ago from Guinevere Q. Plumpheimer, the cook for the Lazy Z outfit. Guinevere is all fed up with Christmas shopping and says she is in hock for the rest of the year already.

She avers that Christmas has become an ultra-zaney season when everybody rushes out like mad to buy things for other folks which they wish they could afford for themselves.

She says prices are out of this world. At least they are so far out of reach that she couldn't hit a price tag with a V-12 rocket. A dollar bill has become so small, Guinevere complains, that she wouldn't be surprised to see people using them for Christmas seals next year.

And turkeys. They're higher than geese flying south over a bunch of hunters after a bad storm in Canada. She says she doesn't know what she'll eat for Christmas dinner, if any.

It's the same with all meat, according to Guinevere. Beef has gone so high, she reports, that even the stockmen are going to have to put their calves on stilts next spring to keep them from starving to death.

She said she took her Christmas shopping list, multiplied the names by what she thought she could afford for each, divided that figure in half then went looking for a long rope and a rafter.

She finally wrote a letter to Santa Claus, addressed it in care of the White House, Washington, D. C., and got a reply from the

Marshall plan directors asking how she voted at the last meeting of the United Nations.

Her Uncle Herkimer, she wrote, had scared the daylights out of all the kids on neighboring ranches. He told them that Santa Claus had to come out by way of Denver and that Henry Barnes, the traffic engineer, was putting up signs and parking meters on all the rooftops.

Guinevere came to Denver couple weeks before Christmas and said she got into a line to get neckties. Three days later she finally got out of the queue but only after she had her credit okayed twice, paid for overtime parking, got a free chest X-ray, was told she had no mail in general delivery and learned the conga.

It was the biggest crowd she said she had seen since her hometown in Kentucky was flooded and the Red Cross offered to shelter the homeless in the state's largest distillery. Uncle Herkimer was there, too. He brought his own bed and a gallon jug.

First thing she did when she got back to the ranch, she said, was to take off her shoes and make sure they had the right feet in them. They had been stepped on more times than a department store escalator.

Guinevere is glad the shopping rush is over. Now she can't wait until the exchange season is over and congress is back in session so she can have something to divert her attention from the time payments and the income tax deadline.

Speaking of taxes, she noted in a postscript, the gift levies imposed by the federal government have caused her to wonder if our congressmen are all heathens. They could not discourage Christmas any more, she observes, if they made it illegal.

All Hail the Horse

With very little more than a couple of whinnies up at Joe Dekker's livery stable, National Save the Horse week came and went a few days ago as silently as did its founder, old Harry Galbraith of Colorado Springs. This isn't to say that the week went unobserved. Some horse magazines carried articles, saddle clubs that help sponsor it took special note and there were plans to perpetuate it.

If I didn't do my part to help promote the annual period of homage to man's most dependable transportation, I'd expect to wake up some night and see the ha'nt of old Harry, God bless him, looking me right in the eye with that accusing stare he used to give scoffers.

Before Harry died a few years back, he sort of charged me with responsibility for seeing to it that horses were never forgotten. He had spent a lifetime and his own meager fortunes in doing that.

It was funny the way Harry got the government to set aside a whole week honoring horses. I've told the story before. But it can stand re-telling. He had written to each president of the United States for years seeking a "horse week." Harry had been a cowpuncher at one time. He understood, as few men nowadays are privileged to understand, the bond of affection that springs up between a man and a saddle or work horse.

Each time Harry would write a letter to the White House, he would get a polite thank-you from some secretary. Never did he get close to realizing his purpose.

When the horse cavalry was disbanded, Harry was deeply disturbed. Sure that horses were doomed to extinction, Harry stepped up his campaign. He wrote letters to foreign governments, to saddle clubs, newspapers and magazines.

I'll bet Harry spent $60 on postage writing to me, alone. That was because I sympathized and encouraged him.

Then one day the old rannie hurried to the post office for his annual copy of the bulletin put out by the U. S. department of commerce, listing all the weeks proclaimed officially by the president. National Save the Horse Week was not there—again!

This time, however, Harry pulled what he called a "rannie-ke-boo," rangeland parlance for a "fast one." He telegraphed the department and called attention to what he termed their "oversight." He didn't *say* the president had never proclaimed the week. He just said it was not listed in the book.

Back came a telegram of apology asking for more information. Not wishing to risk the embarrassment of admitting to the president that they had committed an oversight, the department next year listed the week as official. It has been official ever since.

251

And now that the government has discontinued the bulletin, the U. S. Chamber of Commerce has decided to issue it. They wrote me about it not many weeks ago. Next year National Save the Horse Week will be observed Oct. 10 through 16.

Godiva of the Corrals

Bonnie Gray is probably the only woman in history, aside from a gal named Godiva, ever to do a striptease on horseback. Bonnie didn't exactly plan it that way, either. It certainly was not a part of the program. But there she was, bare as a babe from the waist down and the audience whistling and applauding like sailors at a burly-Q.

It happened at Kiowa, Kan., a good many years ago when Bonnie Gray was the "queen of the rodeo circuit." Bonnie was held in high esteem by rodeo performers. She was as leathery as the best of them albeit as lovely a woman to look upon as ever wore war-paint.

Her feature stunt was a high jump on her famous horse, King Tut, over an open touring car. Said touring car usually contained all the dignitaries that could be rounded up to risk their skins under King Tut's hooves and thereby win public approbation.

On the Kiowa occasion, Bonnie was galloping King Tut at the car full tilt when she felt a front foot plunge into a gopher hole. King Tut stumbled, righted himself and made a half-hearted leap at the auto. Four feet flying, he landed astraddle the car full of public officials. State representatives, the mayor and city alder-men tumbled out of the car as if they had just thought of a new source of tax revenue and were in a hurry to collect.

King Tut pawed for footing. Bonnie was thrown forward and her leather skirt caught on the saddle horn. She hung there help-less, head down, feet waving in the direction of the Diomede galaxy.

At that instant a thoughtful cowboy raced to her aid, knife in hand. With one deft stroke he sliced through the leather skirt. Bonnie slipped to the ground, rose to bow, realized her predica-ment and dived under the automobile.

Bonnie also was the first woman performer to "go under a

horse"—completely circumnavigate the animal at a full gallop. The stunt has since been emulated, but Bonnie was first and for several years the only woman to do it. Ed Wright, my old pal and world's greatest rodeo clown, back in Denver again for the season at Centennial park, taught Bonnie the trick. He also arranged for her to make the first ride on a fighting bull in Mexico back in the 1920's. She was almost trampled to death.

What becomes of oldtime rodeo performers? Well, Bonnie is working in a defense plant at Burbank, Calif. Thelma Hunt, rodeo girl and former Denver dancer, is selling hosiery in Venice, Calif. Vera McGinnis had a spill several years ago, retired, now lives in San Fernando valley.

And Mabel Strickland? She lives on a ranch somewhere out west, but Strickland park, named for her late husband, Hugh Strickland, is just across the way from Bonnie's home in Burbank. And April Strickland, the little blond-headed toddler who used to be seen at all the rodeos with her rodeo-ing dad and mom, is in show business, too. But no horses for her—she's an ice skating star and appears frequently on west coast television.

How to Get Along With Horses

He's a real pal, that horse of yours. Out there on the trail in the high mountain country, or out on the endless stretches of hot prairie, he's mighty important to you, too.

He'll pay you back in kind for the treatment you give him— good or bad. Treat him well and he will reward you with good behavior and alert response to your every whim. Well tended and properly handled, he will be a congenial companion and a strong friend, exulting with you in each new adventure and sharing with you the delights of the great outdoors—cool water, mighty vistas, the challenge of the climb, mountain breezes.

Neglect him, mistreat him, abuse him or ignore him and you'll regret it. He can be superlatively surly, obstinate and unresponding.

Perhaps you will be fortunate enough to take part in a group trail ride this summer. If you are, here are a few tips on horse care as practiced by that peer of all trail riding groups, the Round-up Riders of the Rockies:

First, master the rudiments of horsemanship. Learn how to mount and dismount properly. Get the knack of neck reining. Acquire some "horse savvy." Learn to shift your weight for the horse's greatest comfort. Know how to adjust the cinch, and be sure you can pick up your horse's feet for periodic inspections.

Although a good horse will enjoy an occasional burst of speed, it should be of brief duration and only after the horse is already warmed up in the walk, trot, canter succession.

Hold your position in the group, and don't ride close on the heels of the horse ahead of you. One kick can put your horse out of the ride and you afoot.

Use a Johnson rope halter with an eight-foot long, half-inch lead rope tied, not snapped, onto it. Snaps break, so do some halters. Don't use a neck rope. You can't control a horse with one. It's dangerous.

Remember, wet ropes shrink. Leave enough space in the halter for your horse to work his jaws.

When you tie your mount to a picket line, allow just enough halter rope for him to eat off the ground. Long shanks mean rope burns on your horse. Learn to tie a halter rope knot.

If you tie your horse to a tree or bush, tie him high and so the rope won't slip down. Also tie him so he cannot walk around. If he does he probably will shorten his tie, get excited and break loose.

If your horse won't stand tied, use hobbles. Never hobble to the head.

Use a breast strap in the high country. It holds your saddle in place. It should be high and loose, however. If short and low it can cause cinch sores.

Tie-downs (a strap going from the cinch up between the front legs to the bridle) are pretty in the movies, but don't use one on the trail. Your horse has better balance in a fall or in any other pinch if he has control of his head.

Carry a good, sharp pocket knife. Don't be hesitant about cutting equipment such as a rope or bridle in an emergency.

Don't tie your reins together while riding. If thrown you may lose your horse and tack or get a foot caught. That's a shortcut to the cemetery.

End the day's ride at a walk. Learn to unburden your horse slowly so as not to take all the weight off at once. Any old-timer will be glad to show you how to blanket your horse, water-cool his back and bandage his legs if necessary.

Look for stones in his feet at the end of the ride. Know when to allow him to drink (*never* while he's hot!). Let him graze when you stop. Watch for wrinkles, sticks, stones or bulges in your saddle blanket.

If your horse throws his head on the trail, something's wrong. Maybe the bit is too far up or down, the curb strap too tight. But when his ears are up, his eyes alert and there's snap in his step—you and he are in the pink.

Good for a Man

HRB

There we were, looking silly and grinning from ear to ear. It was 1:30 of a frosty morning. The rest of the seventy-five Roundup Riders of the Rockies were snoring in their sacks. But not the crowd in our tent. Oh, no.

Stark naked and half frozen, we shivered behind a screen and daubed Indian war paint on each other. One of the fierce

"Apaches" wore a painted tech sergeant's stripes on his arm. Bare bellies bore various slogans and a few suggestions we'd best just overlook here.

In the bunch were such otherwise reserved gentlemen as Roy Miller, Denver department store executive; Ray Davis, theater boss; Capt. Donald Kemp of Eldora; Montie Montana, the trick rider and roper, and his son, Montie Jr. There also were Rudy Paulson, rancher; Col. Bud Anderson, Union Pacific publicity; Don Starnes, Cheyenne county attorney, and some others.

Pretty soon we sneaked out the back of our tent. Two fellows jumped on bareback horses. I hammered a tom-tom and we began a low-toned war chant.

Then all hell busted loose and we swooped down on the defenseless camp. We built up the fire, yelled our lungs out and leaped in the air. Then we hauled Frank H. (Rick) Ricketson out of his sack squealing and kicking.

Just for fun, we intended to burn Rick at the stake but changed our mind when he gave back our Indian squaw—a life-size store window dummy presented to me with ceremony by Hollywood movie friends Dick Dickson, Tim Tyler and Rocky Rockriver.

He didn't give her back until after we had shaved him with a straight edge razor, it should be added.

That incident was typical of the fun enjoyed annually by the most exclusive riding club in America. Along the 125 miles of Colorado mountain trails past glaciers, through snow banks along mighty ridges, beside roaring torrents and over bald rock in sun and rain, there's time for all sorts of high jinks. There are some solemn occasions, too.

For instance there was the Sunday morning we sat our horses with heads bared and listened to Dave Dekker, Denver baritone, sing *The Lord's Prayer*. I'm here to say that only a heathen would have missed the inspiration of that moment. Looking out on the sweeping view before us at towering, snow-clad peaks and green carpeted valleys, we knew we were in the greatest church in the world—God's own.

In eight days of riding, fighting mosquitoes, getting soaking wet and trying to conceal saddle stiffness, a great many impressions are formed. Now they rush in on my mind so fast I can't type them.

Fellows calling Chrysler Sales President D. A. Wallace "Dave";

Frank Johns, Denver Dry Goods president, washing the mud out of his palomino's tail on the picket line; Blackie Trainor, camp boss who has tended camps here and in California for twelve years, being served a drink by Oil Millionaire John Eastman of Denver; Dr. Paul Isaacson using surgeon's hands to saddle a horse; three fellows singing Viking songs with Harold Dahl, Denver businessman.

It's a grand experience, that ride. Steaks two inches thick, night around a campfire from which female critters are barred, a bed under the stars, a nip on the trail and a big one at night, brushing your teeth with beer when the camp water runs out. Boy!

Joe Dekker, Denver theaterman, sums it up this way: "You'll never get closer to heaven on a horse than here."

Formality falls off at the camp entrance on the first night and stays in the dust the rest of the trip. Friendships spring up and endure. Good fellowship is topmost. And in all four years of the ride, not one cross word has been spoken man to man. The outside of a horse is good for the inside of a man.

Saddle Savvy

Before this summer is over a great many vacationing Americans are going to acquire at least a standing acquaintance with saddle leather—standing, that is, after the first ride is finished. For city folk it will be their first experience with a kack (saddle, to you tenderfoots) and horse. And for some it probably will be slightly painful.

It is interesting to observe, therefore, that ever since the knights of yore, Genghis Khan and the Spanish Conquistadores, men have been striving, futilely, you may say at first, to make that seat atop a broomtail a little easier on the fundament.

Evolution of the saddle is an old story to the stockman, but to some others it may be interesting. So hunker down, you visitors and you young buckaroos, and let's talk saddle.

By and large the western saddle is nothing more than an improved adaptation of the earliest known types used by ancient warriors. Some fancy do-dads have been added, some varying types of cinches have developed, but mainly the saddle remains a device by which a rider most comfortably and efficiently may use a horse. To the cowman the saddle is a tool, one that has to represent the maximum in efficiency.

Long before the big herds moved north out of Texas to graze on the buffalo grass of the great plains, cowpunchers were riding the old Spanish rig saddle. It was simply utilitarian, had a horn for roping and had saddlebags but no skirts.

Oh, yes, the horn is that thing at the top and front of the saddle which you will find a convenient hand hold for mounting or when your mount decides he doesn't like the parts he is in and sets out for greener pastures. The skirt is the broad piece of leather down by your knees.

Those pretty things which cover and suspend from the stirrups are tapaderos (abbreviated to "taps" by the cowpuncher). The gismo that holds the saddle onto the horse is the cincha. The thing against the rear of your Levis is the cantle, and those lumps between your thighs where the blisters develop along toward afternoon, are the swells. The entire seating part of the kack is known as a tree.

It is in the tree that perhaps the greatest evolution has taken place. Some riders preferred a bulge they could grip with their thighs when riding bucking horses. So the old slick tree without swells gradually began to be replaced by larger and still larger swells. Finally the association saddle came into being and is the one used at all rodeos today.

The earlier saddle had an open seat. A little slit ran from back to front right at the top, but a closed seat was developed in the twentieth century because of the greater comfort it afforded.

At one time you could just about tell what part of the country a rider hailed from by the type of rigging he rode. There was the California saddle, the Pony Express saddle, the Texas and other types.

One of the old standbys is the De Walker roper which originated in the 1870's, was improved in 1894 and perfected in years to come. It is one of the most popular types today, having weathered the years of change to remain largely as it was originally.

A variety of riggings exist. There's the Spanish rig with the cincha well to the front, even exposed in the Texas version; the three-quarter rig with the cincha three-quarters of the way toward

258

the front of the saddle; the center fire which is exactly as it sounds, and the double rig with a cincha to the front and a back strap toward the rear.

With all the improvements, however, no saddle maker has ever devised a sure-fire outfit for eliminating all the agony from the first day in the saddle. If a built-in pain eliminator is ever devised, I'll be the first to report it.

Science Goes Too Far in Aiding Fair Sex

They used to say there is a destiny that shapes our ends. Today it's the three-way stretch that does the trick. Science and invention have changed the shape of things considerably. And, oddly, the brainy boys who think up the revolutionary mechanical wonders of our day seem to be making a bid for the woman's vote. Each day they put new and more diabolical devices in the hands of the fair sex. Now it's electronics! Don't be surprised, men, if you come home to your little love nest some night after a hard day at the office, to find a pair of electrician's pliers hanging next to the can opener in the kitchen pantry. If you do make this shocking discovery, look up on the shelf where the gal keeps her cook book. There you will find a volume dealing with electronics and—heaven forbid—a treatise on Home Application of Atomic Energy.

The electronics boys say there is no telling what may be achieved in this new field. Applied to the domestic scene it may completely rework man's conception of home life.

Picture yourself tiptoeing in at 3 a.m. There is the little female. Instead of holding a rolling pin she has a Buck Rogerish gadget bristling with wires and radio tubes. It's not a lie detector—it's a thought wave receiver set tuned in on your active brain cells if you have any left by this time.

She asks where you have been. You say at the office helping the boss. She, who has had the thought wave machine on you for the last four hours, inquires why you raised the ante with nothing but a pair of jacks. There you are. Whipped.

Now I have been hoping ever since the first time I gazed into a radar screen that some social-minded mental giant would come

259

up with a device for locating submarged bars of soap in bathtubs. But think what Sally Snoop could do with such equipment.

Electronics will make possible the ten-minute meal. Domestically applied it will enable you to leave junior in his crib while you go off to the show, certain that should he become restless the electronic beam will: (a) Start the record player giving out with soft jive. (b) Warm up a bottle of milk and feed it to said youngster. (c) Set in motion a robot which will tap the squawling rascal on the head with a soft hammer should all other remedies fail.

Electronics may eliminate the annoying household chore of dusting by the simple expedient of making furniture electrically dust repellant.

Picture the little bundle of sweetness crawling into the kip at night. She sleeps between electric blankets. Her hair curlers are wired for power. On her head is a set of earphones attached to the thought wave receiving set tuned in on your quarreling neighbors. Her body is bundled in an electrically operated reducing device. She bristles with wires, buzzes with ohms and vibrates with alternating current.

She is a frightful, nightmarish creature from Mars—an atomminded, electrically energized robot who receives her corpuscles from the power company and her heartbeat from Los Alamos.

Thank goodness, fellows, we, out here in the great Rocky Mountain Empire, live in a richly endowed region where the towering pinnacles of the Rockies create radio "dead spots" which are impenetrable to even the keenest short wave.

At least we can go fishing on Sundays and have our thoughts of the good old days without fear of mental intrusion by some inquisitive female. Don't think me an irascible old woman-hater. Quite the contrary, I am on occasion, a soft touch for the soft touch. But this thing can be carried too far. When it becomes necessary to get marriage license and birth certificates from the atomic energy commission—by George, I quit. To heck with science!

Pal Had Faith in Ab, and Bet $4 on It

Each year about this time the leading lights around the news-room rack their brains and come up with this and that yearend roundup. There are the ten biggest stories, the worst disasters of the year, not including, however, that New Year thing, the "derndest woman" yarn of the year, business and production fig-ures and all that.

But to be different this time, I am setting down here what is in my mind one or two of the best yarns of the season. This one comes from Lusk, Wyo. It seems that a somewhat bleery-eyed jasper from out on the ranch showed up at Barney's bar one morning bright and early to inquire how in the name of four digits did he get so busted up the night before. It seems he was slightly more than somewhat bruised here and there about the anatomy and had a deep-seated aversion to alcoholic spirits.

Well, about that time another jasper from the same ranch showed up and was instantly questioned by the first jasper.

"What happened? How'd I get this way?"

"Oh, don't you remember, Ab? We wuz all in that there hotel room last night and you wuz bragging about a stunt you could do. You bet one of the fellers you could jump through one win-dow, circle around in the air like a chicken hawk on a string and come back in that next window."

"Well, why in the name of the great horned toad didn't you stop me?"

"Shucks, Ab, I had up $4 that you could do it."

Then there's the old Wyoming rancher who had never been outside Natrona county. Old Bill was so rich he could have poured his dollars into the Platte river and stopped the thing.

One day he was riding the range when he ran into his old friend, Tom. To make a short story long, let us begin right here by saying that Tom talked Bill into visiting Washington, D. C.—his first trip—and persuaded him that inasmuch as he had no relatives, he had better just spend some of that money and, "by George, Bill, get the best of everything."

Bill arrived in Washington, carpet bag in hand, boots shined and his Levis freshly washed. He shucked off a $20 bill, ordered a limousine and instructed the driver to deliver him to "the finest place there is in this town for strangers to put up."

The reluctant driver took the man to the newest and best hostelry in the city. Bill called the manager, flashed his roll, ordered the best room in the place—and got it!

Then he set out to eat some of the "strange vittles" he had been told about. He took on a tremendous cargo of seafood, drank champagne, consumed numerous sweets and topped the whole thing off with some straight bourbon. But he was still hungry.

He returned to the hotel, called the headwaiter and told him he was a "Wyoming ranchman, and I want the best derned steak you've got in the place."

The waiter took the order and solicitously asked what kind of soup Bill wanted. No, he didn't want any soup.

"But we always serve soup with out best meals."

No. No soup.

"We're very proud of our soup here, sir. Oxtail, consomme. . ."

"By Jupiter, I don't want any soup. I c'n get that out in Wyoming. Bring me that steak."

Bill dined, started up stairs to his room and fainted. When he regained consciousness two orderlies, a nurse and a doctor were holding him and giving old Bill the first enema he ever had.

Bill went home. Next day he met Tom.

"Tom, you and the missus going back to Washington this fall like you said? You ever been there before? Well, it's a nice place. They got a mighty fine hotel there. But lemme give you one tip, Tom.

"When you go into that dining room to eat—by guppies eat that derned soup when they want to give it to you."

Those are my nominations for the season's big stories.